ARIZONA

ARIZONA

DON AND BARBARA LAINE
AND LAWRENCE LETHAM

THE MOUNTAINEERS BOOKS

THE MOUNTAINEERS BOOKS
is the nonprofit publishing arm of The Mountaineers Club, an organization founded in 1906 and dedicated to the exploration, preservation, and enjoyment of outdoor and wilderness areas.

1001 SW Klickitat Way, Suite 201, Seattle, WA 98134

First edition, 2005

Published simultaneously in Great Britain by Cordee, 3a DeMontfort Street, Leicester, England, LE1 7HD

Manufactured in the United States of America

Acquisitions Editor: Deb Easter
Project Editor: Laura Drury
Copy Editor: Paula Thurman
Cover and Book Design: The Mountaineers Books
Layout and Profiles: Mayumi Thompson
Cartographer: Barbara Laine
All photos are by the authors unless otherwise noted

Cover photograph: *Grand Canyon National Park, Arizona* © Corbis
Frontispiece: *Catalina Canyon Loop Trail*

Library of Congress Cataloging-in-Publication Data
Laine, Don.
Best short hikes in Arizona / Don and Barbara Laine and Lawrence Letham.-- 1st ed.
p. cm.
Includes bibliographical references and index.
ISBN 0-89886-948-X (pbk.)
1. Hiking--Arizona--Guidebooks. 2. Trails--Arizona--Guidebooks. 3. Arizona--Guidebooks. I. Laine, Barbara. II. Letham, Lawrence. III. Title.
GV199.42.A6L35 2005
917.9104'54--dc22
2005026137

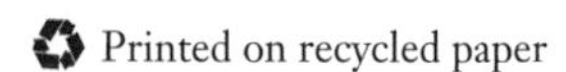

Printed on recycled paper

CONTENTS

ORGAN PIPE CACTUS NATIONAL MONUMENT

CHIRICAHUA NATIONAL MONUMENT

GRAND CANYON NATIONAL PARK

FLAGSTAFF AND NORTHERN ARIZONA

THE SEDONA AREA

PETRIFIED FOREST NATIONAL PARK

Cactus in bloom along the Wind Cave Trail

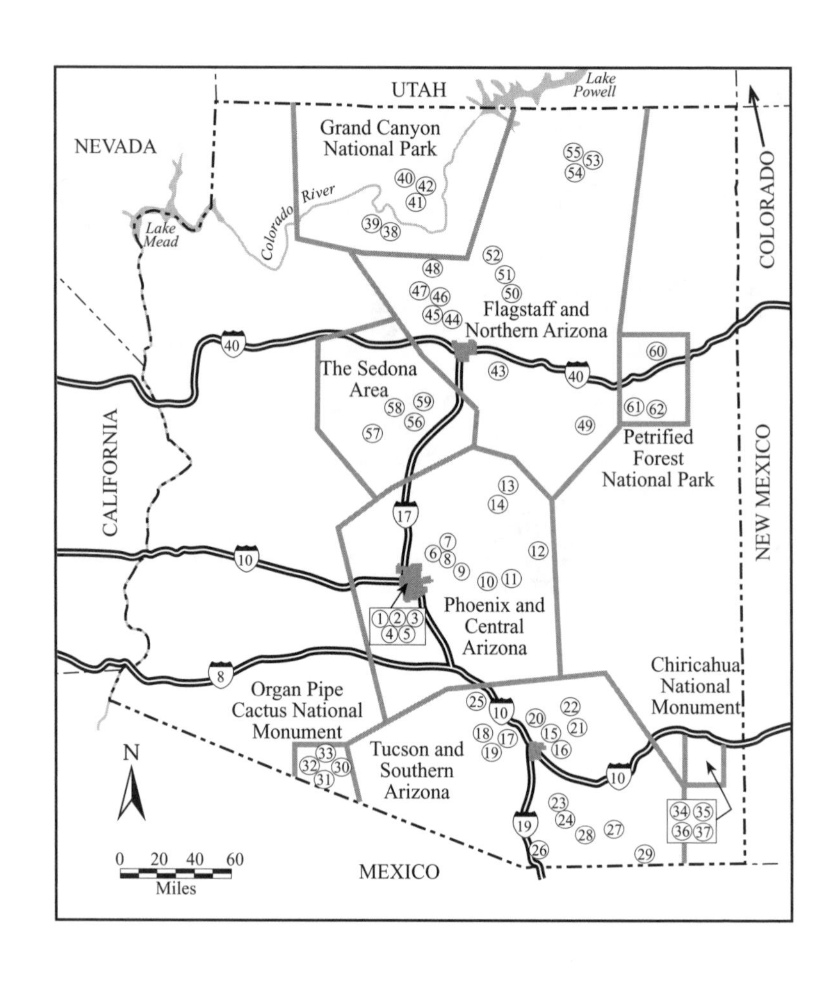
UTAH
Lake Powell
NEVADA
Grand Canyon National Park
Colorado River
Lake Mead
COLORADO
Flagstaff and Northern Arizona
The Sedona Area
Petrified Forest National Park
CALIFORNIA
NEW MEXICO
Phoenix and Central Arizona
Chiricahua National Monument
Organ Pipe Cactus National Monument
Tucson and Southern Arizona
MEXICO
N
0 20 40 60
Miles

LEGEND

Main road
Interstate
Paved road
Unpaved road
River, lake, waterfall
Arroyo, wash
Trail
Secondary trail
USFS or other government boundary
Canyon rim or ridge
Ranger station/visitor center
Mine
Mountain peak, butte, etc.
Tunnel

17 Interstate highway
70 US highway
80 State highway
4653 USFS road
P Parking area
T Trailhead
R Restroom
City or town
Point of interest
Campground
Picnic area
Bird-watching area
Scenic view
Turnaround point
Gate

HIKES AT A GLANCE

HIKE	DISTANCE (MILES ROUND TRIP)	ELEVATION GAIN (FEET)	DIFFICULTY	FEATURES
1 Papago Park Loop Trail	3	225	Easy	Rock formations
2 Nature Trail	1.5	420	Moderate	Desert plant life
3 Lookout Mountain Circumference Trail	2.6	150	Easy	Desert plant life
4 North Mountain National Trail	1.6	845	Moderate to strenuous	Scenic views
5 Camelback Summit Trail	2.3	1500	Strenuous	Scenic views
6 Wind Cave Trail	3	785	Moderate	Desert plant life
7 Pass Mountain Trail	7.1	660	Strenuous	Wildlife
8 Merkle and Vista Trail	1.2	200	Easy	Good for kids
9 Treasure Loop Trail	2.4	525	Moderate	Scenic views
10 Peralta Canyon Trail	4.5	1365	Moderate to strenuous	Scenic views
11 Boulder Canyon Trail	5	900	Moderate to strenuous	Rock formations
12 Lower Cliff Dwelling Trail	1.0	410	Moderate	Historic sites
13 Gowan Loop Trail	0.5	185	Moderate	Riparian area
14 Pine Creek Trail	1	300	Moderate to strenuous	Riparian area
15 Mica View Trail	2	85	Easy	Good for kids
16 Freeman Homestead Trail	1	150	Easy	Desert plant life
17 Valley View Overlook Trail	0.8	250	Easy	Desert plant life
18 Signal Hill Trail	0.5	35	Easy	Good for kids

19	Brown Mountain Trail	2.4 or 4.8	775	Moderate	Scenic views
20	Canyon Loop Trail	2.3	325	Easy to moderate	Wildlife
21	Sycamore Reservoir Trail	4.8	400	Moderate	Wildlife
22	Butterfly Trail	5.2	1700	Strenuous	Springs
23	Dutch John Trail	1.9	960	Moderate	Wildlife
24	Madera Canyon Nature Trail	2.7	425	Easy	Riparian area
25	Hunter Trail	4	1600	Strenuous	Scenic views
26	Juan Bautista de Anza National Historical Trail	9	75	Easy to moderate	Bird-watching
27	Creek and Railroad Loop Trail	1.75	92	Easy	Good for kids
28	Sonoita Creek Trail	2	100	Easy	Wildlife
29	Coronado Cave Trail	2	700	Moderate	Good for kids
30	Campground Perimeter Trail	1	50	Easy	Desert plant life
31	Victoria Mine Trail	5	65	Moderate	Historic sites
32	Desert View Trail	1.2	285	Easy to moderate	Desert plant life
33	Red Tanks Tinaja Trail	1.2	50	Easy to moderate	Water catch-basin
34	Natural Bridge Trail	4.8	700	Moderate to strenuous	Rock formations
35	Echo Canyon Loop Trail	3.3	1100	Moderate to strenuous	Rock formations
36	Sugarloaf Mountain Trail	1.8	570	Moderate	Scenic views
37	Massai Point Nature Trail	0.5	100	Easy	Good for kids
38	Rim Trail	Up to 11.75	200	Easy	Scenic views
39	Bright Angel Trail	3	1065	Moderate to strenuous	Scenic views
40	Bright Angel Point Trail	1	350	Easy	Good for kids
41	Cliff Spring Trail	2	310	Moderate	Springs

HIKE	DISTANCE (MILES ROUND TRIP)	ELEVATION GAIN (FEET)	DIFFICULTY	FEATURES
42 Cape Royal Trail	1	70	Easy	Scenic views
43 Island Trail	0.9	185	Moderate	Historic sites
44 Lamar Haines Memorial Wildlife Area Loop Trail	1.8	220	Easy	Good for kids
45 Lava River Cave Trail	2	120	Easy	Volcanic tunnels
46 Kendrick Park Watchable Wildlife Trail	1.5	160	Easy	Good for kids
47 Red Mountain Trail	2.4	350	Easy to moderate	Good for kids
48 Ledges Trail	2	180	Easy	Scenic views
49 Red Butte Trail	2.4	885	Moderate	Scenic views
50 Lava Flow Trail	1	85	Easy to moderate	Good for kids
51 Wupatki Pueblo Trail	0.5	90	Easy	Historic sites
52 Doney Mountain Trail	1	230	Easy to moderate	Scenic views
53 Sandal Trail	1	215	Easy	Historic sites
54 Aspen Forest Overlook Trail	1	300	Moderate to strenuous	Good for kids
55 Betatakin Trail	5	700	Strenuous	Historic sites
56 Huckaby Trail	5.8	600	Moderate	Rock formations
57 Devils Bridge Trail	1.8	400	Moderate	Rock formations
58 West Fork Trail	6.8	1145	Moderate	Riparian area
59 Red Rock State Park Trail	5	300	Easy to moderate	Riparian area
60 Blue Mesa Trail	1	90	Moderate	Rock formations
61 Giant Logs Trail	0.4	30	Easy	Petrified wood
62 Long Logs and Agate House Trail	3	175	Moderate	Historic sites

THE BEST OF THE BEST—AUTHOR FAVORITES

HIKE	DIFFICULTY	WHY
2 Nature Trail	Moderate	A close-up view of the Sonoran Desert along a hilly trail
6 Wind Cave Trail	Moderate	Panoramic views, wildlife and desert plants galore, plus a shallow cave
10 Peralta Canyon Trail	Moderate to strenuous	Spectacular views reached via a steep, boulder-strewn path
19 Brown Mountain Trail	Moderate	A trip through a cactus forest and up along a rocky ridgeline for wonderful views of the surrounding mountains and valleys
20 Canyon Loop Trail	Easy to moderate	A picturesque stream, tall saguaro, fascinating rock formations, and panoramic mountain views
31 Victoria Mine Trail	Moderate	Splendid views of surrounding mountains along a pleasant hike through rolling desert to the ruins of an historic silver mine
35 Echo Canyon Loop Trail	Moderate to strenuous	Fascinating rock formations on a trip through desert and forest
39 Bright Angel Trail	Moderate to strenuous	Dramatic views from within the Grand Canyon and a great feeling of accomplishment
47 Red Mountain Trail	Easy to moderate	Bizarre rock formations in an eroded volcanic cinder cone
54 Aspen Forest Overlook Trail	Moderate to strenuous	From barren sandstone cliffs down a winding switchback to a great view of a lush forest in a scenic valley
56 Huckaby Trail	Moderate	A shady walk along pretty Oak Creek plus breathtaking views of Sedona's famous red rocks
58 West Fork Trail	Moderate	A shady hike along (and through) an appealing creek in a beautiful canyon filled with oak, maple, box elder, and pine trees

INTRODUCTION

A rugged land of deserts, canyons, mountains, and forests, Arizona is an absolute paradise for hikers. There are thousands of miles of established trails on over 30 million acres of public lands. Some trails lead to the peaks of mountains with spectacular views, while others meander through forests, among weird rock formations, through cactus gardens, along and sometimes through creeks and streams, past prehistoric ruins, and even down into the colossal Grand Canyon. Hikers who live in or are visiting metropolitan areas do not even have to travel far to enjoy the outdoors. For instance, many trails are found right in the metropolitan Phoenix area, where city and county governments have developed large, beautiful preserves of many thousands of acres.

One of the striking aspects of Arizona is the amount of public land that is available for outdoor recreation, with national parks, national monuments, national forests, and state, city, and county parks. While many of these public lands offer practically unlimited opportunities for overnight backpacking trips through remote wilderness areas, there are also a surprising number of easy-to-reach short hikes. Pack a light lunch or snack, take a liter or two of water, head out, and be back in time for dinner.

The purpose of this book is simple—to gather within its pages all the information you need to hike the very best short hikes in Arizona. We have included trail descriptions, maps, trail profiles, and photos. More than sixty hikes are included, and there are good reasons to take any of them—beautiful scenery, panoramic views, historic or prehistoric ruins, ancient rock art, a shady stream or cool lake, or the chance to see birds and wildlife. The hikes range from a fraction of a mile to just over 7 miles round-trip, and although the majority of these hikes are rated easy or moderate, there are also some strenuous trails.

THE LAND

A physically large state—sixth in the nation in terms of square miles—Arizona is far from its Hollywood image of being one big barren desert, flat and hot, with nothing in sight in any direction but cactus. Certainly Arizona has its deserts, and unquestionably parts of the state are hot and dry, but Arizona also has tall snow-capped mountains, forests of

Opposite: *Hiking among the giant saguaro at Saguaro National Park*

fir and pine, oak-shaded river canyons, and vast grasslands. About 40 percent of the state is technically desert, 25 percent is grasslands, and the rest is forest or woods.

There are six distinct life zones in Arizona, and the climate and altitude determine the plant and animal life of each zone.

Lower Sonoran Life Zone. In the southwest portion of Arizona is the hot, arid desert that receives a maximum of 12 inches of rain from July to September and December to February. It starts at 100 feet elevation and continues to 3500 feet. It is too dry to support grasses, but there are many small-leafed bushes such as creosote, mesquite, paloverde, brittlebush, bursage, and Joshua tree. Numerous varieties of cactus, including saguaro, cholla, prickly pear, organ pipe, and barrel, live here, and animals in this hot, dry desert include the white-tailed deer, desert bighorn sheep, coyote, jack and cottontail rabbits, and a variety of snakes, lizards, spiders, and scorpions. Birds of prey are frequently seen soaring high overhead. The collared peccary—better known as the javelina—is a very nearsighted piglike animal that eats the prickly pear cacti, spines and all. Although the desert may look barren, it is a wonderland to the careful observer.

Upper Sonoran Life Zone. The next zone lies between 3500 and 7000 feet, primarily in the state's northeast corner but also in other mountainous areas. It too is an arid region, but it is a cooler desert that receives between 7 and 22 inches of annual rainfall. There are grasses, sagebrush, scrub oak, manzanita, and even juniper, piñon, and oak trees. Along the banks of streams, riparian trees such as cottonwood, willows, and walnut are common. Even though the area is a desert, there are fewer cacti because of the cold temperatures. Deer, porcupines, black bear, rabbits, and gray fox are common in this zone, as well as in some of the higher zones.

Transition Life Zone. The ponderosa pine tree is the predominant plant of the life zone that occurs between 7000 and 8000 feet. The Kaibab Plateau near the Grand Canyon, and the Mogollon Rim, a clifflike ridge that crosses the entire state, are good examples of the Transition Life Zone; however, it also occurs on mountains in any part of the state that reach that altitude and receive no less than 18 inches of precipitation each year. There are also plants like buckbrush, manzanita, and even hedgehog cactus. Elk and various squirrels are found here.

Canadian Life Zone. The Douglas fir and white fir trees found in this life zone grow 150 feet high and live from 200 to 400 years. The zone, stretching to altitudes of between 8000 and 9000 feet, receives approximately 25 inches of rain per year. Other plants include Gambel oak, aspen, and various grasses and shrubs.

Hudsonian Life Zone. This life zone, between 9000 and 11,500 feet, supports primarily spruce and alpine fir trees.

Arctic-Alpine Life Zone. This life zone is above tree line at 11,500 feet and higher. In Arizona, this zone is found only on the upper reaches of the San Franciscan Peaks near Flagstaff. The trees at timberline are twisted by strong winds and heavy snows, while their growth is stunted by poor soil conditions. The plants above tree line are of an arctic variety like moss, lichens, and grasses. The tundra pipit, a bird, is the only animal that makes its home in such a hostile environment.

THE PEOPLE

Nomadic peoples roamed this area more than 10,000 years ago, and by the first few centuries AD began creating communities—first of pit houses and then multistory pueblos, either in cliff-side caves or free-standing. Spanish explorers arrived in the mid-1500s, and although they did not find the cities of gold they sought, they were the first to

A prehistoric pueblo on the Wupatki Pueblo Trail

record their impressions of the Grand Canyon. By the mid-1700s the Spanish established missions at Tubac and nearby Tumacácori, which are considered the first permanent European settlements in Arizona.

Most of Arizona became part of the United States in 1848 with the Treaty of Guadalupe Hidalgo, although Tucson and points south waited five years until their purchase from Mexico. The second half of the nineteenth century saw an influx of white settlers, resulting in numerous conflicts with the Navajos and Apaches, until U.S. forces defeated them in the late 1880s. Also during this period mining boom towns such as Tombstone sprang up, and Arizona began to acquire its Wild West image. Arizona became the United States' forty-eighth state on February 14, 1912.

Today, thanks in large part to the development of air conditioning and various water projects that have helped turn the desert green, the state is one of the fastest growing areas in the United States, a bustling mix of agriculture, industry, and tourism. Its population includes a large number of retirees seeking relief from the cold of northern states, and quite a few—known locally as snowbirds or simply winter residents—spend winters in the Phoenix and Tucson areas, returning north when temperatures start to climb.

OUTDOOR ETHICS

The general rule of thumb for those spending time in public lands is to use planning, knowledge, and most of all common sense to have as little impact on the land as possible. The ideal situation is that every visitor would see no evidence that anyone had been there before, but even here in the relatively empty Southwest, that's a bit too much to hope for.

Our goal should be to minimize human impact by staying on trails, properly disposing of all trash—many of these areas are Pack It In–Pack It Out—and being especially careful to avoid polluting lakes, streams, and rivers. A number of the sites contain American Indian ruins and artifacts, or relics from Spanish colonial times or the pioneer days of the 1800s. These irreplaceable artifacts and prehistoric and historic sites should be observed, appreciated, and photographed, but never disturbed. Even touching ancient rock art is damaging, because of the natural oils in our skin.

FEES

Day-use and camping fees are collected at many of the areas discussed in this book, with national parks being by far the most expensive (often

$10 to $20 per vehicle for up to one week), national monuments operated by the National Park Service next highest in cost, then city and county parks, and the least expensive or free are sites operated by the U.S. Forest Service (except in the Sedona area, which has additional fees). In most cases, there are no extra charges for ranger-guided hikes and talks.

The federal government offers several passes that offer discounts or free admission to a number of federal recreation sites, including

Views from Bright Angel Trail

Prickly pear cactus in bloom

many of those discussed in this book. Persons covered by the passes are the pass holder and any accompanying passengers in a personal vehicle. For those traveling in another manner, such as by bike or on foot, the pass admits free the pass holder, spouse, children, and parents. Good for one year from date of purchase, the passes cover entry fees but not what are called user fees, such as camping and boat launching.

Two passes are available to the general public. While they are not usually worth the purchase price to those visiting two or three facilities within a year, travelers who will be visiting six or more, especially the higher-priced national parks, can usually save money by buying one of the passes. The National Parks Pass is valid for entrance fees at all sites operated by the National Park Service. The slightly more expensive Golden Eagle Passport is similar except that in addition to National Park Service properties, it provides free entry to all other federal government fee areas, such as those operated by the U.S. Forest Service.

We also strongly recommend that those who qualify for two special passes take advantage of them. One is the Golden Age Passport, a lifetime pass similar to the Golden Eagle that is available to those 62 years or older, which, in addition to covering site entry also provides a 50 percent discount on user fees for all services and facilities in national parks, such as camping. "Special recreation fees" or fees charged by concessionaires are not covered by the pass. The second is the Golden Access Passport, which provides the same benefits as the Golden Age Passport and is available to those who are blind or permanently disabled, regardless of age.

The Arizona State Parks Department also offers several types of annual day-use passes, which may save money for those planning to spend a lot of time in state parks. Some counties that charge entrance fees also offer annual passes, and members of the Nature Conservancy receive discounts on fees for Nature Conservancy properties.

Camping costs vary according to the facilities provided and the popularity of the park, monument, or site, and can range from free or $7 to $15 per night for a primitive site to $12 to $25 per site for more developed campgrounds. Campsite reservations are available at some of the more popular areas. See the appendix for contact information.

REGULATIONS AND PETS

Regulations vary, depending on the agency administering the particular site, with the National Park Service generally being more restrictive than the U.S. Forest Service. Most regulations are common courtesy and common sense, such as staying on established trails, not disturbing the landscape, and quiet hours in campgrounds—usually from 10:00 PM until 6:00 or 7:00 AM, which prohibit loud music, the use of generators, and other noise that disturbs campers.

One of the major differences among federal agencies' regulations, and even among different sites under the same agency, is the way in which pets are regulated. Most National Park Service properties, and especially the larger national parks, are not pet-friendly, and those planning to visit them should consider leaving their pets at home. With some exceptions, dogs are prohibited on hiking trails and in the backcountry, and must always be leashed. This means that if you take your pet into these parks and monuments they can be with you in the campgrounds and inside your vehicle, and you can walk them in parking areas, but that's about it.

Lands administered by the U.S. Forest Service, Arizona State Parks, and city and county parks are generally less restrictive, and you will usually find that dogs are permitted on trails, although they must be leashed and most agencies now require that you clean up after your pets. In the following pages, we have assumed that dogs are prohibited on trails in properties operated by the National Park Service and permitted on trails under the jurisdiction of the U.S. Forest Service and Arizona State Parks. We have noted the exceptions to these generalities, and also included information on pets in most city and county parks.

However, we cannot emphasize too strongly that just because a

Squirrels seem to be everywhere along Sonoita Creek Trail.

government agency permits pets on its trails does not mean that it is a good idea. Many trails have sharp rocks that will cut the pads on dogs' feet or overhanging cactus that can dig into the dogs' fur or skin. Also, it may be too hot. If you do hike with your pets, be sure to take a portable water bowl—they need water just as much as you do—and realize that pets need to take breaks on the trail just as people do. Also, never leave pets locked in a closed vehicle in the sun; it is a sure way to kill them. Local government agencies or convention and visitor bureaus can usually help you find a kennel or veterinarian where your pets can be kept while you're on the trail.

CLIMATE, HEALTH, AND SAFETY

Arizona's different climatic regions allow people to choose the weather they want to enjoy at practically any time of year. In the summer, the temperature is scorching in the desert, but the days are cool in the mountains. Winter brings deep snow to higher elevations and absolutely perfect days to the desert, so hikers can have it all—usually whenever they want it—though there are bound to be some storms occasionally. Hikers in the winter may see rain in the lower desert, and the monsoon season from July to September may be wet, but the amount of moisture all depends on the overall weather patterns. The weather at higher elevations is typical of mountains: freezing cold in the winter with cool nights and warm days in the summer. Always be prepared for cold and rain at the higher elevations regardless of the time of year. Even after these caveats, it is fair to say that, more often than not, the weather in Arizona is great, and most of the state enjoys more than 300 days of clear skies and sunshine every year.

The same elevation extremes that help produce such climate differences can also slow you down and even cause health problems, because the higher you go, the less oxygen there is. Visitors from lower elevations who have heart or respiratory problems should consult their home physicians before planning trips to the mountains, perhaps anywhere above 5000 feet. Those in generally good health need not take any special precautions, but can ease the transition to high elevations by changing altitude gradually.

Arizona has among the highest skin cancer rates in the nation, so those planning to be outdoors are strongly advised to wear broad-brimmed hats, ultraviolet-blocking sunglasses, and use a good-quality sunscreen. If traveling in the mountains in winter, make sure your

The San Francisco Peaks, a Flagstaff landmark

vehicle has snow tires or chains, and carry extra blankets and emergency food and water—just in case.

Hypothermia is another potential problem, especially in the mountains. Hypothermia occurs when the body's core temperature drops below normal, 98.6° Fahrenheit, and if left untreated it can be deadly. Advanced symptoms of hypothermia are incoherent speech, cold skin, disorientation, or listlessness. It is difficult for victims of hypothermia to recognize the symptoms in themselves, so watch each other carefully.

Hypothermia strikes in surprising conditions. A case in Arizona occurred when a woman was fishing on a warm day. The sky clouded over, the temperature dropped quickly, and it rained before she could take cover. Because the storm was brief and it did not seem cold, she did not take any action. In wet clothes at about 50° Fahrenheit, her body temperature could not keep up and she developed hypothermia. Fortunately, her partner recognized the symptoms and helped her.

Sonoita Creek Trail follows a lakeshore and creek, where you're apt to see a variety of waterfowl.

The right clothing helps to keep you warm. Take raingear and find shelter when it rains. Avoid being wet from sweat by wearing clothing in layers. When you are hot, remove layers and as you cool down, put more back on. Choose clothing based on its material. Cotton does not retain warmth when it gets wet, but wool, cotton-polyester blends, silk, and polypropylene retain heat even when soaked. A hat, gloves, and warm shoes are also important in cold weather because most of the body's heat is lost through the extremities. Hypothermia is not often a problem in the lower-elevation deserts during the summer because the nighttime low temperatures are too high. However, there are areas of the state at higher altitudes where it gets cold at night regardless of the time of year. During the monsoon season it can rain unexpectedly, so be prepared with the proper clothing.

Hyperthermia, also known as heat exhaustion and heat stroke, is the opposite condition of hypothermia, and is fairly common in Arizona's southern desert areas. When the body gets hot, it sweats to try to maintain a stable temperature. If the water lost through perspiration is not replaced, the body's temperature rises and makes the person sick. Symptoms include dizziness, pale face, weakness, listlessness, or nausea. If the symptoms appear, put the person in the shade, have him or her lie down, and give sips of water every 10 to 15 minutes until the person feels better. To prevent hyperthermia, be sure to drink water or a sports drink regularly when hiking, even if you don't feel thirsty.

Heat stroke is an acute case of heat exhaustion and is a medical emergency. The symptoms are headache, nausea, skin that is hot and dry (dry because the body has stopped sweating), fever, red face, or even unconsciousness. While waiting to evacuate the person for medical treatment, have him or her lie down in the shade while you cool his or her body with water or ice. If conscious, give sips of water that has a bit of salt in it to replace the salt the person has lost through sweating.

Area health officials warn outdoor enthusiasts to take precautions against hantavirus pulmonary syndrome, a rare but often fatal respiratory disease. Hantavirus was first recognized in this country in 1993, and a large percentage of the almost 300 confirmed cases were reported in the Four Corners states. About half of the cases resulted in death. The disease is usually spread by the urine, droppings, and saliva of deer mice and other rodents, and health officials recommend that campers avoid areas with signs of rodent droppings. Symptoms of hantavirus appear anywhere from three days to six weeks after exposure and are similar to flu—fever, muscle aches, nausea, vomiting, coughing, diarrhea—and can lead to breathing difficulties and shock.

One of the great joys of going into wild areas is the possibility of seeing wildlife, but the last thing you want is a confrontation. Mountain lions, which are nocturnal, rarely bother people, although there have been a few reported cases in recent years. Black bears, however, are another story. Although generally shy, bears have learned that wherever there are humans there is food. In especially dry years when their usual food supplies are low, bears head to public lands, often visiting campgrounds at night. For this reason, those camping or hiking in bear country need to check with park rangers about any current bear prob-

No-trace hiking preserves fascinating ruins for future generations. (Photo by Lawrence Letham)

lems. If hiking at dawn or dusk, when bear encounters are more likely, make noise by talking or singing. Although this goes against the usual ethic of being quiet on the trail so as to not disturb other hikers, it will prevent surprising a bear, or worse, finding yourself between a mother bear and her cub. Campers in bear country should store food away from tents and other sleeping areas and dispose of garbage properly.

Another hazard is the rattlesnake, the most common poisonous reptile of the Southwest. Snakes are cold blooded, and often lie in the sun. Wise hikers always watch where they're stepping and check carefully before putting their hands into spaces between rocks. Snakes enjoy the heat that rocks absorb and take immediate offense when a human invades their space. Also, when hiking after dark, or even walking in a campground at night, use a flashlight to make certain you don't step on a snake. On the other hand, snakes aren't usually aggressive and will avoid people whenever possible. There are other poisonous creatures in Arizona, mostly in the warmer desert regions, and you will often find warnings about them at trailheads and in campgrounds.

Safety is an important concern in all outdoor activities. For even the shortest wilderness excursion, we recommend that you bring along the following Ten Essentials:

1. Extra food
2. Extra water
3. Extra clothing, in case of accidents or weather changes
4. First-aid kit, with tweezers to remove cactus spines
5. Sunglasses and sunscreen, especially in snowy or desert climates
6. Knife
7. Firestarter, such as chemical fuel and matches in a waterproof container
8. Flashlight, with extra batteries
9. Compass and map of your immediate area
10. Emergency shelter

You may also want to bring along water purification tablets or a water filter, raingear, and insect repellant. In addition, it is always a good idea to leave information about your trip (where you will be and for how long) with a reliable person, such as a ranger or family member, so help can be sent if you do not make it home on time.

Modern technology has produced two electronic devices that are being seen more and more on the trail. A cellular telephone can be very helpful, even indispensable in a pinch, although cell phones don't work everywhere in Arizona, especially in deep valleys. A Global Positioning System (GPS) receiver is not only useful but fun. It helps you locate your position and measure distances and speed, and it can also help you get back to the trailhead if you get lost.

HOW TO USE THIS BOOK

The purpose of this book is to help hikers in Arizona find the right short trails for their particular preferences, needs, and physical abilities—to maximize the enjoyment while minimizing frustrations and disappointments. The hikes are arranged geographically by region, and in each region roughly by distance from the major city or destination. Thus, in the chapter on the Phoenix area, the hikes within city limits are first and those farthest from Phoenix are last.

A short regional introduction gives an overview of the area being covered and, we hope, some interesting details about the region. It also includes descriptions of public campgrounds—those operated by government entities—and tells in what communities commercial campgrounds are located. There is also a regional map at the beginning of each chapter.

Each hike begins with an information block that is mostly self-explanatory, but we do want to say a few words about difficulty. Hikes are rated from easy to strenuous, but please keep in mind that these are subjective ratings from the authors and other experienced hikers, and what is easy for one person might be strenuous for another, and vice versa. Also, because of the climate extremes in Arizona, a hike in the lower-elevation desert that might be easy or moderate in January when temperatures are moderate will be strenuous or even foolhardy in July, when temperatures soar well above 100° Fahrenheit. Therefore, before attempting a particular hike, be sure to consider the current weather conditions, elevation change, and your own physical abilities. However, do not ignore a trail just because it is listed as strenuous. There are always turnaround points that make the hike shorter, and it is the wise hiker who knows his or her limitations.

The Early Bird Gets the Best Hike

Time of day is an important consideration when heading out on the trail, and much more important in the desert areas of Arizona than many other places. Hiking in the cool part of the day—usually early morning—is always easier and much more pleasant than hiking the same trail during the hottest part of the day. A bonus is that the lighting is almost always better just after sunrise, providing crystal-clear panoramic views with deep shadows and perfect colors.

Mourning doves are frequently seen at Organ Pipe Cactus National Monument.

Descriptive signs help hikers identify desert flora and fauna.

The information block also contains the total climb. By this we mean the grand total in feet of all the times the trail goes uphill. Therefore, the total climb can easily exceed the difference between the starting elevation and highest elevation, and even the difference between highest and lowest elevations.

The hikes are grouped geographically into eight chapters. Each chapter has a starting point, or home base (Phoenix, Tucson, Organ Pipe National Monument, and so forth), and includes the hikes in that starting point plus, in some cases, hikes that could be accomplished as day trips from that starting point. After the information block, the first paragraph gives driving directions to the trailhead. Entry fee, restroom, and drinking water information is mentioned here. Then the trail is described in detail, including points of interest and mileage points along the way.

Each hike is accompanied by a map and a trail profile. The maps generally provide enough detail to allow you to follow the trail, but if you want more detail, the name of the appropriate USGS topographical map is provided. Unfortunately, the only enduring features on the topographical maps are the land formations. Roads, trails, and even the course of streams change over the years, so the trail you want may not appear on the USGS map. Check with the land management agency for more recent maps or brochures.

Charts at the beginning of this book help make your choice of hikes

Partially restored prehistoric pueblo made of petrified wood

easier. Finally, the appendix provides a comprehensive list of addresses, phone numbers, and websites of the appropriate government agencies and visitor and convention bureaus. We strongly encourage you to check on current conditions and any possible changes before setting out, especially if you'll be traveling a long distance to the trail.

An Additional Note About Safety

No guidebook can alert you to every hazard or anticipate the limitations of every reader. Therefore, the descriptions of roads, trails, routes, and natural features in this book are not representations that a particular place or excursion will be safe for your party. When you follow any of the routes described in this book, you assume responsibility for your own safety. Under normal conditions, such excursions require the usual attention to traffic, road and trail conditions, weather, terrain, the capabilities of your party, and other factors. Keeping informed on current conditions and exercising common sense are the keys to a safe, enjoyable outing.

—*The Mountaineers Books*

PHOENIX AND CENTRAL ARIZONA

Phoenix, the state's largest city with about 1.4 million residents, is at the center of what is appropriately called the Valley of the Sun, a land where the sun shines more than 325 days each year. Summers in this desert climate are hot—average high temperatures are over 100° Fahrenheit from June through August—but the rest of the year is absolutely delightful, with perfect weather for hiking and other outdoor activities from November through March.

The city and its numerous suburbs (the population of the greater Phoenix area is 3.2 million) make a good base for exploring the Superstition Mountains and other nearby public lands. The metropolitan area

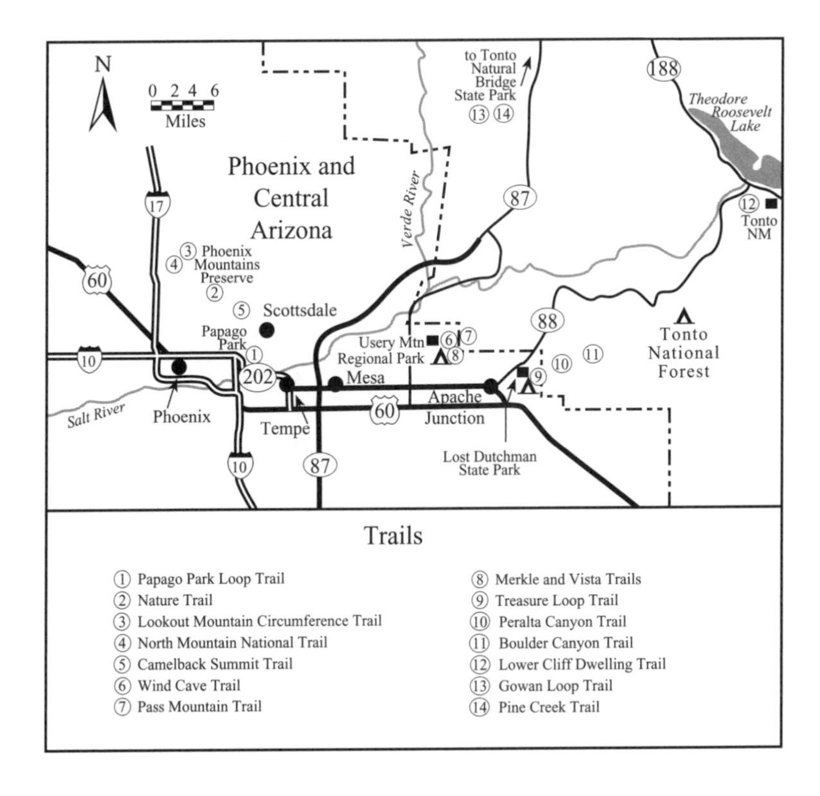

Cactus in bloom along the Nature Trail

has all the lodging, restaurants, and other amenities you could ask for, including more than 200 golf courses. There are numerous museums, spectator sports, and other attractions. A pleasant surprise is to discover that Phoenix has done a commendable job of setting aside open space, and the city, plus Maricopa County of which it is a part, has some excellent public parks. Elevation in Phoenix is just under 1100 feet.

Although there is evidence that the ancient Hohokam people lived here until about 1450, the modern city of Phoenix is relatively new, established in the late 1800s—first as a supply depot and then a rough-and-tumble Wild West town, the type that decent people avoided. It wasn't until the twentieth century that Phoenix took off, and that was in large part because of the arrival of the railroad, various projects to bring water to this desert, and probably most important, the development of air conditioning.

In addition to exploring the hiking trails in the excellent Phoenix city parks, we'll be visiting a nearby county park that was named for a nineteenth-century highwayman and horse thief, a nearby wilderness area that may hide the secret to hidden gold, and a bit farther away we'll see a prehistoric cliff dwelling and a natural rock bridge.

For additional information, contact the various government agencies mentioned below, as well as the Greater Phoenix Convention & Visitors Bureau. You'll find complete contact information in the appendix at the back of this book.

CAMPGROUNDS

There are commercial campgrounds, with RV hookups, hot showers, and all the usual amenities in Phoenix and its suburbs. Many of these are considered RV resorts, with activities, game rooms, swimming pools, and the like, and are often quite busy during the winter when snowbirds—residents of colder areas—invade this region in droves to bask in the sun and warmth. Our choice, however, is to camp at one of the very pleasant campgrounds on nearby public lands.

Usery Mountain Regional Park. A convenient location for those hiking the trails at Usery Mountain Regional Park and the surrounding areas, this very nice campground has spacious sites in a desert environment. There are water and electricity hookups, restrooms with showers, and an RV dump station. It is located on the north edge of the communities of Mesa and Apache Junction off Usery Pass Road, an extension of Ellsworth Road. From Phoenix follow US 60/Superstition Freeway east to exit 191, then head north on Ellsworth and Usery Pass roads for a little over 7 miles to the park entrance, which will be on your right. There are 73 RV sites. Open year-round; reservations not accepted. A moderate fee is charged.

Lost Dutchman State Park. In the shadow of the Superstition Mountains, Lost Dutchman State Park does not have RV hookups, but there are spacious sites, restrooms with showers, and an RV dump station. The park is 5 miles north of Apache Junction (which is about 25 miles east of Phoenix) via AZ 88, also called Apache Trail. There are 35 RV and tent campsites plus one hike- or bike-in campsite. Open year-round; reservations not accepted. A modest fee is charged.

Tonto National Forest. Excellent campgrounds are located throughout the Tonto National Forest, and dispersed camping—no established campground, no facilities, and no fee—is permitted in many parts of the forest. The forest service campgrounds do not have RV hookups, but many have restrooms with showers. Some of the higher elevation campgrounds, such as those near Roosevelt Lake east of Phoenix, are open year-round, while some of the lower elevation ones are closed during the summer. Reservations are available at some but not others. Modest fees are charged at established campgrounds. Contact the Tonto National Forest for information.

1. PAPAGO PARK LOOP TRAIL

Distance	3 miles round trip
Difficulty	Easy
Features	A convenient walk around large red rock buttes
Starting elevation	1244 feet
Highest elevation	1370 feet
Total climb	225 feet
Location	Papago Park
Map	USGS Tempe
Hiking season	Fall through early spring

Getting there: The city-run Papago Park is located in Phoenix, north of Loop 202, also called the Red Mountain Freeway. From Loop 202, go north on Priest Drive about a mile to the park, where it becomes Galvin Parkway. Turn left onto West Park Drive and follow it until it ends at a parking area. The road used to continue but has now been closed to vehicles, so you'll have to walk on either the closed road or an adjacent dirt path to the Eliot Ramada and the beginning of the actual loop around the Papago Buttes. Drinking water and restrooms are nearby. The park is open daily from sunrise to sunset.

This trail, also called the Eliot Ramada Trail, is a great place for a short walk when you're in Phoenix. It's dry as dry can be, so carry a little water as you take a pleasant walk around some prominent red buttes, colored by iron oxide-hematite. The buttes contain large, strange-looking holes, called tafoni by geologists, that were created by water seeping into the rock and dissolving the minerals.

Because this city park is crisscrossed with trails, it is difficult to be sure you're on the right one until you actually start circling the buttes. But it doesn't really matter. The buttes dominate the skyline, so simply follow the nearest path heading in their direction. The trails here are open to mountain bikers—some apparently trying to follow in the footsteps of Evel Knievel—and also to leashed pets. Glass beverage containers are prohibited.

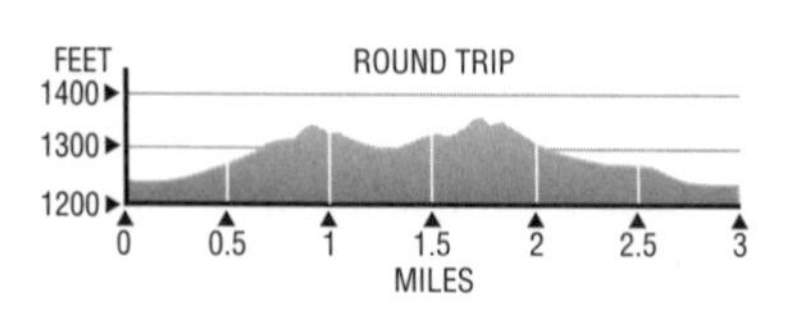

From the Eliot Ramada, walk north along the obvious dirt trail and turn either right (east) or left

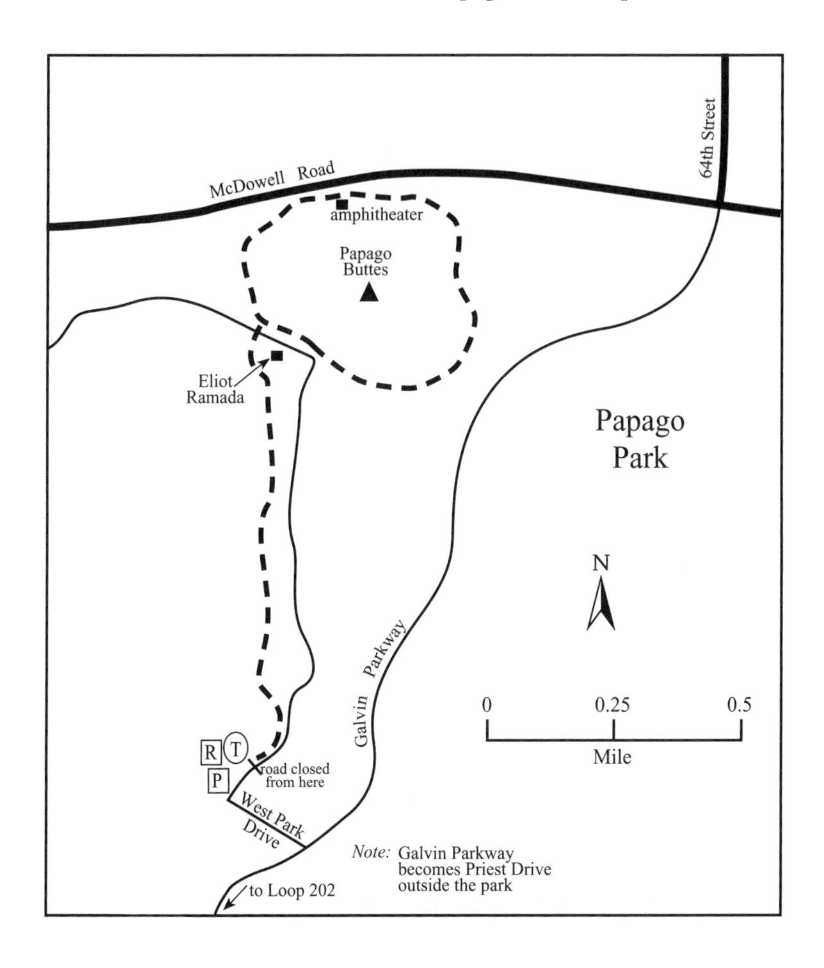

(west) when you get to the loop section. As you circle the 1663-foot sandstone buttes you'll cross a few washes and walk through typical desert terrain of creosote bush—a lot of creosote bush—plus mesquite, ironwood, and paloverde. There are also a few saguaros, mostly on the east side. The north side of the buttes parallels McDowell Road, and about halfway around the buttes, on the north side along the road, is an amphitheater.

From the amphitheater, continue around the buttes, heading south back to the parking area. If too many trail choices lead to confusion, look out over the park toward the south for a large square building, several stories high. This is Papago Park Central, and if you aim for it you'll soon find yourself in the parking lot.

Red rocks with strange-looking holes called tafoni

Prisoners Escape Papago Park

What is now a 1200-acre city park in east Phoenix, Papago Park has been many things—an American Indian reservation, a national monument, and then, during World War II, a camp to house German prisoners of war. From 1943 to 1946 more than 400 German POWs were held there, and in what is believed to be the largest POW escape in the United States, more than two dozen of the Germans escaped through an underground tunnel they had dug. It is reported that they told guards they were using the shovels to construct a volleyball court.

9. NATURE TRAIL

Distance ▪ 1.5-mile loop
Difficulty ▪ Moderate
Features ▪ An excellent trek through the rugged Sonoran Desert
Starting elevation ▪ 1550 feet
Highest elevation ▪ 1790 feet
Total climb ▪ 420 feet
Location ▪ Phoenix Mountains Preserve
Map ▪ USGS Sunnyslope
Hiking season ▪ Fall through early spring

Getting there: The trail is located in Phoenix Mountains Preserve, operated by the Phoenix Parks and Recreation Department.

From AZ 51, exit onto Lincoln Drive east to the park entrance road. Turn left (north) into the park and follow this road to Apache Picnic Area, where there is a parking lot, restrooms, and drinking water. The park is open daily from sunrise to sunset.

Among our favorite short hikes within the Phoenix city limits, this loop trail through rugged Sonoran Desert terrain offers a close-up view of the desert as it meanders through hills and valleys, with enough relatively steep hilly sections that you get a good feeling of accomplishment. There are panoramic views of Piestewa Peak to the east, occasional signs identifying the desert plants, and brown signs displaying the number 304 in white to keep you on track.

Until recently, 2608-foot Piestewa Peak was called Squaw Peak, and you may still find that name on some maps and trail descriptions. The name of the mountain and several trails near and on it was changed to honor U.S. Army Pfc. Lori Piestewa, recognized as the first female American Indian soldier to be killed in combat. A Hopi, and the mother of two children, she died March 23, 2003, when her company was ambushed near Nasiriyah, Iraq.

Because the trail is a loop, you can go in either direction; here we describe the hike going clockwise. The trail starts at a brown sign with the number 304 on it, which is located to the left of a large informational sign. There's another trailhead, where you'll return, a short distance to the right. Be sure to carry water (glass beverage containers are prohibited) because this hike is surprisingly hilly for an urban nature trail. It's open to leashed pets and mountain bikes.

The trail starts heading downhill, with a short amount of paving, and then turns to dirt. It enters a deep wash, climbs up a hillside, and then follows a ravine. The trail is rocky, fairly narrow, and lined with a variety of cacti, including prickly pear, cholla, and a lot of little barrel cacti, which have wonderful purple flowers in spring. Paloverde, mesquite, some ocotillo, creosote bush, brittlebush, and saguaro, dot the hillsides. Keep an eye out for Gambel's quail, cactus wrens—watch for their nests in holes in saguaros—mockingbirds, and turkey vultures. There are also a lot of lizards, and be sure to avoid the rattlesnakes.

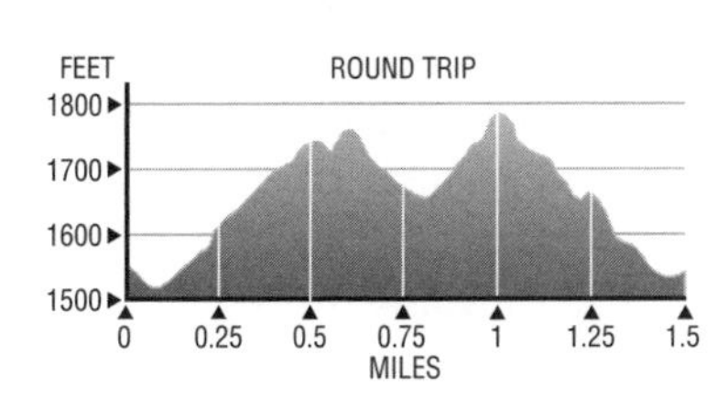

Looking to the west you'll see rocky Piestewa Peak, formed from a type of granite called schist

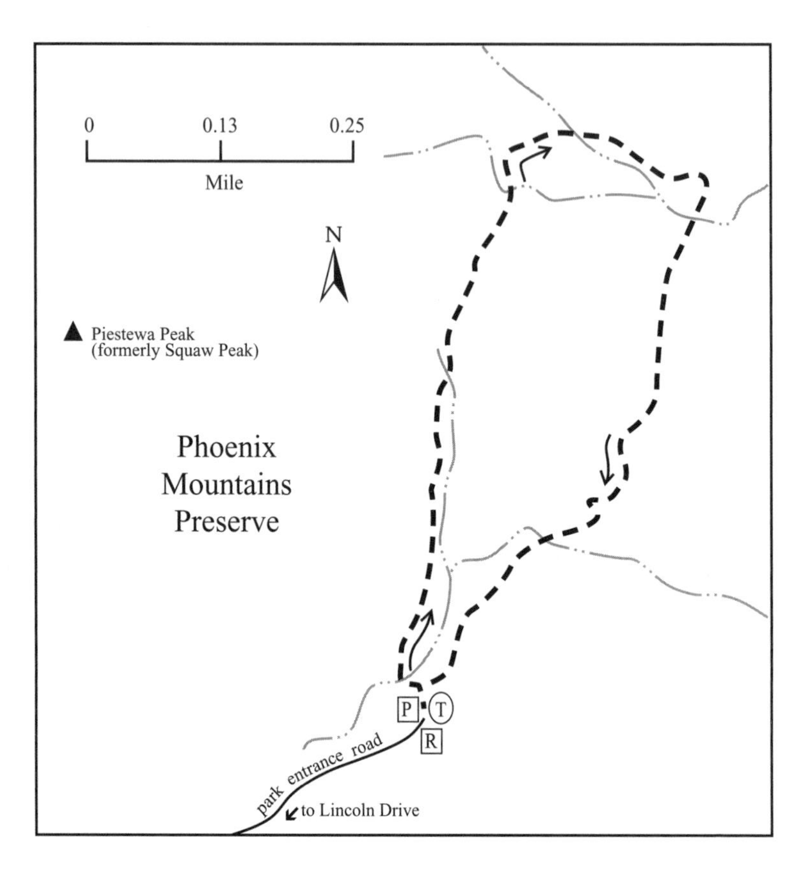

some 14 million years ago. The strenuous Piestewa Peak Summit Trail, which we do not describe in this book, takes you to the top. Information is available from preserve officials.

The trail, which has now become somewhat rocky, continues to climb as it heads north. A bit before the halfway point you'll find yourself in a wide saddle where, depending on weather conditions at the time, you'll have either a crystal-clear view of downtown Phoenix or an unpleasant scene of brown haze masking the skyline. The trail gradually makes a right turn, now heading generally east, starts dropping a bit—what goes up must come down, especially on a loop trail—and leads you away from city views into an area that deceptively appears to be out in the middle of nowhere, far from civilization.

There is an abundance of cholla and other cacti, including some

Opposite: *Cactus in bloom*

stately saguaros, as the trail crosses several rocky washes and heads south back toward the parking lot. It's especially hilly here, and the trail eventually ends in the Apache Picnic Area parking lot, about 100 feet east of where it started.

3. LOOKOUT MOUNTAIN CIRCUMFERENCE TRAIL

Distance ■ 2.6-mile loop
Difficulty ■ Easy
Features ■ An enjoyable walk around a rocky mountain
Starting elevation ■ 1550 feet
Highest elevation ■ 1700 feet
Total climb ■ 150 feet
Location ■ Phoenix Mountains Preserve
Map ■ USGS Sunnyslope, Union Hills
Hiking season ■ Fall through spring

Getting there: The Circumference Trail is located in the Lookout Mountain Area, a section of Phoenix Mountains Preserve, operated by the Phoenix Parks and Recreation Department. In Phoenix, from I-17 take exit 212 and go east on Bell Road for about 3.5 miles to 16th Street, turn right (south) and follow 16th Street a little under 1 mile into the park and to the trailhead. There are restrooms and drinking water. The park is open from sunrise to sunset. Glass containers are prohibited; leashed pets are allowed.

Lookout Mountain offers desert solitude in the middle of the city of Phoenix. The Circumference Trail circles the entire park, as well as the mountain itself, with a number of short climbs and descents, and it is one of Phoenix's lesser-used trails. There are good views of the rocky, basalt Lookout Mountain, with a desert terrain of cholla, brittlebush, creosote bush, and paloverde. Rabbits, lizards, and an occasional rock climber add a bit of variety to the hike. The trail is marked with brown posts that have the number 308 in white.

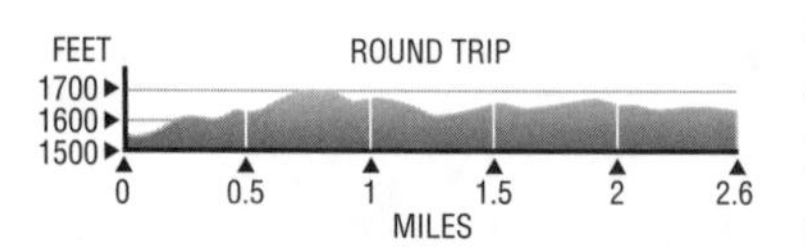

From the trailhead, go to the right to hike the loop counterclockwise, which is easier to follow. At unmarked intersections, always take the lower-altitude

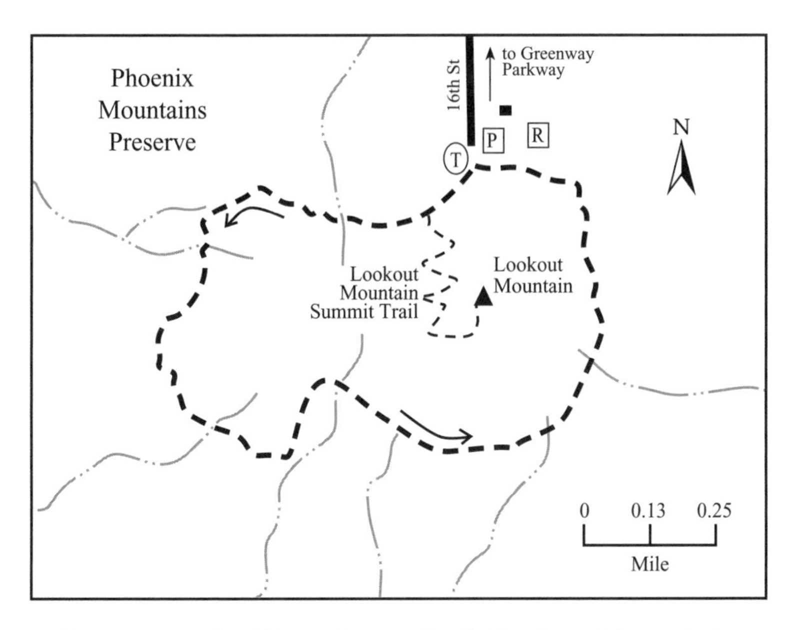

trail to stay on the Circumference Trail. Lookout Mountain is on the left as you go around it. The trail has an open feeling, with few saguaros, and the abundant brittlebush and creosote bush color the landscape with yellow blossoms in the spring. There are two types of rabbits to watch for here: the smaller cottontails with white cotton ball-like tails, and the much-larger black-tailed jackrabbits, with long legs and gigantic ears.

As you approach the north side of the mountain, you will pass the intersection with the Lookout Mountain Summit Trail. This 1.2-mile round-trip side trip to the 2054-foot summit provides wonderful views, on a moderate to strenuous hike with a climb of over 500 feet. Assuming you don't give in to the temptation to hike to the top, continue southwest on the Circumference Trail.

The trail will drop gently into a wash. Then, at the next marked intersection, stay to the right until you begin a short climb to a saddle between two peaks. Over the saddle, the walk around the westernmost mountain takes you almost into the backyards of some exclusive houses that highlight the purpose of the preserve lands—to provide open space for humans and wildlife in an otherwise crowded area. Soon the trail turns left around a mountain, with the mountainside dotted with teddybear cholla, and heads toward a shallow wash.

At about 1.2 miles you reach another saddle, which offers a good view of the twin peaks that comprise Lookout Mountain. Continuing, you'll see a sheer basalt cliff, about 70 feet high that is a favorite of rock climbers. The trail now proceeds down and along the south edge of Lookout Mountain. It seems to be littered with rocks from the cliffs above. If a rock shines a little, it may be covered with a thin coat of baked-on dust called desert varnish. At almost 2 miles the trail starts turning north, following Lookout Mountain's eastern slope. There are more plants here—suggesting that this area gets a bit more rain—and soon the trail turns west to return to the trailhead.

4. NORTH MOUNTAIN NATIONAL TRAIL

Distance	1.6-mile loop
Difficulty	Moderate to strenuous
Features	A rugged hike to a ridge offering great views of Phoenix and the nearby mountains
Starting elevation	1450 feet
Highest elevation	2100 feet
Total climb	845 feet
Location	Phoenix Mountains Preserve
Map	USGS Sunnyslope
Hiking season	Fall through spring

Getting there: The trail is in the North Mountain Recreation Area, part of the Phoenix Mountains Preserve, operated by the Phoenix Parks and Recreation Department. From Interstate 17 in Phoenix, take exit 210 and go east on Thunderbird Road about 4 miles to 7th Street, turn right and take 7th Street south just under 2 miles to Peoria Avenue, where you turn right to enter the recreation area. Turn right onto the park loop road and follow it to the Maricopa Ramada, where you'll find the trailhead, restrooms, and drinking water. Leashed dogs are permitted on the trail; glass containers are not. The recreation area is open daily from sunrise to sunset.

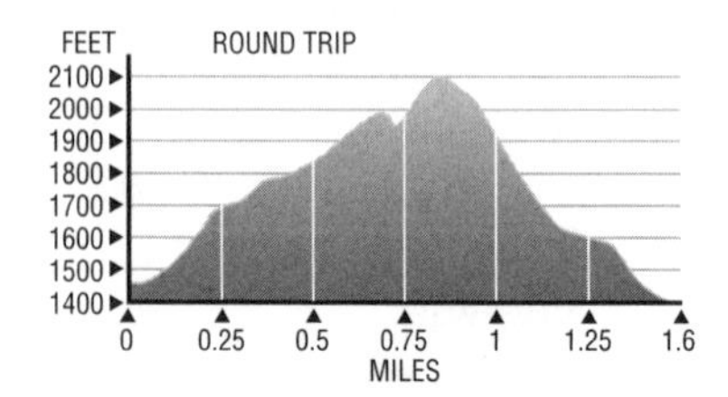

The rise and fall of the terrain give the relatively short National Trail the feel of a much longer expedition. The trail climbs one side of North Mountain, passes outcrops of black, broken volcanic rock, and

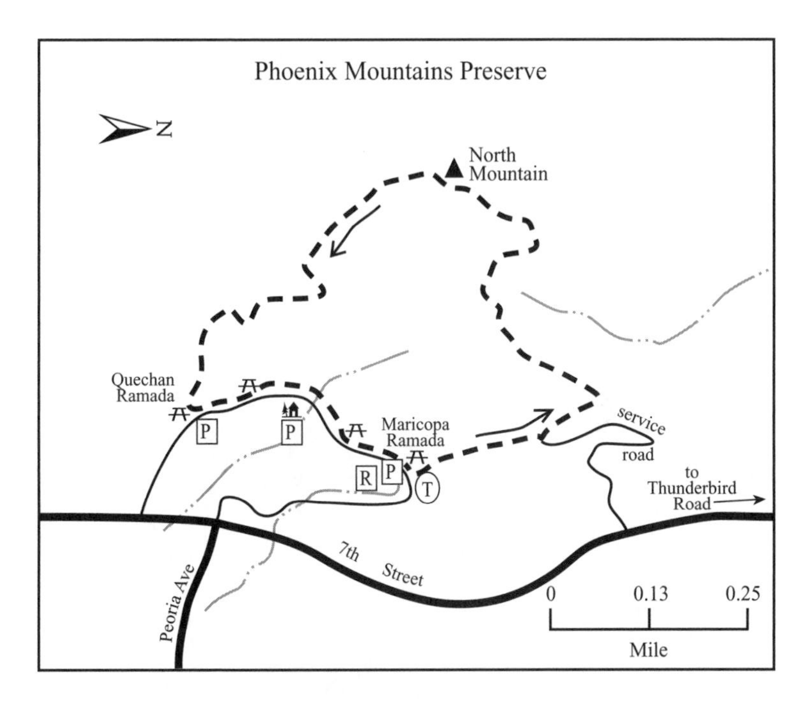

drops down the other side. It offers a lot of brittlebush and creosote bush, hard quartz rocks, the violet blossom of desert lavender (which bloom year-round), and beautiful views of the desert and city. Chipmunks and birds are often seen along the trail.

The National Trail is easy to follow, marked with square posts with number 44. It begins with a fairly gentle incline and some natural stone steps that lead to a landing, where it veers to the right to connect with a paved service road, which you will follow up the northeast side of the mountain for about 0.5 mile. The road climbs past small cliffs on the left. There are several overlooks along the way, and the road ends at a high viewpoint just below a forest of antennas and transmission towers. Here a sign shows the trail going to the left, where it turns once more to dirt—rocky, rough, and narrow in spots. A brief incline takes you to the top of a ridge that provides good views of the surrounding area.

About 0.1 mile along the ridge, an outcropping of white quartz attracts the eye because it is so white compared to the black volcanic rock that lies everywhere else. At 0.8 mile the trail reaches the summit. The actual mountaintop is fenced off, so the trail ends on a ridge to the south. From here you have a splendid view of downtown Phoenix and 2608-foot Piestewa Peak.

The trail now goes mostly south and soon begins to drop down the steep, rocky mountainside. At about the 1-mile mark, it drops past some large rocks to a fork. The path to the left goes directly to the ranger station. Stay straight on the National Trail and within 0.1 mile, a trail marker appears. The trail descends again to a three-way intersection. Take the trail to the left, which leads to the Quechan Ramada. From there, walk north along the park loop road for 0.3 mile to the trailhead at the Maricopa Ramada.

Descending North Mountain (Photo by Lawrence Letham)

5. CAMELBACK SUMMIT TRAIL

Distance ■ 2.3 miles round trip
Difficulty ■ Strenuous
Features ■ A tough climb up a mountainside rewarded with wonderful views
Starting elevation ■ 1425 feet
Highest elevation ■ 2700 feet
Total climb ■ 1500 feet
Location ■ Echo Canyon Recreation Area
Map ■ USGS Paradise Valley
Hiking season ■ Fall through spring

Getting there: The trail is in Echo Canyon Recreation Area, a Phoenix city park that lies between Paradise Valley, Scottsdale, and the Phoenix Mountains Preserve. From US 60 in Phoenix, take Rural Road, whose name later changes to Scottsdale Road, north for 11 miles. Turn left at McDonald Drive, then in 3 miles, just before the light at Tatum Boulevard, turn left onto Echo Canyon Parkway. The road dead-ends in the parking lot. Camelback is a popular place, especially on weekends, and you may have to wait for a parking space. Park only in designated spaces to avoid tickets. There is water, but no restroom, at the trailhead. Pets and glass containers are not permitted on the trail.

Not for everyone, this is a short hike on rough terrain practically straight up the side of a mountain. But it offers wonderful views for experienced hikers in excellent physical condition, and along the way there are a variety of Sonoran Desert plants, sandstone cliffs, boulders, and some strangely shaped rocks. Cottontail rabbits, Harris' antelope squirrels, lizards, and rattlesnakes are often seen.

A prominent landmark in the Phoenix area, 2704-foot Camelback Mountain has two summits that some say make it look like a kneeling camel. The camel's head (the lower summit to the west) is composed of layered sandstone, while the taller hump (to the east) is made of much older granite.

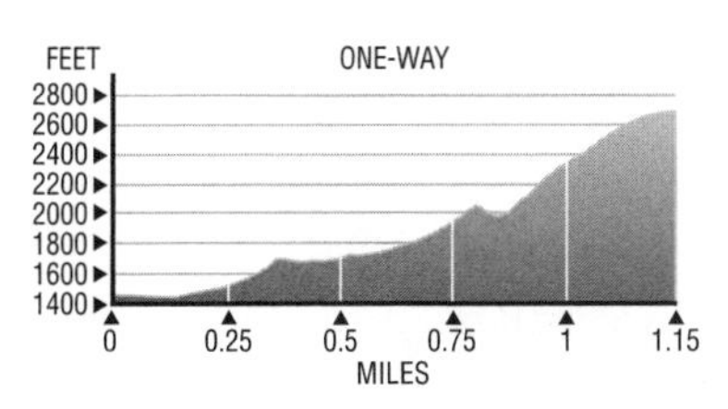

The trail starts at the covered picnic shelter at the east end of the parking lot. Follow the stairs to the left that climb the hill, where

Moon rising over Echo Canyon (Photo by Lawrence Letham)

squirrels live in the brush, and watch for the Praying Monk, a towering red-rock formation high above the trail. At an intersection at 0.25 mile, continue straight ahead, where the trail goes between a tall irregularly shaped cliff of volcanic tuff on the right and a fence to the left. Below you is Echo Canyon Bowl. At just under 0.4 mile there is a handrail to help on a very steep section of the trail. From here, continue up the hill with special care, because the rock around the handrails is slick from so much wear.

Soon there is another handrail and then a short landing, at about the 0.5-mile mark, where you can catch your breath. Near the trail are rocks with indentations cut by wind erosion. The views of the expansive city are contrasted by these strange rock formations, composed of granite, schist, and gravel, which represent the three different classes of rocks: igneous, metamorphic, and sedimentary, respectively.

At the halfway point, 0.6 mile, a rough cliff rises to one side while large boulders lie piled in the trail. Notice the branches of the paloverde tree growing in the middle of the trail. They are smooth and polished by the thousands of hands that grab them each year for support. From here the trail to the summit is steep and rocky, with numerous boulders to climb over as the route follows a series of gullies.

Once on top, the view is beautiful. You can see all the mountains of the Phoenix Mountains Preserve, dense housing, and, farther in the distance, the Superstition Mountains and a large checkerboard of plowed and planted fields. Swifts fly around the summit, and occasionally a helicopter whisks by at a low altitude.

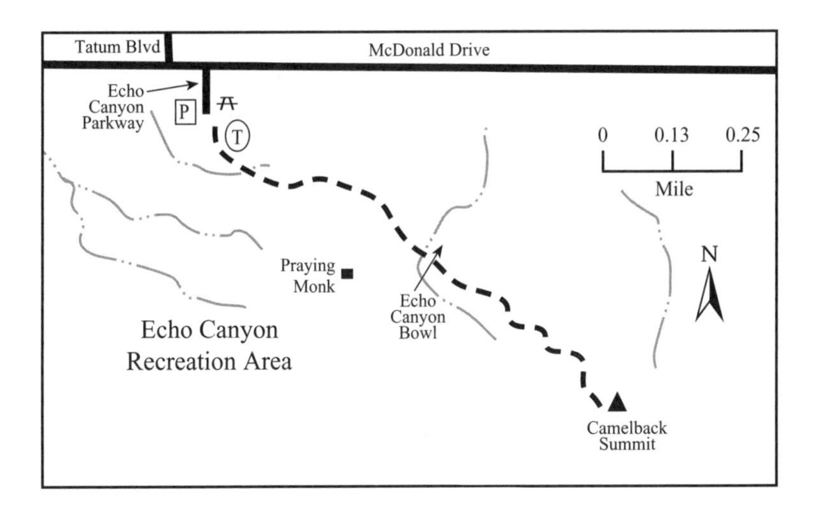

Return by the same route. When you reach the railings, it is usually easier to go down backward.

6. WIND CAVE TRAIL

Distance	3 miles round trip
Difficulty	Moderate
Features	Distant views, desert plants, and a shallow cave
Starting elevation	2049 feet
Highest elevation	2835 feet
Total climb	785 feet total
Location	Usery Mountain Regional Park
Map	USGS Apache Junction (trail not shown); park trail map
Hiking season	Fall through early spring

Getting there: The trail is in Usery Mountain Regional Park, managed by Maricopa County, which is located on the north edge of the communities of Mesa and Apache Junction off Usery Pass Road, an extension of Ellsworth Road. From Phoenix follow US 60/Superstition Freeway east to exit 191 and head north on Ellsworth and Usery Pass roads for a little over 7 miles to the park entrance on your right. At the entrance station you can get a map showing the trail location. The hike takes off from a parking

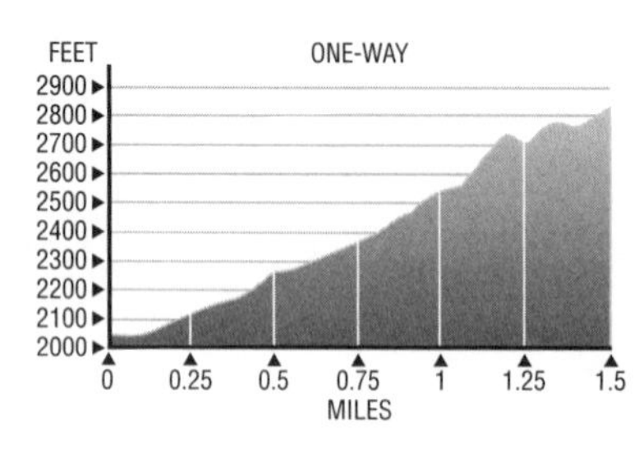

area at the top or north end of Wind Cave Drive, where there's a restroom and water available. A nominal fee is charged to enter the park. Leashed dogs are permitted; glass containers are not.

Wind Cave is one of the most popular trails in Usery Mountain Regional Park—and deservedly so. It offers panoramic views, plus wildlife and desert plants galore, and takes about 1.5 to 2 hours.

After a moist winter and spring, you'll see blooms on almost every plant, and the ocotillo may even boast small round leaves up and down its spindly arms. Be sure to watch for the lovely soft red blooms of the barrel cactus, the pale yellow of the prickly pear, and the stunning hot pink of the cholla blossoms, brilliant in the sun. Watch, too, for hummingbirds and butterflies flitting about seeking nectar and pollen.

The beginning of the hike is a stroll through a desert garden scattered with saguaro, prickly pear, barrel, hedgehog, and cholla cacti, plus ocotillo, brittlebush, creosote bush, paloverde, and desert agave. This short stretch of trail is hard-packed earth and fairly level. At about 600 feet you'll pass through the forest service boundary, and soon the trail descends into an arroyo, becoming both sandy and rocky—watch where you step as the rocks are favored hideouts for rattlesnakes. At the arroyo's bottom you'll switchback to the left and gradually emerge onto the *bajada*, or plain.

The next 0.5 mile is a gradual ascent toward the base of Pass Mountain, where the trail gradually changes from sand to gravel and becomes increasingly rock-strewn. As you climb, pause occasionally to look up, down, and around, so you don't miss the variety of vistas unfolding around you. Above and to the east is an expanse of yellow-green lichen-covered rock, which houses the cave that is your destination.

Lizards abound along this rocky trail, so keep your eyes peeled for their sudden darting moves. As the trail continues, zigzagging its way up to the cave, you'll find yourself climbing over the occasional boulder.

After about a mile there's a stone bench where you can sit and catch your breath before continuing. It faces southwest, but the view is at least 180 degrees, so relax and look about. On the hillside to your

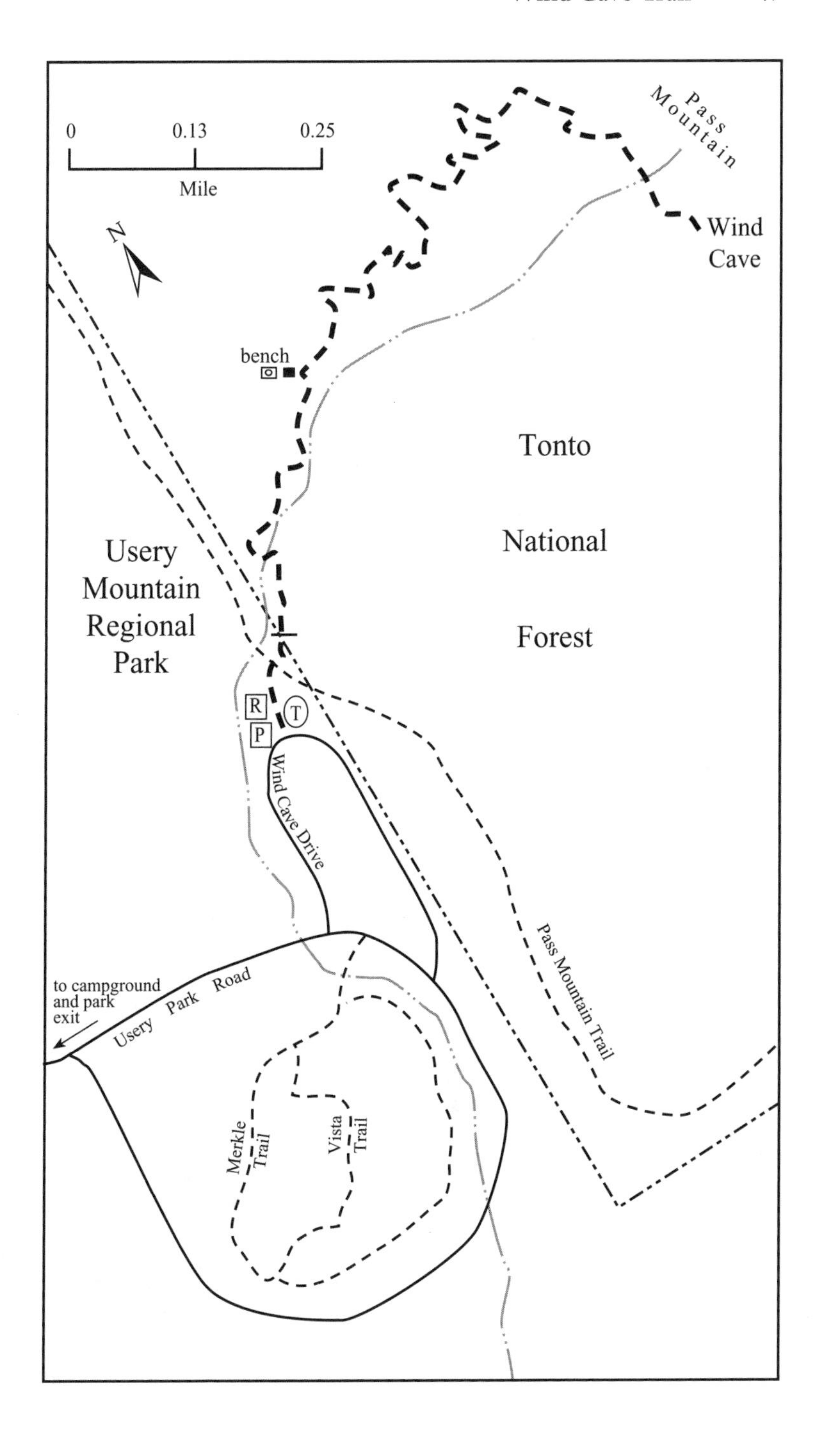
0
0.13
0.25
Mile
N
Pass Mountain
Wind Cave
bench
Tonto
National
Forest
Usery
Mountain
Regional
Park
R
T
P
Wind Cave Drive
Pass Mountain Trail
to campground
and park
exit
Usery Park Road
Merkle Trail
Vista Trail

right there's an intriguing "sign"—apparently made from white-painted rocks—pointing the way to Phoenix. Looking southwest you can see the parking area where you began, then by lifting your eyes just a bit you can see beyond that to the Merkle Hills trails, and then lifting a bit more you can see out over the park to the city of Mesa and the horizon beyond.

Back on the trail, you continue hiking over rocks, among cacti and other desert plants, climbing steadily toward your goal. In another 0.2 mile you'll find yourself moving along the face of the overhanging lichen-covered wall you saw from below. Watch for large birds emerging from above and behind the wall, soaring on air currents while eyeing the desert floor for food.

You will notice small holes and indentations in the rock face, harbingers of the cave to come. The last bit of the trail is a short steep climb to the cave, which is really little more than a larger indentation in the stone face. But it boasts a few plants clinging to its walls and

Desert views along Wind Cave Trail

ceiling, plus a busy band of bees living in numerous little holes in the wall. Ground squirrels have made their home here as well. And of course the view is grand.

Once you've looked your fill and rested a bit, retrace your steps to the trailhead.

7. PASS MOUNTAIN TRAIL

Distance	■	7.1-mile loop
Difficulty	■	Strenuous
Features	■	A rugged hike around a mountain through the desert
Starting elevation	■	1900 feet
Highest elevation	■	2550 feet
Total climb	■	660 feet
Location	■	Usery Mountain Regional Park
Map	■	USGS Apache Junction; park trail map
Hiking season	■	Fall through spring

Getting there: The trailhead is in Usery Mountain Regional Park, managed by Maricopa County. The park is located on the north edge of the communities of Mesa and Apache Junction off Usery Pass Road, an extension of Ellsworth Road. From Phoenix follow US 60/Superstition Freeway east to exit 191 and head north on Ellsworth and Usery Pass roads for a little over 7 miles to the park entrance on your right. A small fee is charged to enter the park, and at the entrance station you can get a park map. Once in the park, take Usery Park Road to the turnoff, on the left, for Wind Cave Drive, where you turn left and proceed a short distance until you see the restrooms. The trailhead is to the right and behind the restrooms, and you can also get drinking water here. Glass containers are not allowed. Mountain bikes, horses, and leashed dogs are allowed.

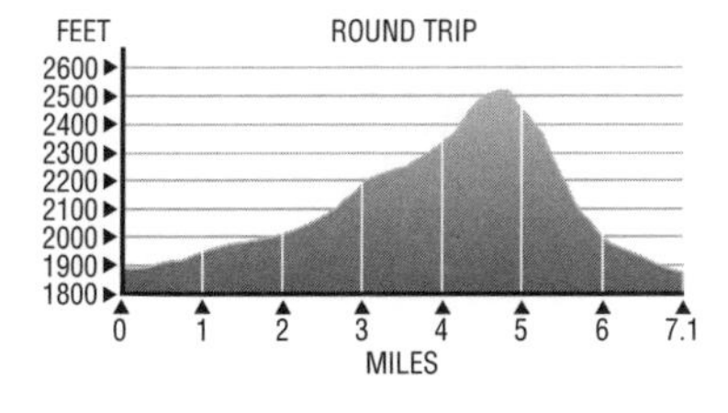

This rugged hike through the desert circles 3312-foot Pass Mountain. It is a good hike during any of the cooler months, but especially nice from February through April when the Lower

Sonoran Life Zone is in full bloom. All varieties of desert plants will be seen, especially cacti, which seem to prosper from the water they get in the more than a dozen washes you'll be crossing along the trail. Watch for the odd-looking saguaro that has six arms that bend down and around its body. Spring is also a good time to see a variety of birds here, ranging from turkey vultures to Costa's hummingbirds.

At the trailhead, Pass Mountain—known as "Scarface" to locals—stands directly ahead with a band of yellow rock cutting across its face, and the barren rock of the mountain is a stark contrast to the abundance of desert plants along the trail. A sign shows the Pass Mountain Trail to both the left and the right. Go to the left to travel clockwise around the mountain so that you'll be taking the gentler slope up and the steeper slope down. The trail is hard earth covered with decomposed granite in some places. From the beginning of the trail, there are a variety of plants, including the round, squat barrel cactus, which does not grow

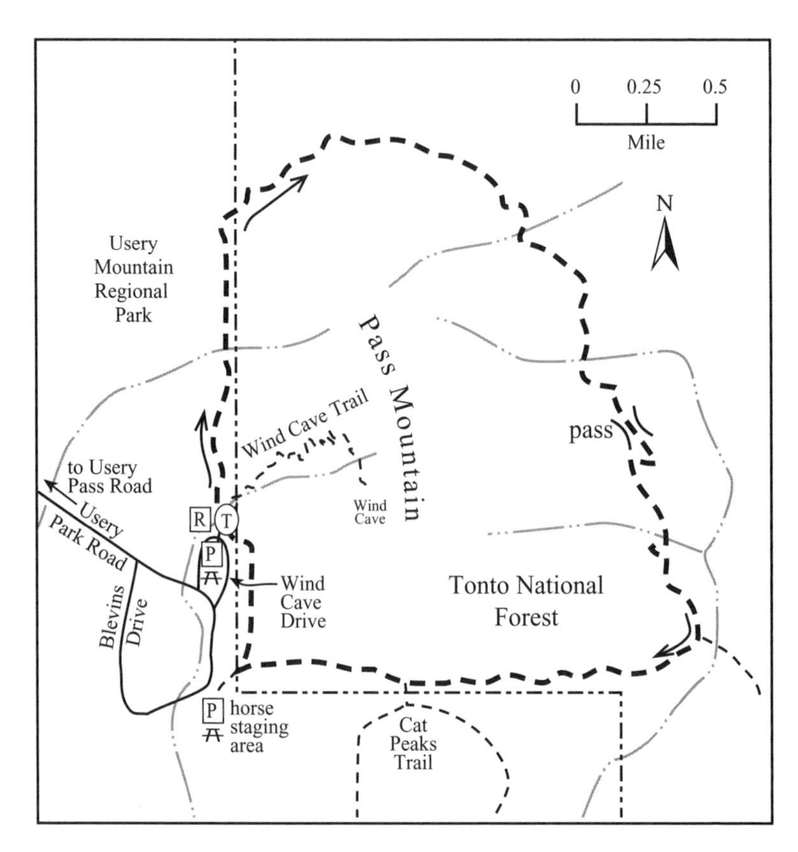

A small cavern formed by boulders (Photo by Lawrence Letham)

straight up into the air but leans noticeably southward because it grows toward the most constant source of sunlight.

The first of many washes cuts across the trail at 0.15 mile, and then, at about 0.7 mile, there is a deeper wash with 8-foot-high rocks lining its sides that protect it from the gouging, erosive force of rainwater. Just beyond that wash the trail begins to climb fairly steeply. A dead saguaro cactus lies next to the trail. Although the roots of a saguaro spread out as far as the cactus is tall, they do not grow deeply. Shallow roots have the advantage of collecting any scarce rain that may fall, but they cannot provide the support necessary to keep the cactus from blowing over in strong winds.

Buckthorn, brittlebush, and teddybear and chain-fruit cholla grow abundantly next to the trail, along with prickly pear cactus and some saguaros. You'll also likely see plenty of lizards and birds such as rock wrens, cactus wrens, verdins, black-throated sparrows, black-tailed gnatcatchers, and Gila woodpeckers. As the trail begins to curve around the mountain, a sign at 1.2 miles marks the boundary to the Tonto National Forest. Once around the north end of the mountain, the plant life and terrain change. There are fewer saguaros, and other cacti and scrub bushes like creosote, as well as boulders, dominate the scene. By the 2-mile mark, a large valley opens to the left, with tall mountains in the distance, including Four Peaks. The trail soon hugs the mountain on the right as it drops into a gulch.

At about 3 miles, the trail appears to break off to the left to go around some small mountains, but actually continues straight ahead. The trail begins a steep descent through a pass between two hills, and at about 3.5 miles, as the trail passes through a wash, watch for a saguaro that has six arms twisting down and around its body—an unusual pose for a cactus. At a little under 4 miles, the trail climbs to a pass—the hike's high point—and then starts to drop dramatically, becoming rocky with loose gravel. About 0.2 mile farther an old trail takes off to the left; be sure to stay to the right. As the trail continues around the southeast corner of the mountain, the plants grow closer together and the washes appear with more frequency. Several more trails take off to the left, but you'll want to stay to the right to return to the trailhead.

Mountain and Park Named for Thief

Usery Mountain Regional Park, east of Phoenix, is named for Usery Mountain, which took its name from a nineteenth-century cattleman-turned-outlaw named King Usery (also sometimes spelled Ussery). Apparently Usery was not doing too well in the cattle business, so in late 1891 or early 1892, he and an accomplice held up a stagecoach, stealing two bars of silver bullion valued at $2,000. To make matters worse, it seems that Usery had stolen a horse to use in the robbery. He was captured, convicted, and sentenced to seven years in the Territorial Prison in Yuma. One bullion bar was recovered, but it is not clear whether Usery's accomplice was ever captured or if the other bullion bar was recovered. Usery was pardoned two years later, but soon wound up in jail again for horse stealing. After serving that term, he wisely disappeared.

8. MERKLE AND VISTA TRAILS

Distance ▪	1.2 miles round trip
Difficulty ▪	Easy
Features ▪	A level nature trail combined with a trek over two small hills
Starting elevation ▪	1910 feet
Highest elevation ▪	2050 feet
Total climb ▪	200 feet
Location ▪	Usery Mountain Regional Park
Map ▪	USGS Apache Junction; park trail map
Hiking season ▪	Fall through spring

Getting there: The trails are in Usery Mountain Regional Park, managed by Maricopa County. The park is located on the north edge of the communities of Mesa and Apache Junction off Usery Pass Road, an extension of Ellsworth Road. From Phoenix follow US 60/Superstition Freeway east to exit 191 and head north on Ellsworth and Usery Pass roads for a little over 7 miles to the park entrance on your right. A nominal fee is charged to enter the park. At the entrance station you can get a map showing the trail location. Once in the park, continue straight on Usery Park Road to covered picnic shelter #6, on the right side of the road just past Wind Cave Drive. The trailhead is obvious; nearby there are restrooms and drinking water. Glass containers, mountain bikes, and horses are not permitted; leashed dogs are allowed.

The Merkle and Vista Trails, when combined, are especially rewarding for those hiking with children. The Merkle Trail loop is a nature trail with signs marking and describing the plants of the Lower Sonoran Desert, and the two rocky hills crossed by the Vista Trail provide a bit of adventure and a feeling of accomplishment.

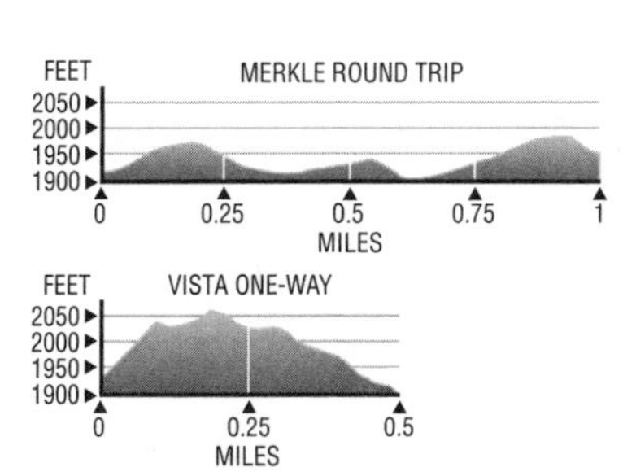

A short spur trail from the parking lot leads through a wash, where there is a prominent dead saguaro, to the Merkle Trail, which loops around the two small hills. Both trails are packed gravel; the Merkle Trail is wheelchair accessible. Because it is impossible to get lost, you can go in either direction on the Merkle Trail until you find either end of the Vista Trail going up the side of the hill. The hike described here takes the Merkle Trail to the right to first go over the low mountains on the Vista Trail and then return on the west portion of the Merkle Trail.

At about 0.2 mile from the trailhead the Merkle Trail junctions with the Vista Trail. Take the Vista Trail to the left and follow it as it heads uphill in a somewhat zigzag fashion. Once on top—which doesn't take very long—the peaks offer a good view of the entire area, including the Phoenix suburb of Mesa to the west and the Superstition Mountains to the east, and the desert plants that grow as far as the eye can see. The trail leads from the first peak to a valley between the small mountains at 0.4 mile, where boulders ranging from 2 to 6 feet high provide a place to sit and watch for birds and the numerous small lizards that populate the area.

Continue across the saddle to the other peak, and head down the Vista Trail to its other end's intersection with the Merkle Trail at 0.6 mile. Go right on the Merkle Trail. Orange and green lichens add splashes of color to the rocks scattered across the hillsides, and barrel cactus, cholla, saguaro, ocotillo, paloverde, and other desert plants dominate the landscape. In one section there is an abundance of fishhook cacti, named because their spines resemble large, barbed fishhooks. Benches are placed at intervals along the trail, and the plants, animals, and geology of the Lower Sonoran Desert are discussed in trailside signs.

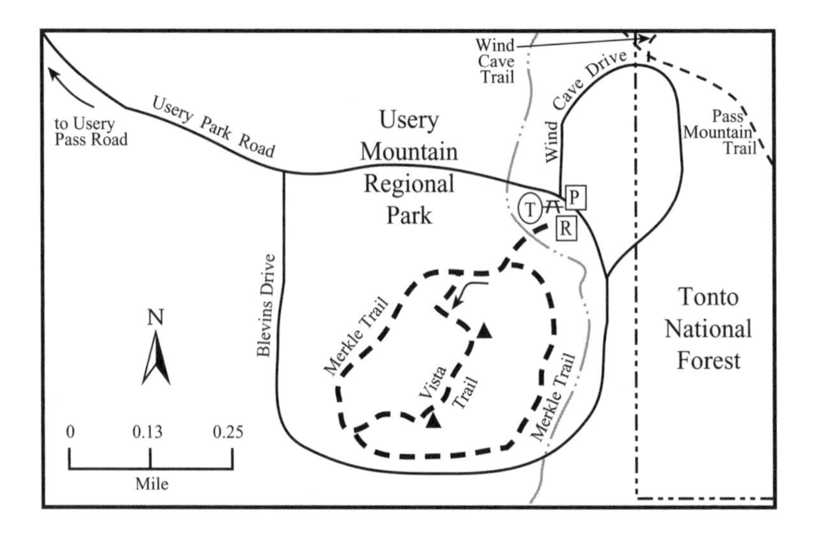

Cholla, barrel, and saguaro cactus

In another 0.4 mile, the trail reaches the intersection of Merkle and Vista Trails where you first ascended via the Vista Trail. Stay left on the Merkle Trail and head back to the parking lot. An alternative, which will add a bit over 1 mile round-trip, is to continue around the east side of the Merkle Trail to the far end of the Vista Trail, and then turn around to return to the parking lot via the same route.

9. TREASURE LOOP TRAIL

Distance	2.4-mile loop
Difficulty	Moderate
Features	A desert hike among saguaro cacti offering panoramic views
Starting elevation	2100 feet
Highest elevation	2590 feet
Total climb	525 feet
Location	Lost Dutchman State Park
Map	USGS Goldfield
Hiking season	Fall through spring

Getting there: The Treasure Loop Trail begins and ends in Lost Dutchman State Park, but practically all of the rest of it is outside the park, in the Mesa Ranger District of the Tonto National Forest. The state park is 5 miles north of Apache Junction (which is about 25 miles east of Phoenix) via AZ 88, also

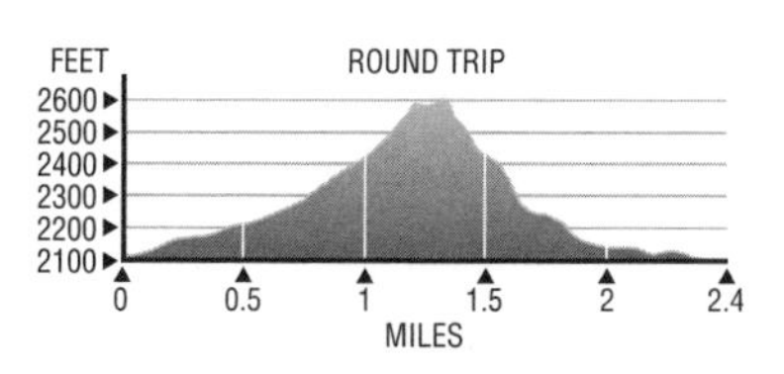

called Apache Trail. After entering the park, follow the park road to an intersection, turn left and continue to the Cholla Day Use Area, which has restrooms, drinking water, and picnic tables. The trailhead is on the north side of the parking lot. Although mostly easy, the trail does have a few steep sections.

Splendid up-close views of the mysterious Superstition Mountains, accented by tall saguaro cacti, plus sweeping panoramas to the west make this a very worthwhile hike at any time, but especially late in the day, when the setting sun turns the rocky landscape blood-red. Desert wildflowers can be beautiful from February through April, and cacti are usually in bloom from April through June, with May the best time to see blooming saguaros. Stumbling upon a large cache of gold would be a bonus, of course. See the sidebar "Thar's Gold in Them Thar Hills (Maybe)" below.

Almost immediately after starting, the trail passes through a gate as it enters the national forest. The wide dirt trail rises gradually, passing numerous stately saguaros and other cacti, plus jojoba and paloverde. At about 0.4 mile the trail crosses the north-south Jacob's Trail and then begins to climb more steeply as it follows a rocky ridge that overlooks two washes. You are now at the base of the Superstition Mountains. Looking to the north-northeast is a volcanic rock formation—a pinnacle that is called Praying Hands.

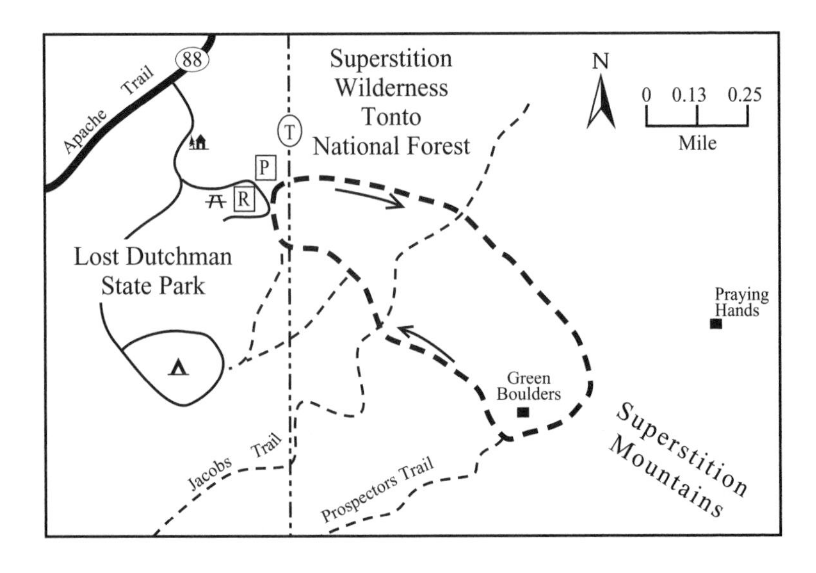

Hiking the Treasure Loop Trail

At about 1.2 miles the Treasure Loop Trail reaches its highest point, which offers spectacular views off to the west—a series of mountains with the city of Phoenix at their feet. The trail passes the Green Boulders—rocks covered with algae—and then at 1.3 miles junctions with Prospectors Trail. Continue right to stay on Treasure Loop Trail as it drops fairly quickly down switchbacks and steps, past some huge boulders, before again crossing Jacobs Trail. From here it gradually levels out and you walk through a forest of saguaro, paloverde, and cholla cacti. The trail reenters Lost Dutchman State Park. Several trails branch off Treasure Loop Trail, but stay to the right to return to the Cholla Day Use Area.

Thar's Gold in Them Thar Hills (Maybe)

Lost Dutchman State Park sits quietly at the foot of the Superstition Mountains, providing not only spectacular views but a handy base camp for hikers heading out into the mountains, perhaps in search of the Lost Dutchman Gold Mine. Legend has it that in the 1840s a prospecting family from northern Mexico named Peralta developed a rich gold mine in the Superstitions, but during a trip to haul gold back to Mexico they were ambushed by Apaches, and almost the entire party was killed. Then, in the 1870s, a German immigrant named Jacob Waltz, known as "the Dutchman," is said to have found the mine, worked it, and stashed piles of gold in the mountains. Waltz's partner, Jacob Weiser, died mysteriously, killed by Apaches or, some say, by Waltz. Waltz died in the early 1890s and on his deathbed revealed somewhat vague directions to the mine and caches of gold. Although numerous people have searched the Superstition Mountains through the years, nothing has been found.

10. PERALTA CANYON TRAIL

Distance	4.5 miles round trip
Difficulty	Moderate to strenuous
Features	Panoramic views reached via a steep, boulder-strewn trail
Starting elevation	2400 feet
Highest elevation	3766 feet
Total climb	1365 feet
Location	Superstition Wilderness, Tonto National Forest
Map	USGS Weavers Needle, Tonto National Forest
Hiking season	Fall through early spring

Getting there: The trail is in the Superstition Wilderness Area, in the Mesa Ranger District of the Tonto National Forest. To get to the trailhead, drive east from Phoenix on US 60 (Superstition Freeway), passing through the community of Apache Junction, and just past mile marker 204 turn left (north) onto Peralta Road. Follow Peralta Road through a fairly new subdivision, where the road is paved for the first mile, and then continue for 6 miles on dirt to a parking area for the trail. A small fee is charged.

This popular hike—in our opinion one of the state's best—has something for everyone: enough of a challenge to work up a sweat and make you feel you've accomplished something, a variety of flora and scenic views along the way, and spectacular panoramic views at the turnaround point.

The dirt road is passable for all types of vehicles, but is washboard in spots, so motor homes will likely be going very slowly. It's a very popular trail, so there will probably be a lot of activity in the parking area. Vehicle break-ins here are fairly common, so be sure to lock your vehicle and keep valuables out of sight. There are vault toilets but no drinking water available at the trailhead.

The trail into Peralta Canyon begins as a typical gravel path, but it soon becomes evident that there are more rocks and boulders than dirt, and by the time you reach the higher elevations much of the trail is over large sections of bare bedrock. However, the trail has an adequate supply of shade as well, provided by oaks and sumacs, and in some spots you'll find almost-comfortable chair-shaped boulders.

Those hiking in spring, especially after a wet winter, will likely see a plethora of wildflowers such as yellow spiny daisies, Mexican gold poppies, desert phlox, globemallow, wild heliotropes, Indian paintbrush, and several species of cactus. Hikers in most seasons will also see numerous small lizards.

Almost immediately the hike offers splendid views of a variety of rock formations, ranging from arches and windows to pinnacles and balancing rocks. Much of this is from tuff—rock created of ash from volcanic activity—and some is colored a rich brown by iron oxide. The scenery is good all along, but there is a genuine photo op of some great rock formations to the north at about 1.75 miles into the canyon.

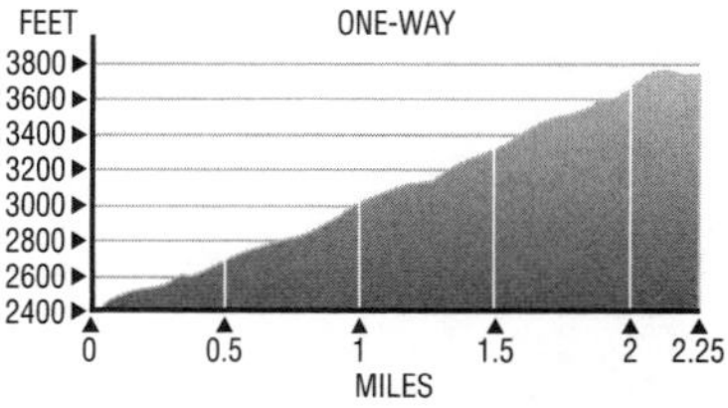

After about 2 miles the vegetation changes a bit, with an abundance of agave and prickly pear cacti. This is also a good spot to look back down the canyon—the splendid views are somewhat like

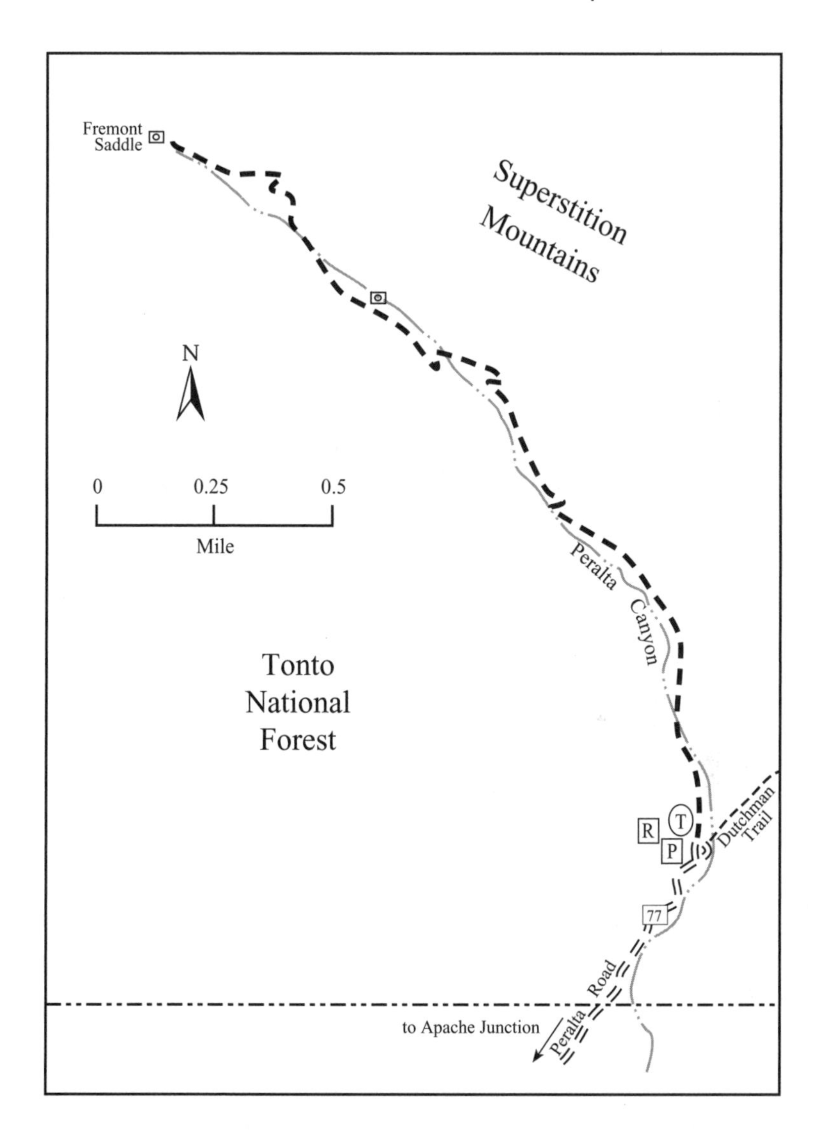

the Grand Canyon. From here there is less shade and the trail seems a bit steeper.

Fremont Saddle offers panoramic views in practically all directions. Most prominent is Weavers Needle, a towering volcanic pinnacle believed to have been named for nineteenth-century mountain man and

Opposite: *Weavers Needle, a towering volcanic pinnacle*

scout Pauline Weaver (yes a man, despite the name), who was born in Tennessee about 1800 and came to Arizona in the late 1820s.

Legend has it that the shadow of Weavers Needle marks the spot where German prospector Jacob Waltz—known as the Dutchman—discovered an old and very rich Spanish gold mine in the late 1800s, and killed anyone who attempted to find it. Over the years, many people have searched for the gold and a number of them have died, often under mysterious circumstances, or have simply disappeared, but the mine has never been found.

From Fremont Saddle, head back down the trail to the parking area.

11. BOULDER CANYON TRAIL

Distance ■ 5 miles round trip
Difficulty ■ Moderate to strenuous
Features ■ A rugged trail offering views of impressive rock formations and a man-made lake
Starting elevation ■ 1700 feet
Highest elevation ■ 2325 feet
Total climb ■ 900 feet
Location ■ Superstition Wilderness, Tonto National Forest
Map ■ USGS Mormon Flat Dam
Hiking season ■ Fall through spring

Getting there: This trail is located in the Superstition Wilderness Area in the Mesa Ranger District of the Tonto National Forest. From Phoenix take US 60 east to exit 196 north, Idaho Road/AZ 88, which you follow north until AZ 88 turns right (east) onto Apache Trail. Follow Apache Trail/AZ 88 northeasterly about 13 miles to the Canyon Lake Marina. Leave your vehicle in the marina parking lot and cross the road for the signed trailhead, which is near some white posts. Leashed pets are allowed; mountain bikes are not. There is no water along the way, so take all you need. You'll find water and restrooms at the marina.

Boulder Canyon Trail provides spectacular views of the Superstition Wilderness and Canyon Lake as it meanders through rocky washes and a rugged terrain of volcanic rock, where birds of prey soar high

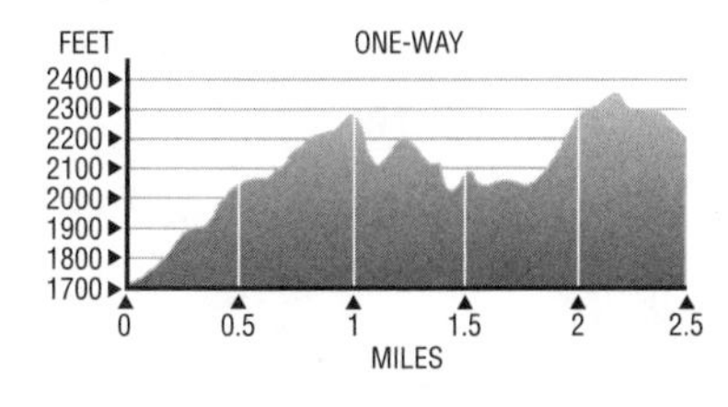

above barren cliffs. The beauty of Weavers Needle, square mesas, and the deep erosion scars of Geronimo Head are the backdrop for wildflowers, cholla, pincushion cacti, and an abundance of black volcanic rock.

As you cross through the white posts, stay to the left as the trail climbs the first of several small hills. The people you see floating in the small arm of the lake below are anglers. Behind the lake is a light-colored mountain with brown rocks spotted across it. This entire area was born of volcanoes: the dark rock was left by basaltic lava that comes from the earth's mantle and the lighter rock comes from either a thick lava composed of silica or from hot volcanic ash that melded together to form tuff.

At 0.35 mile, you arrive at the top of another small hill where

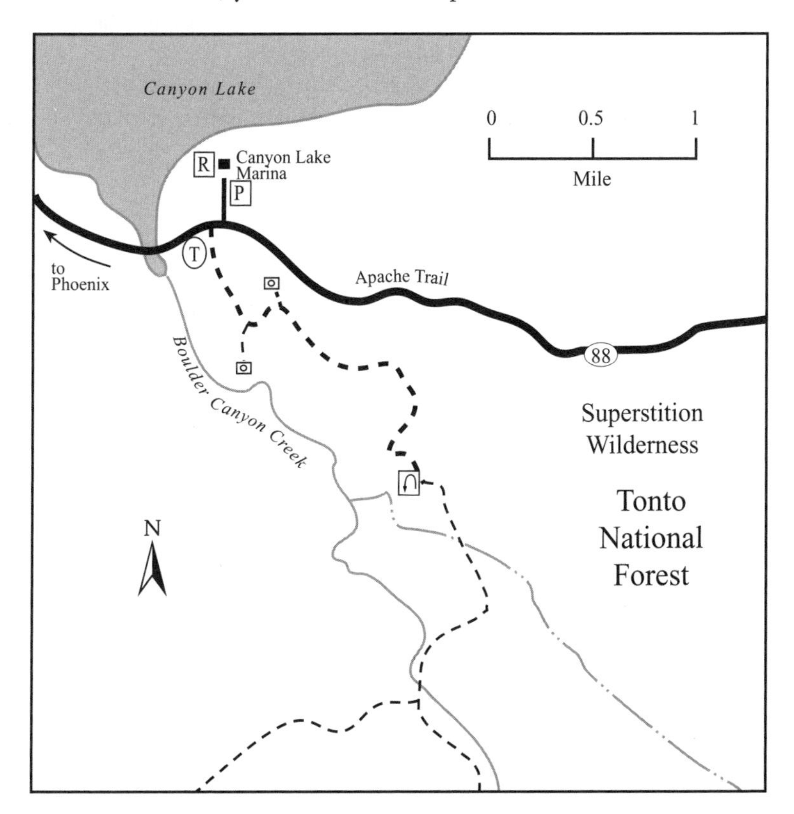

A man-made lake in the desert (Photo by Lawrence Letham)

you see the sheer canyon cliffs rise out of the waters of Canyon Lake, with Four Peaks in the background. The lake was formed by Mormon Flat dam, when it was built in 1925. The first superb view of Weavers Needle is from an outlook at the 0.5-mile point, where a sign marks the Superstition Wilderness boundary. Take a detour here by continuing straight ahead for about 200 feet to the lookout where there is a good view of Weavers Needle framed by two square mesas. A dry riverbed wends its way through the valley far below. This is also a good spot to watch for red-tailed hawks and turkey vultures.

Now return to the wilderness boundary sign, where the trail continues up a hill and then doubles back to offer another view of the lake. At 0.75 mile, a side trail to the left leads to an overview of the lake. Look across the water to see part of the dam at the far end. Return to the main trail, which now climbs and descends over several small hills. At about the 1-mile point the trail ascends a hill where overlooks provide an excellent view of Weavers Needle.

Up to this point the trail is wide with solid rock in many places, but it now narrows and plants crowd the edges. It passes behind some hills that hide the needle and the lake, but new canyons open to view. Continue up and down small hills to a wash of solid rock that rises on the left, where small depressions formed by wind and water erosion are abundant. Past the wash, cholla, saguaros, and other typical desert plants grow freely, and hummingbirds are commonly seen.

At about 2.4 miles the trail appears to fork, but the right branch is blocked with rocks, so veer to the left and follow the cairns. Switchbacks begin to descend into the valley. Just beyond a narrow passage between two large boulders, the vista opens to the deep valley, revealing mesas and faraway piles of huge boulders. To the east, the yellow, deeply furrowed rock of Geronimo Head can be seen rising high into the sky. Although the trail continues down into the valley to the dry riverbed, we recommend turning back here, after enjoying the view, and returning to the trailhead by the same route.

12. LOWER CLIFF DWELLING TRAIL

Distance ■ 1 mile round trip
Difficulty ■ Moderate
Features ■ Hike up a desert hillside to a prehistoric cliff dwelling
Starting elevation ■ 2805 feet
Highest elevation ■ 3155 feet
Total climb ■ 410 feet
Location ■ Tonto National Monument
Map ■ USGS Windy Hill
Hiking season ■ Year-round (hot in summer)

Getting there: The trail is in Tonto National Monument, which is about 110 miles east of Phoenix and 4 miles east of Roosevelt Dam along AZ 188. Follow the monument entrance road to the visitor center parking lot. The monument is open daily (except Christmas) from 8:00 AM to 5:00 PM, but the hike to the Lower Cliff Dwelling must be started by 4:00 PM. A modest fee is charged to enter the monument. Begin your visit in the visitor center to learn a bit about the people who lived here and to get a copy of the Lower Cliff Dwelling Trail Guide. The visitor center also has restrooms and drinking water. Leashed pets are permitted on the trail.

Climbing up a saguaro-studded hillside, this pleasant hike leads to a well-preserved cliff dwelling built some 700 years ago by people of the Salado culture. Along the way you'll see birds and other wildlife and walk through a Sonoran Desert environment of cacti, ocotillo, yucca, paloverde, and cholla.

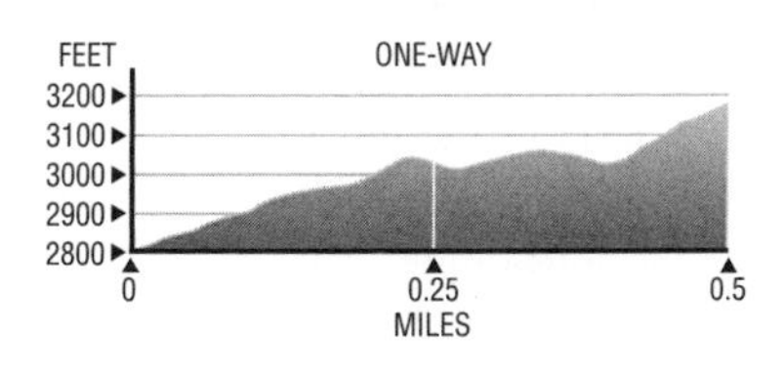

Easily seen from the visitor center parking lot, the Lower Ruin contains about twenty rooms built

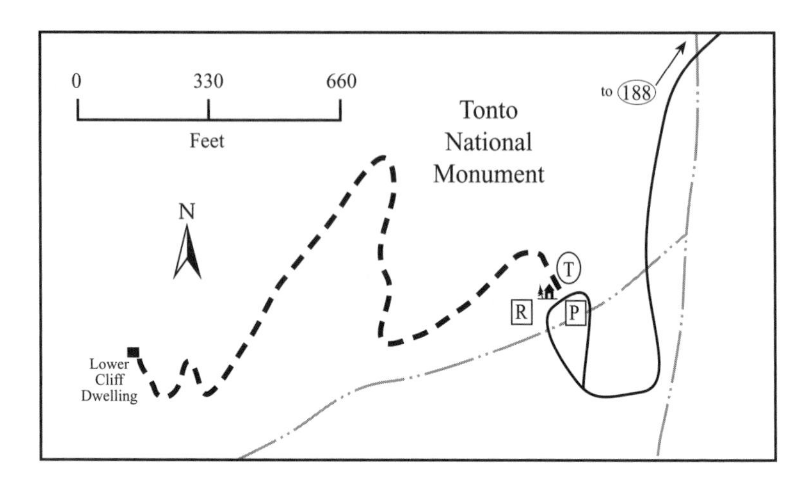

into a shallow cave that allowed the low winter sun in but shaded the rooms from the hot summer sun, which is higher in the sky. Archeologists believe that from forty to sixty people lived here, and along its walls, some blackened by cooking and heating fires, are marks left by the residents' hands and fingers, apparently from smoothing wet mud plaster. About 300 feet north of the Lower Ruin are the much-weathered remains of what is believed to have been an annex of about a dozen additional rooms.

The trail begins at the parking lot, and although it is paved it climbs steadily for 350 feet, with little shade from the desert sun. Benches along the trail offer a welcome respite from the climb, but even if you don't want a breather, it is worth stopping occasionally to look behind you at the panoramic views of the valley stretched out below.

Although the towering saguaros seem to dominate the hillside, as the trail begins to climb you'll notice a number of other plants. These include paloverde, easily identified by its green bark, ocotillo, brittlebush, mesquite, prickly pear and teddybear cholla cactus, agave, and yucca. The trail, which has been heading mostly southwest, switchbacks to the north at about 0.15 mile, then switchbacks back to the southwest at about the 0.25-mile point. From here it continues fairly straight to the base of the cliff dwellings. From the upper elevations of the trail there are wonderful panoramic views to the east, out across the valley and of Roosevelt Lake, created by the construction of a dam in 1911.

The trail leads directly into the cliff dwellings, where you can examine their construction techniques, comment at how small some of the rooms are, and notice the walls blackened by ancient fires.

The walls are made of stone and mud, with roofs held up by beams, poles, and the ribs of saguaro cacti covered with mud. Archeologists say the cliff dwellings were built around AD 1300, and occupied for 100 to 150 years, when the Salado left. We can only guess where they went.

Actually, there is a lot we do not know about the Salado. Evidence suggests they used irrigation for farming and grew corn, beans, squash, and cotton. They also ate the fruits of cacti, prickly pear cactus pads, and the beans and seeds of various desert plants. The Salado hunted, primarily deer and rabbits, but also prairie dogs, gophers, wood rats, birds, and even snakes and lizards. It is believed that the Salado women were the potters, who created beautiful polychrome pottery, and that the men wove sandals and baskets from yucca and agave leaves and clothing from the cotton they grew.

After exploring the cliff dwellings, head back down the trail along the same route to the visitor center parking lot.

Exploring ancient cliff dwellings

Ancient Peoples Made Good Use of Plants

The Salado people, who lived in what is now southern Arizona some 700 years ago, couldn't afford to waste anything. They ate the fruit of the saguaros and used the tall ribs in their home construction, and they made sandals, nets, and cord from the leaves of the agave plant, keeping other parts of the plant for food. But the Salado's top prize for usefulness has to go to the yucca: they ate the stalks and buds, used the roots to produce soap, created sewing needles from the leaf tips, and made sandals, clothing, mats, and cord from the leaf fiber.

13. GOWAN LOOP TRAIL

Distance ■ 0.5-mile loop
Difficulty ■ Moderate
Features ■ A shady hike through a forest with a pretty creek and impressive natural stone bridge
Starting elevation ■ 4533 feet
Highest elevation ■ 4533 feet
Total climb ■ 185 feet
Location ■ Tonto Natural Bridge State Park
Map ■ USGS Buckhead Mesa
Hiking season ■ Year-round

Getting there: The trail is in Tonto Natural Bridge State Park, which is about 10 miles north of Payson (Payson is about 80 miles north of Phoenix) via AZ 87 and the state park access road. Once inside the park, follow the road to the last parking lot—the one closest to the bridge. A path leads to the bridge and Gowan Loop Trail, which starts near an outdoor display that shows how the bridge was formed. Restrooms and drinking water are nearby. There is a fee to enter the park. Pets and glass containers are not permitted on the trail.

This huge stone bridge, formed by eroded deposits of limestone, is believed to be the largest natural travertine bridge in the world. It all began when a series of volcanic eruptions, followed by erosion and uplifts, created the narrow Pine Creek Canyon. Then springs carried carbonate

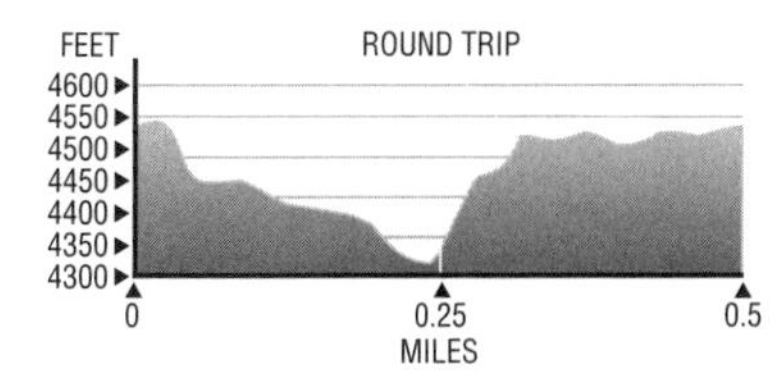

to form a natural dam, and water from Pine Creek eventually cut a hole through the dam to create Tonto Natural Bridge, which is 183 feet high, 150 feet wide, and 400 feet long. The best views of the natural bridge are from the Gowan Loop Trail, which is steep and rough, and leads to an observation deck at the base of the bridge. The water of Pine Creek also supports riparian plants such as oak trees, while the many crevices in the rock provide homes for birds.

Although you can hike the loop in either direction, it is easiest to go clockwise. Start by turning left at the trailhead and going down into the canyon on the steepest part, which includes quite a few uneven rock steps. Then the return to the top will be on an easier grade on the other side of Pine Creek. Hiking boots with good traction soles are advised, since rocks at the bridge tend to be wet and slippery. This trail is a bit of work, but it is particularly pretty, with a lot of trees and impressive boulders, and the views of the natural bridge are spectacular.

From the trailhead, the dirt path heads down through a forest of piñon, juniper, Arizona cypress, and oak. At 0.15 mile, you can see water flowing over the bridge—it was the flow of water that formed the bridge thousands of years ago. After another 0.1 mile the trail turns

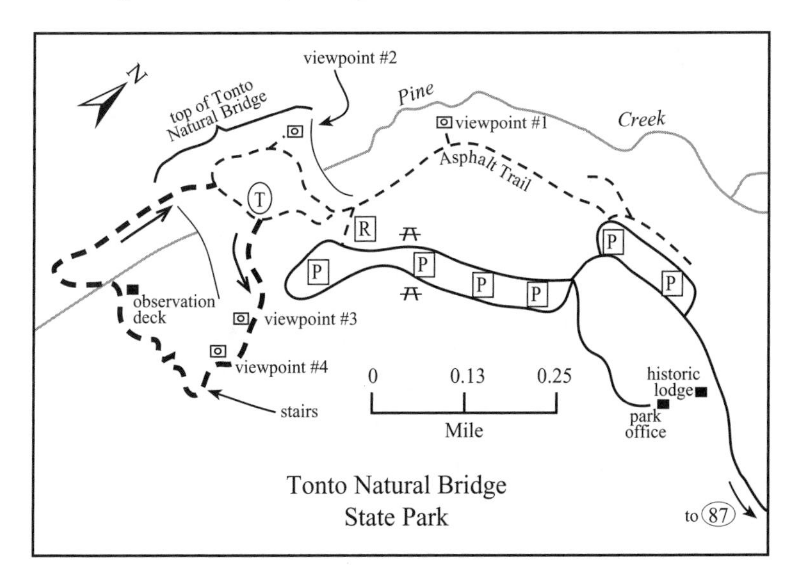

to steep wooden stairs with a handrail. Here you'll notice that the cliff to the right supports red wildflowers frequented by butterflies, while the view to the left is filled with smooth sumac trees that have white blossoms in the spring.

The stairs descend for 0.1 mile to a wooden observation deck at the base of the bridge, a wonderfully scenic spot. The water from the top of the bridge splatters on the rocks and forms a mist in the air that makes rainbows visible when struck by the sun. You may also

Tonto Natural Bridge can be reached by both the Gowan Loop and Pine Creek trails.

see sparrows and larks swooping through the air, then disappearing into their nests in the rock crevices. A gate at the side of the platform leads under the bridge, where there are pools of water, huge chunks of travertine, and large formations covered with a thick moss. It is possible to walk under the bridge, but be careful because travertine and moss are slippery. There is a deep, still pool of water under the center of the bridge.

Swimming is prohibited directly under the bridge, but allowed elsewhere in the chilly creek, which in summer ranges from 62° to 67° Fahrenheit. Although the creek is not deep or wide enough for real swimming, you can wade or at least cool your feet. The best spot is just downstream of a footbridge along the Gowan Loop Trail.

The trail continues from the observation deck over a wooden bridge that spans Pine Creek. Deep pools of water nourish cypress, pine, and sumac trees along its bed. At 0.3 mile, you reach a short set of stairs that fortunately are not as steep as those of the descent. The remainder of the trail is a short, rigorous climb, but the bench at 0.4 mile and the large rock in the shade at 0.45 mile offer places to rest. As the trail climbs away from the creek, the water-loving plants quickly yield to hardier desert varieties. The last few hundred feet of the trail are flat and lead right back to the trailhead.

14. PINE CREEK TRAIL

Distance ■ 1 mile round trip
Difficulty ■ Moderate to strenuous
Features ■ Rock-hopping through a scenic creek to a natural stone bridge
Starting elevation ■ 4475 feet
Highest elevation ■ 4630 feet
Total climb ■ 300 feet
Location ■ Tonto Natural Bridge State Park
Map ■ USGS Buckhead Mesa
Hiking season ■ Year-round

Getting there: Pine Creek Trail is in Tonto Natural Bridge State Park, about 10 miles north of Payson (Payson is about 80 miles north of Phoenix) via AZ 87 and the state park access road. Once inside the park, turn right into the first parking area. The trailhead is at the east side of the parking lot and is marked by a

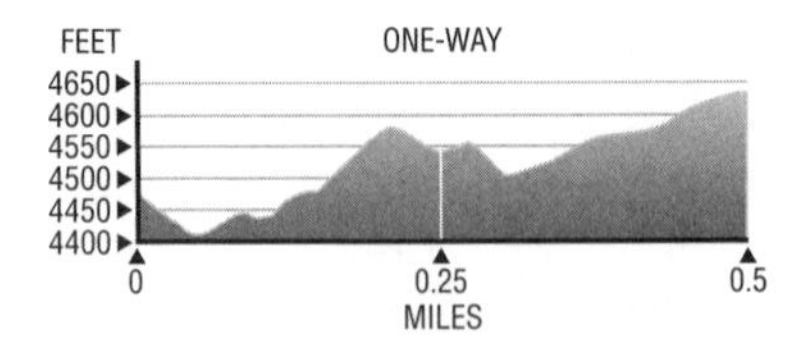

sign. Restrooms and drinking water are nearby. There is a fee to enter the park. Pets and glass containers are not permitted on the trail.

This hike, which is actually more boulder-hopping than hiking, is a lot of work, but it's worth the effort to walk between towering travertine walls, explore a small cave, and view the Tonto Natural Bridge (also see the Gowan Loop Trail, above). The creek flows year-round, and pools of water in the creekbed support frogs, lizards, and dragonflies, while birds of all types chatter overhead. The best view of a waterfall is also seen from Pine Creek Trail. The trail leads under the bridge and, if the creek is low enough, through to the other side.

From the trailhead, a well-worn dirt path leads 0.15 mile through a shady grove of Arizona cypress, alligator juniper, and buckthorn bush over a bridge that spans a dry creek down into a sandbar in Pine Creek's bed. Follow the creek to the southwest to get to Tonto Natural Bridge. The sandbar quickly gives way to large boulders and the real adventure begins. On the first part of the trail, stay to the right side for best passage. Watch for small signs with white arrows on a brown background for direction along the entire length of the trail and even under the bridge.

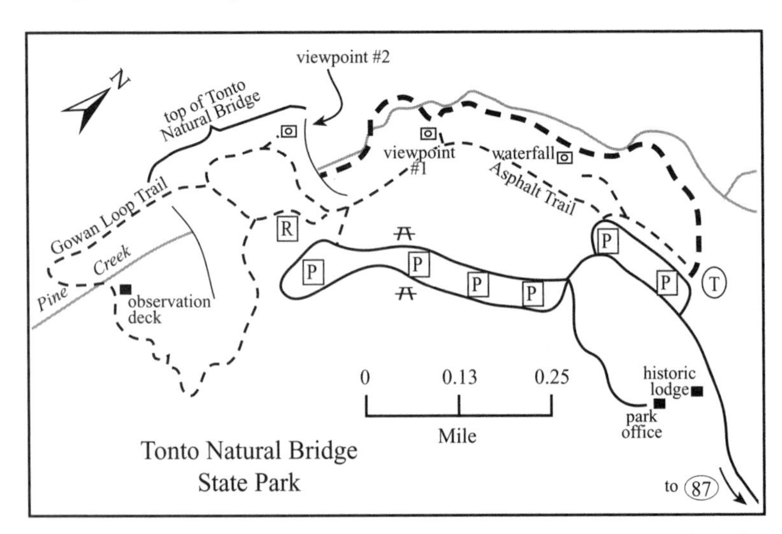

Opposite: *Gleaming white travertine forms a bridge over Pine Creek.* (Photo by Lawrence Letham)

The wetlands along the creek, and particularly under and near the bridge, have created an unusually moist environment that is ideal for wildlife. Among more than one hundred species of birds that are seen here are American dippers, ruby-crowned kinglets, ash-throated flycatchers, Bell's vireo, dark-eyed juncos, Steller's jays, American robins, and mountain bluebirds. Swallows and ravens often nest in protected caves. Also watch for rock squirrels, spotted and striped skunks, raccoons, cottontail rabbits, javelina, white-tailed deer, and elk.

As you move on, the sound of a waterfall becomes stronger until at 0.3 mile it is visible on the left side of the trail. The water splashes down the hill, giving life to a forest of ferns while providing a cool, refreshing atmosphere. At 0.4 mile a tree grows out of the creekbed and curves over to the bank. Two hundred feet later, massive boulders in the middle of the creek signal the best place to move to the south side of the creek, and the small signs with arrows concur. Go as high up on the bank as possible, climb over the exposed roots of an oak tree, and enter the narrow travertine passage formed by two tall walls only 12 feet apart. A close look at the travertine reveals fine crystals, grottos, and crevices.

At just under the 0.5-mile point there is a narrow squeeze between more travertine rocks, and just 75 feet later there is a small cave to pass through. The bridge is seen from the cave exit and is just a few boulders away. Follow the arrows as the trail leads down once more into the creek, then heads directly for the bridge. Under the bridge, there are huge travertine deposits, a deep pool in the middle, and piles of dead branches that sweep under the bridge during seasons of high waters. The travertine rock is slippery, especially when wet.

When the creek is low, it is possible to cross completely under the bridge to the other side. Once again, the signs with white arrows show the way, but one section of the trail is smooth and slippery. From the bridge, return along the same route to the trailhead.

TUCSON AND SOUTHERN ARIZONA

This is what most people think of as the real Arizona—hillsides covered with stately saguaro cacti, tall, rocky mountain peaks, an occasional Spanish mission or cattle ranch, and a lot of broad expanses of hot dry nothingness.

The population and commercial center for this region is Tucson, with a city population of about a half million, and about 800,000 when you include the suburbs. It's an old city—founded in 1775 when this area was part of Mexico—and much of that rich Spanish Colonial history can still be seen today. Tucson also has excellent museums and performing arts, and hosts three major baseball teams for spring training each year. Elevation is about 2400 feet.

The best-known outdoor attraction here is wondrous Saguaro National Park, which is dedicated to the symbol of the American Southwest, the giant saguaro cactus. The park is divided into two parts—the Tucson Mountain District, also called Saguaro West, is primarily Sonoran Desert and is west of the city; the Rincon Mountain District, also called Saguaro East, includes Sonoran Desert plus foothills and mountain terrain on the east side of Tucson. Each section has a scenic drive, a visitor center, trails that wander among the saguaros and other desert plants, plus good wildlife viewing and bird-watching opportunities.

Tucson makes a good base for exploring the nearby desert and mountains, and in this section of the book we'll be heading out of town for hikes in the mountains of Coronado National Forest, which covers some 1,780,000 acres with rugged peaks that rise from the desert floor. We'll also be going to several fine state parks, hiking the path used by Mexican immigrants seeking a new home more than 200 years ago, finding some surprisingly lush areas in this desert land, and exploring a cave down along the Mexican border.

For additional information, contact the various government agencies mentioned below, as well as the Tucson Convention & Visitors Bureau. You'll find complete contact information in the appendix at the back of this book.

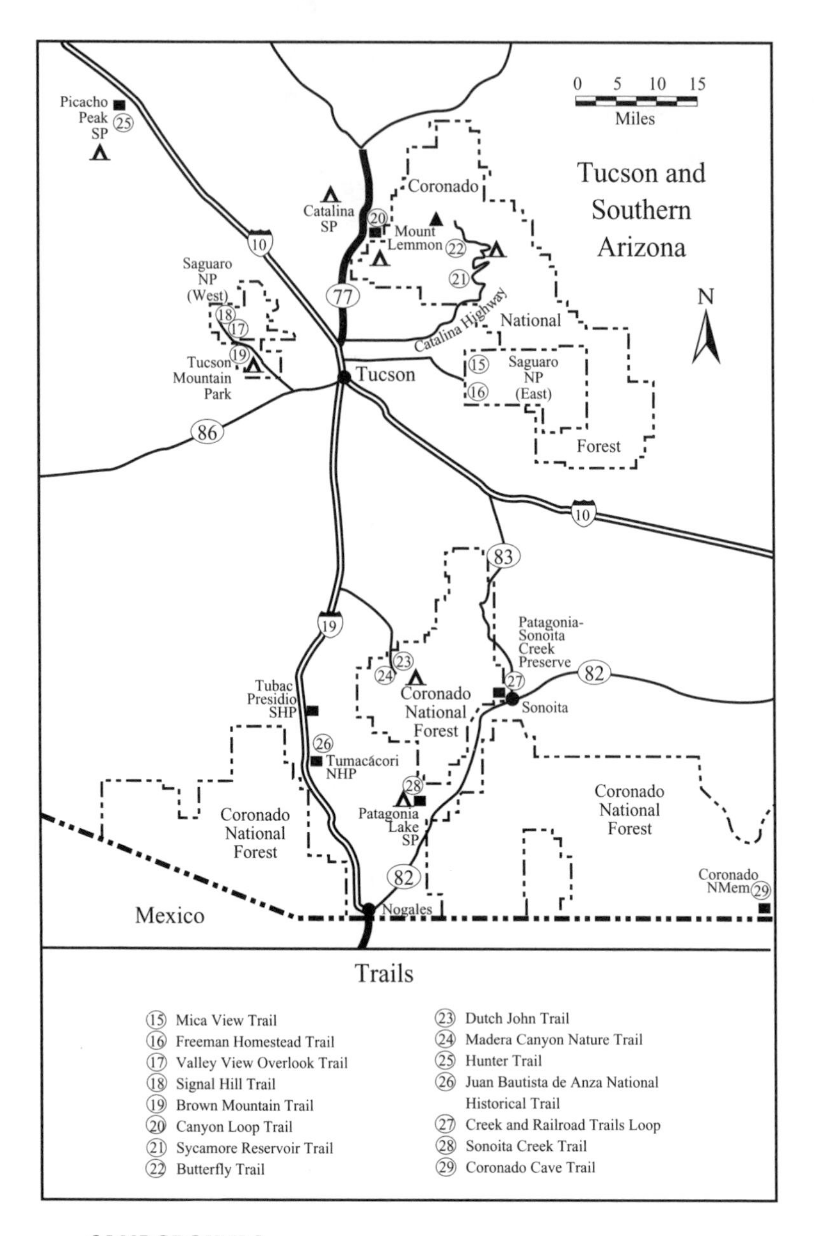

CAMPGROUNDS

There are commercial campgrounds with RV hookups, hot showers, and all the usual amenities in Tucson as well as smaller communities in the region. In addition, there are numerous campgrounds on public

A mature saguaro with multiple arms

lands. Unfortunately, Saguaro National Park does not offer camping. However, there are public lands campgrounds nearby, and moderate fees are charged at all of the following.

Among campgrounds in the **Coronado National Forest** are several that are north of Saguaro National Park's Rincon Mountain District. Located in the forest's Santa Catalina Ranger District, along the Catalina Highway, they include **Molino Basin,** about 18 miles northeast of Tucson, which has 37 sites, virtually no facilities, and can accommodate trailers up to 22 feet only; **Rose Canyon,** about 33 miles northeast of Tucson, which has 74 sites, limited facilities, and offers fishing at Rose Canyon Lake; and **Spencer Canyon,** located near the top of Mount Lemmon about 39 miles northeast of Tucson, which has 68 sites, limited facilities, and can accommodate trailers only up to 18 feet.

In the national forest's Nogales Ranger District, hikers going to Madera Canyon, about 50 miles south of Tucson, might want to consider camping at **Bog Springs Campground.** It has oak-shaded sites, several good trails (Hikes 23 and 24), and is a prime birdwatching area. Take I-19 south from Tucson to exit 63 eastbound for Continental Road. Follow the signs to Madera Canyon, about 12 miles, and to Bog Springs Campground. Reservations are not accepted, and the campground often fills, especially on weekends during the best birding seasons—April through May and September. There are 13 campsites, limited facilities, and a maximum vehicle length of 22 feet. The road to the campground is paved, but narrow, winding, and with some steep sections, and not recommended for RVs. It is sometimes icy in winter. Contact the Coronado National Forest offices for information on these and other campgrounds throughout the forest.

Gilbert Ray Campground. Located in Tucson Mountain Park, 4 miles south of the Saguaro National Park's Tucson Mountain District, this popular county-run campground offers an attractive desert mountain environment of saguaros, prickly pear, cholla, mesquite, and paloverde, with well-maintained gravel sites. Nearby is the Brown Mountain Trail (Hike 19). The campground is located just off Kinney Road on McCain Loop Road. There are about 150 RV and tent sites, including 133 with electricity hookups. The campground has restrooms and an RV dump station, but no showers. Open year-round, reservations are not accepted.

Catalina State Park. This very attractive campground has nicely spaced, well-shaded sites, an abundance of rock squirrels, a fine hike (Canyon Loop Trail, Hike 20), and splendid views of the Santa Catalina Mountains to the southeast. Located 9 miles north of Tucson on AZ 77. There are 120 sites (74 with RV hookups), restrooms with showers, and an RV dump station. Open year-round; reservations are not accepted.

Picacho Peak State Park. The park's campground has well-spaced sites, low desert vegetation, and is quite nice. Hunter Trail, Hike 25, is here. The park is about 40 miles north of Tucson via I-10, exit 219.

The park has restrooms with showers, 85 campsites (60 with electricity hookups), and an RV dump station. Open year-round; reservations are not accepted.

Patagonia Lake State Park. The park has several camping areas. Sites are well-spaced, with some evergreens plus desert plants such as mesquite and cactus, and many sites offer views of the lake. Unlike many of the RV-oriented parks, there are numerous sites here that are well-suited for tenting. The Sonoita Creek Trail (Hike 28) is in the park and the Creek and Railroad Trails Loop (Hike 27) is nearby. Patagonia Lake State Park is located 12 miles northeast of Nogales (which is about 63 miles south of Tucson) on AZ 82 and then 4 miles north on the park access road. It has restrooms with showers, 106 campsites (34 with electricity and water hookups) plus 12 boat-in campsites, boat ramps, and an RV dump station. Open year-round; reservations are not accepted.

15. MICA VIEW TRAIL

Distance	2-mile loop
Difficulty	Easy
Features	Many varieties of cactus and other desert plants
Starting elevation	2812 feet
Highest elevation	2828 feet
Total climb	85 feet
Location	Saguaro National Park (East)
Map	USGS Tanque Verde
Hiking season	Year-round

Getting there: The trail is in the Rincon Mountain District (eastern section) of Saguaro National Park. To get to the park from downtown Tucson, take Speedway or Broadway Boulevards east to Freeman Road, turn right (south) and go about 4 miles to Old Spanish Trail, where you turn left (south) and follow it for about 0.25 mile to the park entrance. A fee is charged to enter the national park. Once in the park, to get to the trailhead take the Cactus Forest Drive and head north on Mica View Road to the picnic area at its

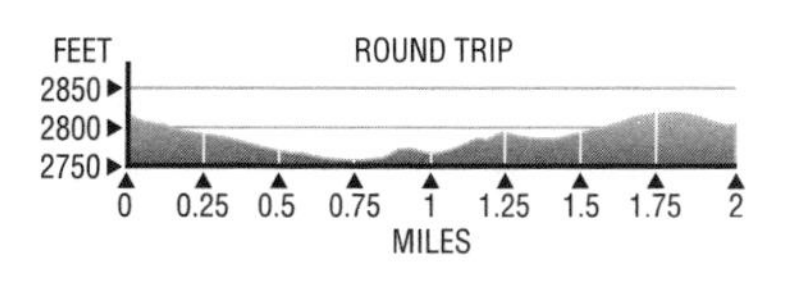

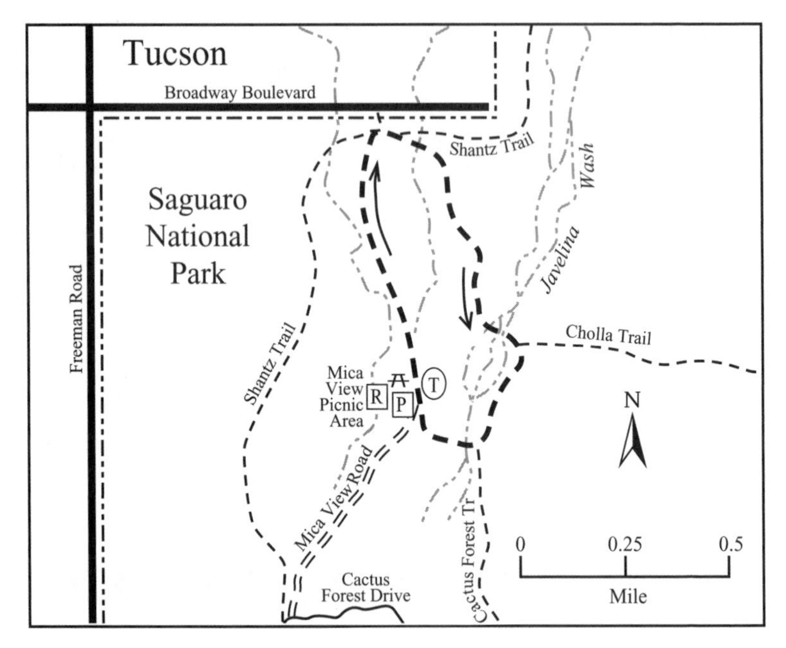

end. There are vault toilets but no drinking water. You'll find the trailhead at the north end of the picnic area, and it heads out almost due north.

This is a great way to see the most desert plants in the shortest period of time. The loop includes parts of three trails: Mica View, Shantz, and Cactus Forest. But it's well marked and easy to follow. The first two are broad, and the last is slightly narrower, but all are packed earth with only one short rocky stretch near the end.

As soon as you start walking down the trail you'll immediately be surrounded by a variety of desert plants. There are saguaros young and old, and most of the younger ones are getting a firm hold on life by starting out underneath a paloverde tree. Hence the nickname "nurse" tree. Not always easy to see are the small pincushion cacti, which boast lovely orange blooms in summer. The larger, fat fishhook barrel cactus also called compass cactus, is easy to spot, and the chain-fruit or jumping cholla seem to glow when the sun is behind them shining through the numerous light-colored spines. The large flat pads of the prickly pear are everywhere, and after a wet spring, their yellow (or sometimes deep red) blossoms are luscious. Non-cactus plants include the state tree—blue paloverde, with its smooth pale green bark—and the rather scruffy-looking mesquite with surprisingly dainty leaves.

After about 0.7 mile you'll bump into Shantz Trail, which goes off to the left and right, and a very short spur goes straight ahead to Broadway Boulevard, where locals sometimes park to walk into the park. Turn to the right on Shantz for about 500 feet, where Cactus Forest Trail branches off to the right. Take this right fork and follow Cactus Forest—a name that is strikingly apropos as the trail is all but overcome with cacti for a while. You're now heading in a southerly direction.

About 0.5 mile farther along you'll cross a couple of small sandy washes, but don't confuse either of them with Javelina Wash. This is a major wash, so broad it has a line of trees growing down its middle! After you cross Javelina, there's a prominent paloverde on your left and a large saguaro at the junction with Cholla Trail. Stay to the right on Cactus Forest for another 0.3 mile where you'll return to Mica View Trail (a right turn). This stretch seems to have more deciduous trees than cacti. Almost immediately you'll find yourself recrossing Javelina Wash. Then it's about 0.3 mile, west and a little north, back to the parking lot and trail's end.

A fishhook cactus

Saguaro, the King of the Desert

The mighty saguaro (pronounced suh-WAR-oh) is undoubtedly the best-known cactus in America, and definitely a plant with a lot of personality. Standing tall, their arms stretching to the sky or pointing the way, saguaros often look human, directing an orchestra or waving to friends. Though saguaros can reach heights of 50 feet and weigh eight tons, they are slow-growing—it often takes 15 years for a saguaro to reach just one foot in height, and about 100 years to reach a height of 25 feet. Their maximum lifetime is about 200 years. At about the age of thirty, a saguaro begins to flower and produce fruit, but branches, or "arms," won't appear until it reaches seventy-five.

16. FREEMAN HOMESTEAD TRAIL

Distance ■ 1-mile loop
Difficulty ■ Easy
Features ■ Panoramic views; interpretive signs describe natural and human history
Starting elevation ■ 3141 feet
Highest elevation ■ 3141 feet
Total climb ■ 150 feet
Location ■ Saguaro National Park East
Map ■ USGS Tanque Verde Peak
Hiking season ■ Year-round

Getting there: The trail is located in the Rincon Mountain District of Saguaro National Park on the east side of Tucson. To get to the park from downtown Tucson, take Speedway or Broadway Boulevards east to Freeman Road, turn right (south) and go about 4 miles to Old Spanish Trail, where you turn left (south) and follow it for about 0.25 mile to the park entrance. A fee is charged to enter the national park. Once in the park, to get to the trailhead, take Cactus Forest Drive to the turnoff for the Javelina Picnic Area. Parking for the trail is about 0.25 mile down the road, shortly before you reach the picnic grounds. There are restrooms at the picnic area, but no drinking water.

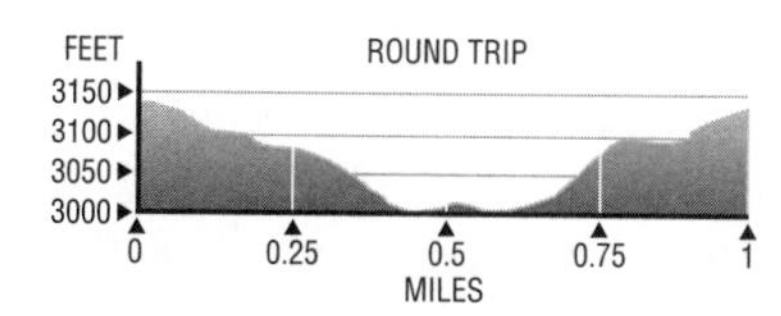

This easy loop through gently rolling desert terrain offers good panoramic views as well as close-up views of saguaros, ocotillo, and other desert plants. Along the way, you'll find several interpretive signs describing desert life and the remains of an early 1900s adobe homestead, now returned to its origins: a mound of dirt with a few rocks strewn about.

The well-marked trail heads almost due south, leading through saguaro, prickly pear, cholla, and barrel cacti for about 0.25 mile to the site of the Freeman Homestead. The Safford Freeman family built a three-room adobe here in 1929, enclosed it with an ocotillo fence, and even dug a well. The only evidence that remains is the hill where the adobe melted back into the earth, but take a few minutes to read the interpretive signs that have been posted around.

The Freemans chose to build above their water source, probably to have advance warning of incomers. But incidentally they had some quite nice views: distant vistas in all directions. Of course today the city of Tucson lies to the north and west. But you can still enjoy some of what they saw—the Tanque Verde Ridge to the southeast and the Saguaro Wilderness of the Coronado National Forest around the north and east.

Leaving the home site, the trail meanders down into the bottom of an arroyo, where you'll see only scrubby mesquite and ironwood bushes, and the quiet can be intense. The going gets a little rough as

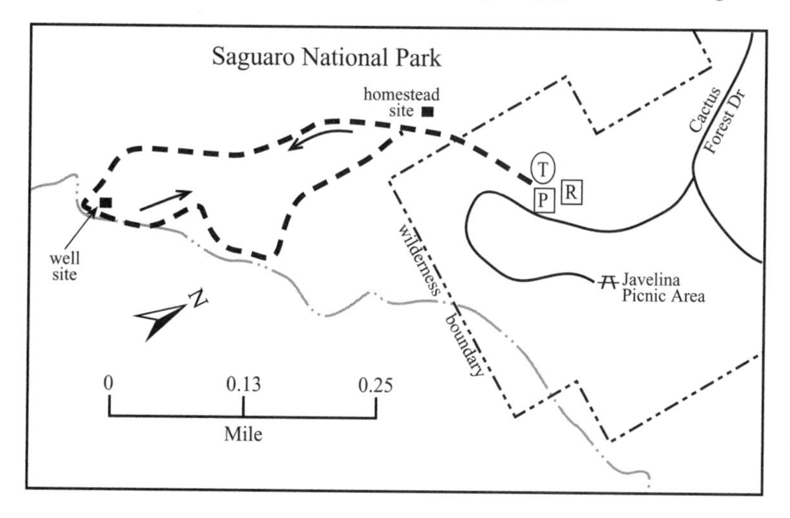

The Freeman Homestead Trail

the trail becomes sandier and your feet sink into it, and in summer it is very hot.

At one point the trail briefly leaves the wash and affords a lovely panoramic view to the south. Once you cross the 0.75-mile mark, you'll begin the short climb out, and soon the air seems to open up a bit and cacti reappear. Back on top, you'll soon complete the loop, returning to the beginning of the trail. From there it's just a short walk back to the parking area and your vehicle.

17. VALLEY VIEW OVERLOOK TRAIL

Distance ▪ 0.8-mile one way
Difficulty ▪ Easy
Features ▪ A saguaro cactus forest and wonderful panoramic views
Starting elevation ▪ 2670 feet
Highest elevation ▪ 2850 feet
Total climb ▪ 250 feet
Location ▪ Saguaro National Park (West)
Map ▪ USGS Avra
Hiking season ▪ Year-round

Getting there: This trail is in the Tucson Mountain District (west side) of Saguaro National Park. From I-10 in Tucson, take AZ 86, also known as the Ajo-Tucson Highway, west for 6 miles to Kinney Road, where you turn right and follow it into the national park. Stop at the Red Hills Visitor Center to learn about the Sonoran

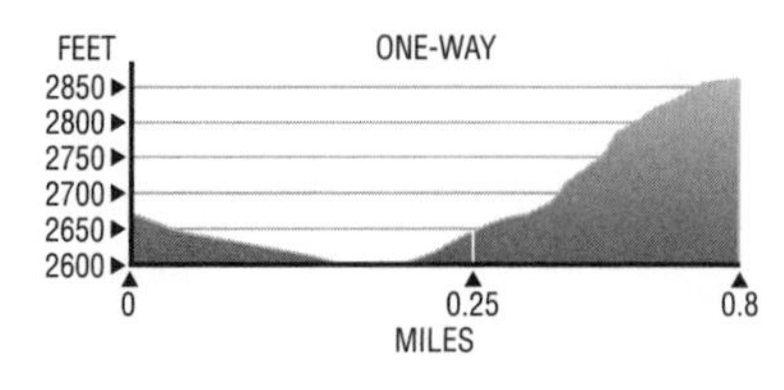

Desert, and where you'll also find restrooms and drinking water. An entrance fee is charged to enter the park. From the visitor center, continue northwest on Kinney Road about 1.5 miles to Bajada Loop Drive, turn right onto Hohokam Road, and drive about 1.25 miles to the well-marked trailhead on the left side of the road.

Forests of saguaro cacti plus numerous other desert plants as well as superb views are the highlights of this short and easy trail. Built by the Civilian Conservation Corps in the 1930s, the trail passes through two washes before climbing to a ridge for panoramic views of the surrounding desert and mountains. A number of interpretative signs discuss the desert's flora and fauna along the way. Of course, the entire Saguaro National Park is a living museum of Lower Sonoran plant life, with the saguaro cactus as its centerpiece. Healthy saguaro cacti at all stages of development represent hundreds of years of growth. Holes in the saguaro, drilled by the Gila woodpecker and gilded flicker, as well as burrows underground, house a variety of desert creatures.

The trail begins with an introductory sign with pictures of thirty plants, birds, and animals that hikers might encounter, and also a warning to avoid poisonous rattlesnakes, Gila monsters, and scorpions, as well as what it labels "prickly plants." It starts down a series of stone steps and then crosses a sandy wash, which abounds with prickly pear,

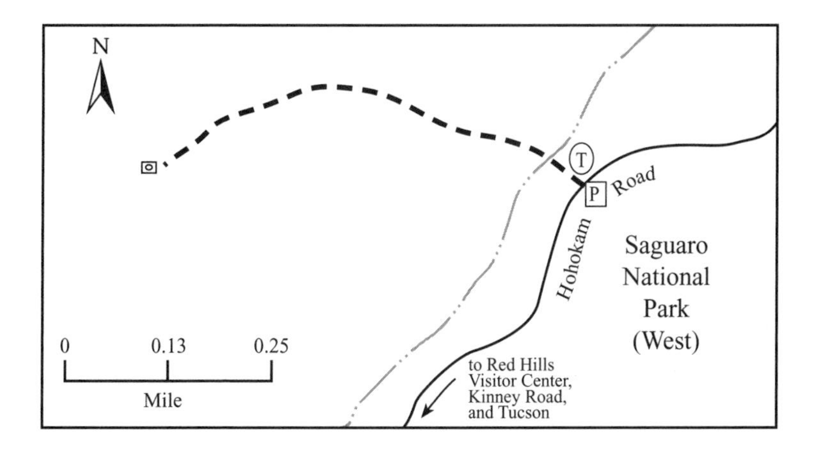

Stopping for a photo of an unusual saguaro

cholla, fishhook, hedgehog, and saguaro cactus, plus ocotillo, mesquite, desert lavender, and other Sonoran Desert plants. Somewhat unusual are the pencil cholla, which, true to their name, have pencil-thin arms, much thinner than the other species of cholla more often seen.

The trail makes its way through the second wash, and then climbs to a small plateau at 0.4 mile, offering views of the sprawling Avra Valley below and rocky Picacho Peak off to the north. When clouds darken the sky, the distant mountains look especially ominous. If the wind is blowing, you'll notice that the taller saguaros are swaying. This is because the thick roots of each cactus spread far to find water, but usually not too deep, so the cacti don't have as much stability as plants with deeper roots.

After enjoying the marvelous view, return to the trailhead along the same route.

Prehistoric Hohokam Were Skilled Engineers

Among the first people to attempt farming in the desert Southwest, the Hohokam people lived in the Sonoran Desert of what is now southern Arizona since at least AD 300. In some areas, including Saguaro National Park, we can see evidence of their time here, such as the curious rock art on the park's Signal Hill Trail. Archeologists tell us that at first the Hohokam built pit houses—holes in the ground with a crude roof—but as their culture evolved they constructed more substantial aboveground structures. By 1450 they were gone. However, at the height of their civilization their communities were spread over 45,000 square miles of the Sonoran Desert. Like other early peoples, the Hohokam learned to make full use of everything the desert offered, from the fruit of the saguaro to the trunks of the paloverde, and they also fished and hunted.

It was their skill at building irrigation systems, however, that enabled the Hohokam to survive here for over 1000 years. Without metal tools, the wheel, or any beasts of burden, they dug over 600 miles of canals and constructed a series of dams and floodgates, sometimes carrying water as far as 10 miles from its source, to grow corn, beans, squash, cotton, and tobacco. So why did they leave? Some archeologists theorize that the Hohokam abandoned their villages to pursue a nomadic hunting and gathering existence. Others believe they just moved, and are seen today in their descendents—the Tohono O'odham and the Pima. But most agree that we really don't know what happened to them or where they went.

18. SIGNAL HILL TRAIL

Distance ■ 0.5-mile round trip
Difficulty ■ Easy
Features ■ A quick trip up a hill to see dozens of ancient petroglyphs
Starting elevation ■ 2455 feet
Highest elevation ■ 2455 feet
Total climb ■ 35 feet
Location ■ Saguaro National Park West
Map ■ USGS Avra
Hiking season ■ Year-round

Getting there: This trail is in the Tucson Mountain District (west side) of Saguaro National Park. From I-10 in Tucson, take AZ 86, also known as the Ajo-Tucson Highway, west for 6 miles to Kinney Road, where you turn right and follow it into the national park. Stop at the Red Hills Visitor Center to learn about the Sonoran Desert and the people who have lived here, and where you'll also find restrooms and drinking water. A fee is charged to enter the park. From the visitor center, continue northwest on Kinney Road about 1.5 miles to the Bajada Loop Drive, turn right onto Hohokam Road, and drive about two-thirds of the way around the loop, turning left onto Golden Gate Road, to the well-marked trailhead. Just to the south is a stone picnic table and barbecue grill built by the Civilian Conservation Corps in the 1930s.

This is a fun hike for kids, but it's also interesting for adults who want to learn about the prehistoric people who lived in this area or just check out some ancient art. The trail zigzags up the side of a small hill to an area containing dozens of examples of American Indian rock art, believed to have been left by the Hohokam people between 550 and 1300 years ago. The hilltop also offers wonderful views of saguaros against rocky mountainsides. Along the way are giant Arizona barrel cacti, also called compass cacti (which almost always lean south or southwest); prickly pear cacti with bite marks made by rodents, rabbits, and javelina; green-barked paloverde; a stone dam; and pencil cholla.

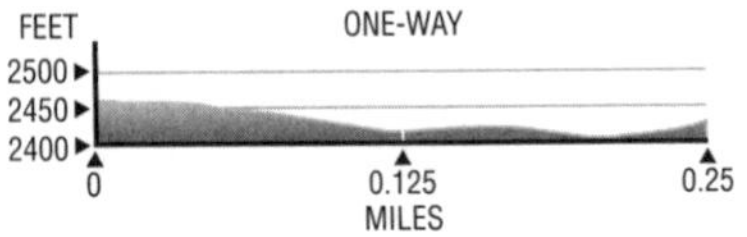

The trail up to Signal Hill is dirt with stone steps. You pass through a wash loaded with paloverde, and

Petroglyphs cover many rocks along the trail

then climb a bit more. Just before a set of descending steps there is a large prickly pear cactus with bite marks, most likely made by a javelina (also called collared peccary), a nearsighted piglike animal with an extremely tough mouth! The trail then crosses a wide, very sandy wash before starting to climb up the hill. To the left of the trail, beyond some steps, is a huge compass cactus, about 2 feet in diameter.

Finish the short jaunt to the top, where black rocks provide the medium for numerous petroglyphs (designs carved into rock) created by the Hohokam people, who lived here from about AD 300 to 1450. The images depict figures of animals plus many abstract designs, such

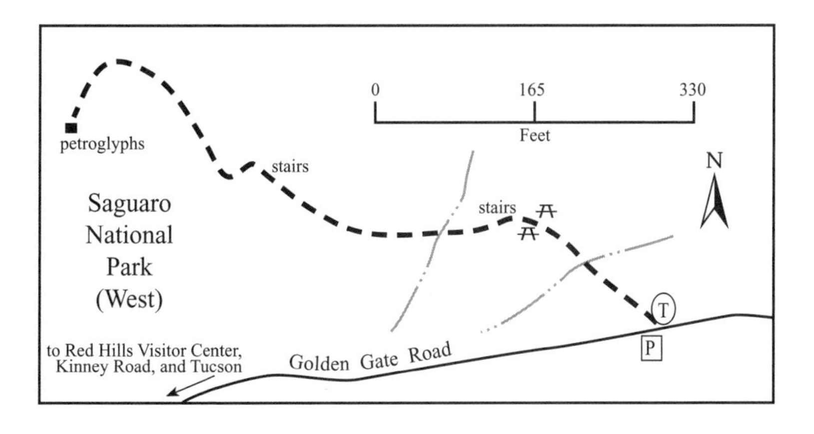

as wavy lines and combinations of circles and spirals. Archeologists believe that the Hohokam did not have a settlement here, but only visited, perhaps on hunting trips or for ceremonies. However, there is evidence that Hohokam villages were established in the eastern section of the park. The name Hohokam was given to these prehistoric people by people in one of southern Arizona's modern tribes, the Pima, and translates to "those who are gone."

After you have seen the petroglyphs and admired the view, return along the same fun path.

Be Kind to Our Scaly Friends

The sound will chill you to the bone. Walking down a rocky trail, listening to the birds singing and watching puffy white clouds sailing across a deep azure sky, you couldn't be more at peace, and suddenly you hear it—a hiss and buzzing rattle—and you freeze in your steps. It's a rattlesnake, ready to strike with its poisonous venom! Arizona has seventeen different species of rattlesnakes. The largest, which seems to be especially prevalent in the Tucson area, is the western diamondback, which can grow to more than 6 feet long. All rattlesnakes have a broad, triangular head and their telltale rattle—made by bony segments at the end of their tails. Diamondbacks are named for their diamond-shaped markings. A myth about rattlesnakes is that the number of segments on its rattle shows its age in years; in fact, a new rattle segment is added every time the snake sheds its skin, which usually occurs two to four times each year.

To avoid unpleasant encounters with rattlesnakes—and they are just as anxious to avoid you as you are to avoid them—stay on established trails, wear sturdy shoes or boots, watch where you put your hands and feet, and always use a flashlight at night to avoid stepping on them. If you do meet a rattlesnake, stay calm and move away slowly. If you are bitten, get medical help immediately, but don't panic. About 25 percent of all rattlesnake bites are dry, meaning no venom was released, and only 2 to 3 percent of the estimated 150 rattlesnake bites in Arizona each year result in death. In fact, Arizona wildlife experts say that more people are killed by lightning in Arizona than by snake bites. There, now we have something else to worry about!

19. BROWN MOUNTAIN TRAIL

Distance	2.4 miles one way (with a shuttle); 4.8 miles round trip
Difficulty	Moderate
Features	A rocky trail along a ridgeline with panoramic views of the Tucson area
Starting elevation	2660 feet
Highest elevation	3095 feet
Total climb	775 feet
Location	Tucson Mountain Park
Map	USGS Brown Mountain
Hiking season	Late fall to early spring

Getting there: The trail is located west of Tucson in Tucson Mountain Park, 4 miles south of Saguaro National Park's Tucson Mountain District. From I-19 in Tucson, take exit 99 for AZ 86 and go west for just over 5 miles. Turn right (north) onto Kinney Road and go about 6 miles to McCain Loop Road, where you turn left. The marked trailhead is a bit over 0.25 mile on the right. Tucson Mountain Park, which includes Gilbert Ray Campground, is operated by the Pima County Parks and Recreation Department. Restrooms and drinking water are available in the park visitor center across McCain Loop Road from the trailhead, and also at the Juan Santa Cruz Picnic Area at the end of the hike. Leashed dogs are permitted on the trail, but the trail has sharp rocks that can cut the pads on their feet. Diamondback rattlesnakes are frequently seen, so watch where you put your hands and feet. Trail markers help keep you on course.

This very rewarding hike leads through a veritable forest of cacti and up along a rocky ridgeline that offers wonderful views of the surrounding mountains and valleys. There are often wildflowers blooming in spring, and you'll also likely see a variety of birds, ranging from mourning doves and cactus wrens to red-tailed hawks and turkey vultures. The hike is best if you can arrange for transportation at the Juan Santa Cruz Picnic Area, where the trail ends, but even if

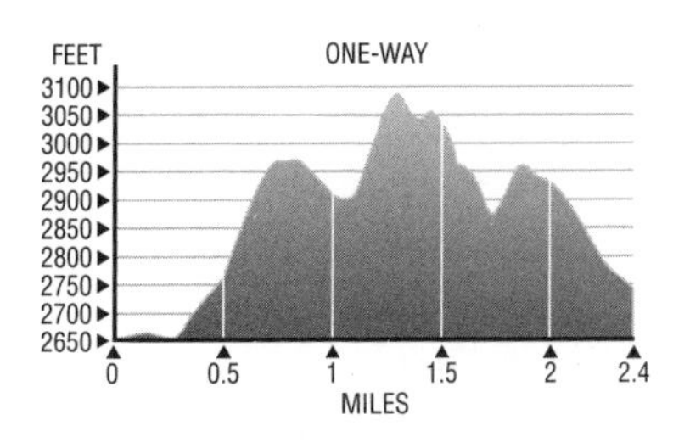

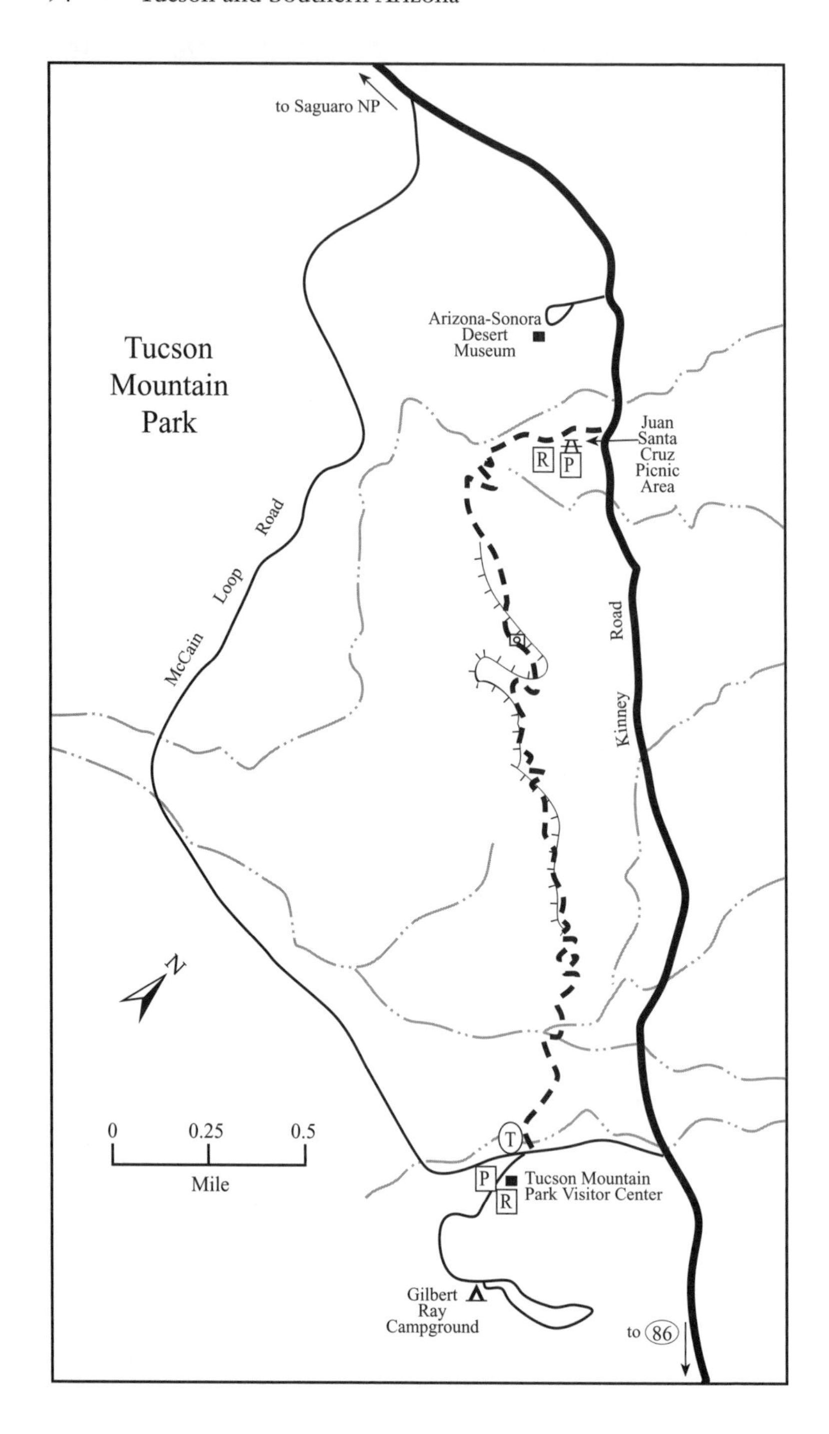
to Saguaro NP
Arizona-Sonora
Desert
Museum
Tucson
Mountain
Park
Juan
Santa
Cruz
Picnic
Area
R
P
McCain Loop Road
Kinney Road
N
0
0.25
0.5
Mile
T
P
R
Tucson Mountain
Park Visitor Center
Gilbert
Ray
Campground
to 86

you hike back along the ridge the views are worth seeing twice.

The hike begins as an easy walk along a narrow dirt path through a forest of cacti—saguaro, tall chain-fruit cholla, prickly pear, fishhook, plus some brush, ocotillo, and paloverde—and soon crosses the first of several washes. There are occasional views of ragged peaks to the east, and plenty of reddish brown rocks along the hillsides. Although the mountain does appear a rich reddish brown, that does not account for the name. Brown Mountain is named for Cornelius Brown, a county agricultural agent who is credited with helping to create Tucson Mountain Park in 1929.

Views along the Brown Mountain Trail

After about 0.33 mile of being surrounded by walls of cacti, the terrain opens up considerably, and at about 0.45 mile the trail drops down into a small valley. It crosses a fairly wide, dry riverbed at about the 0.5-mile point—watch for a brown post to mark the trail on the other side—and then starts to seriously climb up the mountainside. Another trail cuts off to the right, but continuing straight you cross another wash and continue climbing. The desert plant life becomes thicker, and the trail gets rocky—very rocky—as it switchbacks up the hillside.

At about 0.9 mile the trail reaches the first ridge, which offers splendid views over Gilbert Ray Campground behind you and panoramic views of the Tucson Valley to the east. From here the trail mostly follows the ridge, alternating between ascending and descending, including a series of switchbacks. At just under 1.5 miles from the trailhead, the trail ascends a hill, at about 3100 feet elevation, that affords fantastic panoramic views, especially to the southeast. You drop a bit, crest another hill, and then the trail drops sharply, reversing direction and dropping down the north side of the ridge, first east and then switchbacking to go west.

Although it seems that the trail is now heading down to its finale at the base of the mountain, it is not ready to quit just yet and climbs to another hilltop, again offering great views, at just over 2 miles. From here you can see the Juan Santa Cruz Picnic Area, where the trail ends. The trail now rapidly heads down the mountainside, depositing you at the picnic area. If you arranged for transportation this is the end of the hike; if not, follow the trail back over Brown Mountain to the trailhead. You can also walk back to the trailhead along Kinney and McCain Loop roads, and avoid the mountain climbing, but it is dangerous because there are no shoulders.

20. CANYON LOOP TRAIL

Distance ■ 2.3-mile loop
Difficulty ■ Easy to moderate
Features ■ A picturesque stream, rock formations, tall saguaros, and panoramic mountain views all crammed into one very pleasant hike
Starting elevation ■ 2700 feet
Highest elevation ■ 2865 feet
Total climb ■ 325 feet
Location ■ Catalina State Park
Map ■ USGS Oro Valley
Hiking season ■ Year-round (hot in summer)

Getting there: The trail is in Catalina State Park, at the foot of the majestic Santa Catalina Mountains, about 9 miles north of Tucson via AZ 77 (Oracle Road). After entering the park, follow the main park road to where it ends at the communal trailhead. The park has day-use and camping fees; restrooms and drinking water are available. The trail crosses a wash several times, so if you are hiking when it is flowing—usually from late winter into spring—you may end up wading through 6 inches of water or hopping from rock to rock.

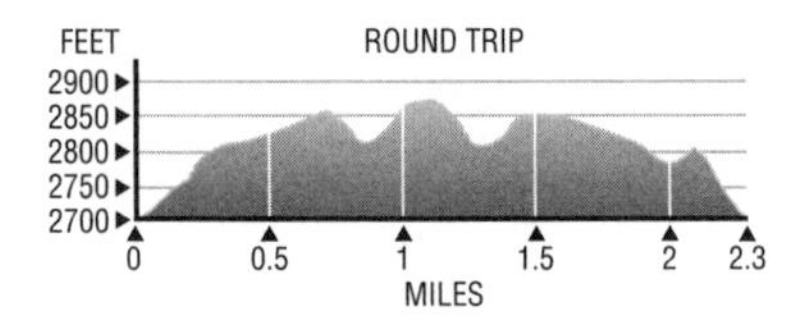

A wide variety of terrain and views make this loop trail among our top hiking choices in this area, and without a doubt the best hike at Catalina State Park. The trail,

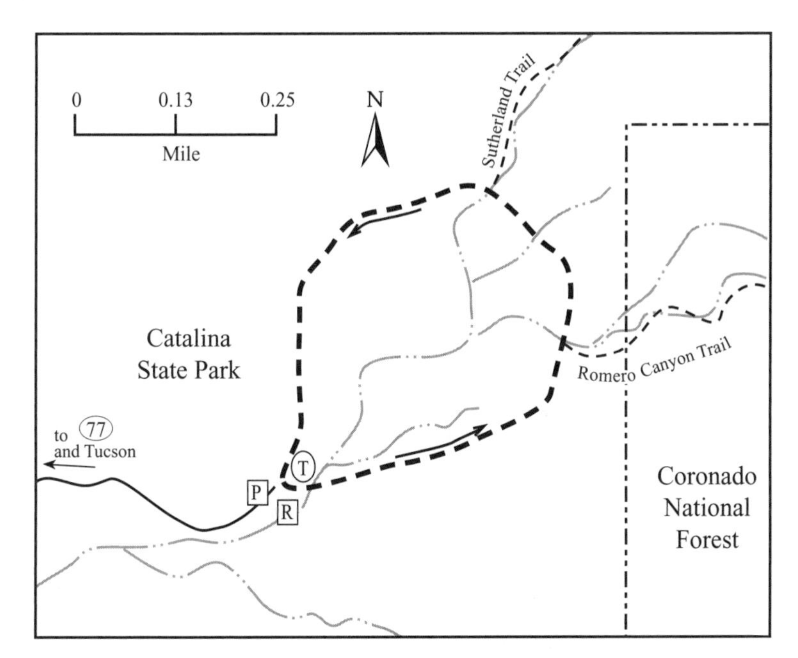

which connects short sections of two longer trails to create a loop, combines Sonoran Desert terrain with mesquite woodlands, has a picturesque stream, and also offers wonderful views and the possibility of seeing birds and other wildlife.

The loop can be hiked in either direction; this description assumes the hike is done counterclockwise. From the trailhead, go to the right (east), following the Romero Canyon Trail for 0.6 mile, then head north and west on what is marked as the Canyon Loop Trail for another 0.9 mile, before connecting with the Sutherland Trail, which you follow west and then south for 0.8 mile back to the trailhead.

The trail begins by almost immediately crossing a wash and then climbs steeply. It soon levels off and changes from packed dirt to sandy soil with a few rocky stretches. Wandering through a typical Sonoran Desert environment, you see mesquite, cholla, prickly pear, and barrel cactus; but there are also magnificent stands of giant saguaros, with tall sotol and ocotillo. As you continue, you'll see some beautiful rock formations, a picturesque stream, and from its higher elevations the trail offers spellbinding panoramic views of the surrounding mountains and desert. The trail is mostly level, except for the steep beginning climb, a 50-foot drop into Romero Canyon before you join Sutherland Trail, and another fairly steep descent near the end.

Hikers are apt to see mule deer, desert cottontail rabbits, rock squirrels, and plenty of lizards, including the poisonous Gila monster. There are also occasional sightings of javelina, coyotes, kit and gray foxes, and badgers. Ringtail cats also live here, but they are usually out only at night. Among the most commonly seen birds are Gambel's quail, red-tailed hawks, common poorwills, roadrunners, mourning doves, northern cardinals, and ladder-backed woodpeckers. The best time to see most of the park's wildlife is during the cooler times, from October through April. The exceptions, however, are lizards and snakes, which tend to be more active during the summer.

The Cat That Isn't a Cat

Seldom seen but usually present in this area, including Catalina State Park, is the ringtail cat, also sometimes called a miner's cat. To be correct, though, we should refer to them simply as ringtails because despite the fact that they are often called cats, ringtails are not cats at all, but relatives of the raccoon. They received their nickname "miner's cats" because they were brought into mines in the late 1800s and early 1900s to eliminate problems with mice and rats, which they apparently accomplished with great enthusiasm. Ringtails have foxlike faces with big, round, dark eyes, but their most prominent feature is their long, bushy, black-and-white tails. They usually sleep all day and come out only at night, when their super-sharp claws and catlike agility enable them to catch rodents, small mammals, and birds.

Rock-hopping at the beginning of the trail

21. SYCAMORE RESERVOIR TRAIL

Distance	4.8 miles round trip
Difficulty	Moderate
Features	Hike from the ruins of a prison camp to a lush riparian area
Starting elevation	4860 feet
Highest elevation	5020 feet
Total climb	400 feet
Location	Coronado National Forest
Map	USGS Agua Caliente Hill
Hiking season	Year-round

Getting there: This trail is in the Santa Catalina Ranger District of the Coronado National Forest, about 24 miles northeast of Tucson. From I-10 in Tucson, take East Grant Road east 10 miles to the Tanque Verde Road intersection. Turn left onto Tanque Verde Road, travel 2 miles, and turn left onto Catalina Highway. Drive about 12 miles, passing milepost 7, to the Hirabayashi Recreation Site turnoff to the left. Follow Prison Camp Road through the recreation site to the trailhead parking area. You'll follow an old jeep road for the beginning of the trail. There are restrooms but no drinking water. There may be water in the reservoir, but it must be purified.

Built to supply water for a long-gone federal prison camp, Sycamore Reservoir is now mostly a marshy riparian area, with alder, willow, and sycamore trees, a sandy beach, and a variety of birds and other wildlife. The hike, part of the Arizona Trail System, starts at Hirabayashi Recreation Site, at the site of the old prison camp, where you'll see the remains of foundations, twisted pipes, and concrete pylons.

The prison camp operated from 1939 to 1967 and had more than fifty buildings, but these were razed by the U.S. Forest Service after the camp was shut down, and mostly what you see here today are concrete foundations. The camp had housed the prisoners who built the road from Tucson to the top of Mount Lemmon; it took 8000 inmates a

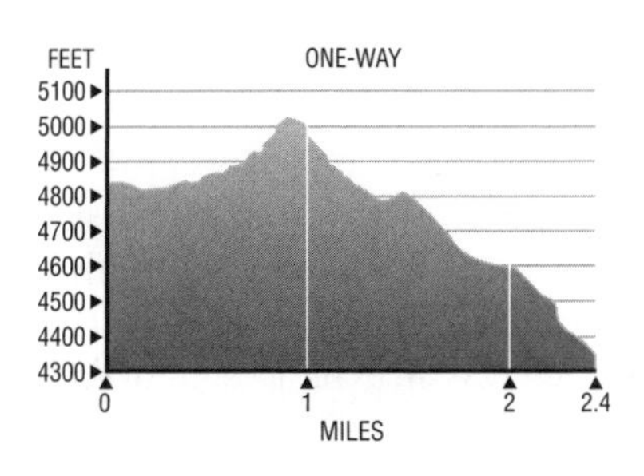

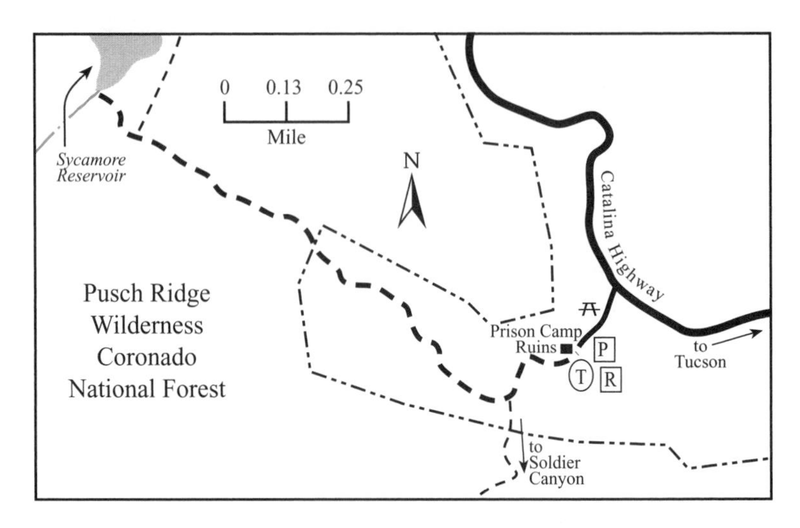

little more than 11 years to complete the 25-mile stretch.

Just past the foundations, the dirt road forks. Continue straight, along a low stone structure that looks like a bridge, over a shallow wash. The road leads to another fork, where you ignore the right branch and continue straight ahead to cross a small wash that then runs parallel to the road. Cypress, oak, and manzanita grow alongside the road, but its width makes them seem far away. Bear grass appears as the road crosses a rocky, dry wash. There are several other forks off of the main trail, but stay straight on the main road. At about the 1-mile point, the road begins a climb that continues for about 0.25 mile to the saddle at the mouth of Sycamore Canyon. A sign marks the boundary of the Pusch Ridge Wilderness Area.

The now-narrow trail, which follows a rocky wash, passes several four-sided, pyramid-shaped pillars of concrete and stones cemented together—these are the old pylons that held the pipes that brought water from the reservoir to the prison camp. On the other side of the wash, after about another 0.25 mile, a near-round boulder 6 feet in diameter sits on the right side of the trail. After a while the trail rejoins the old road that once led to the reservoir.

As the road descends, the lush green of the many plants growing around the water comes into view. It is a contrast to the sparser desert plants on the nearby mountains. Near the trees, the trail goes either to the right around the reservoir or to the left to go to the actual dam. The dam spans a narrow canyon between two small mountains of dark volcanic rock, and the reservoir has filled with sand and silt over the years while still providing nourishment for the riparian cottonwood and oak trees and other water-loving plants.

When you are ready to leave the cool shade, return along the same path.

22. BUTTERFLY TRAIL

Distance ■ 5.2 miles round trip
Difficulty ■ Strenuous
Features ■ A hike down (and then back up) through forest and desert to a lush spring
Starting elevation ■ 7720 feet
Highest elevation ■ 7720 feet
Total climb ■ 1700 feet
Location ■ Coronado National Forest
Map ■ USGS Mount Bigelow
Hiking season ■ Spring through fall

Getting there: The trail is in the Santa Catalina Ranger District of the Coronado National Forest, about 30 miles northeast of Tucson. From I-10 in Tucson, take East Grant Road east for 10 miles to Tanque Verde Road, turn left and go 2 miles, where you turn left onto the Catalina Highway. Stay on the Catalina Highway just beyond mile marker 22, where a sign marks the parking area for the Butterfly Trail. There are no restrooms or drinking water at the trailhead. The trail begins as a paved road past a gate at the end of the parking lot.

This hike, which is just a section of the entire Butterfly Trail, is a pleasant change of pace from the many desert hikes—with nary a drop of water in sight—that are found in this part of arid Arizona. From the trailhead, you'll head to the gurgling waters of Novio Spring, winding through thick trees and brush where there are wild raspberries growing in steep mountain drainages, abundant wildflowers, and chipmunks and other wildlife. The hike, which starts at its high point and then drops 1000 feet, goes from pine trees into an oak woodland environment,

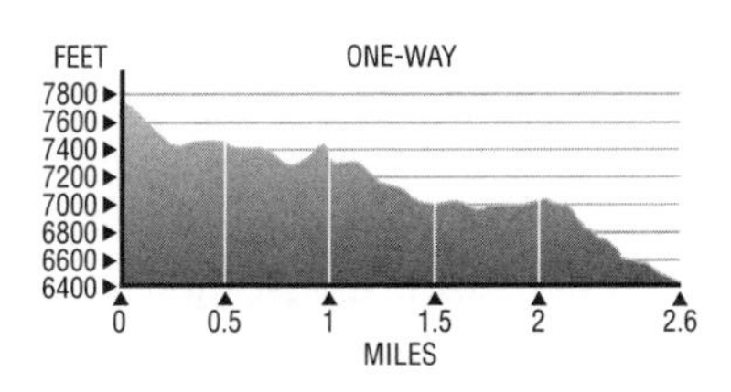

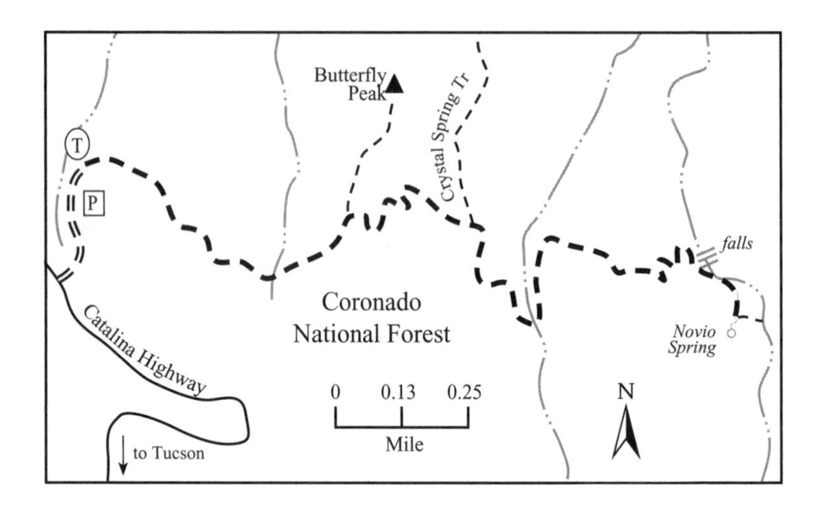

then back into thick pine trees once again. However, be warned. The Butterfly Trail was dramatically affected by a wildfire in 2002, and although it is healing, it will probably take several decades to recover. In the meantime, erosion caused by vegetation loss produces seasonal changes that may make the trail difficult to follow and may result in hazards such as loose rocks and falling branches. The water in Novio Spring flows the entire year except for the very hottest days of summer. Purify the water before drinking.

Within a few hundred feet, the paved road turns into a wide dirt track that soon arrives at an intersection. Take the left fork as the level trail passes majestic trees up to 3 feet in diameter and parallels a deep ravine. At the intersection at 0.15 mile, again take the left fork where the broad road narrows to a single-file mountain trail and begins to descend the side of the steep mountain through tall ponderosa pines with thick undergrowth. The trail frequently crosses valleys between ridges that drain water from the mountain. Fast-running water has cut deep ravines in some valleys, and in others has formed areas where plants, including wild raspberries and flowers, grow abundantly. The drainage at 0.4 mile supplies enough water for bigtooth maple, and later, at 0.9 mile, thick patches of oak and maple shade the trail. The broad intersection at the 1-mile mark provides access to Butterfly Peak to the left, but for this hike, take the right fork to continue on the Butterfly Trail's descent toward Novio Spring.

The thick forest gives way to a clearing near the intersection with the Crystal Spring Trail at 1.4 miles. Stay straight, on the Butterfly

Trail, as yucca and several types of oak become more abundant. At just beyond 1.5 miles the trail becomes less clear as it begins to cross a dry streambed, but a large pine tree and a cairn mark the way and the trail soon becomes well defined once more. The steep descent of the trail, which is rocky at times, is mitigated by switchbacks that cut through thickets of Gambel oak, across gorges, and past large granite boulders among the trees.

A sunnier section of the trail, at 2 miles, has a more oak woodlands environment, where you will likely see lizards climbing on the rocks among the yucca, but the thick forest returns a mere 0.4 mile later. Then, at 2.5 miles, an immense black rock rises next to the trail. Walk through the depression at its base, which fills with water when it rains, and past the rock to an intersection a few hundred feet later. The left fork leads down a hill to pools of water, but continue straight 0.1 mile as the trail begins to parallel the small stream formed by the springs.

A turnoff to the waters of Novio Spring is marked by a large fallen tree to the right of the trail and a 3-foot-high rock that is almost square and nearly 4 feet across. Take the path to the left, just beyond the boulder, down to the jumble of rocks that form myriad small pools

Along the Butterfly Trail (Photo by Lawrence Letham)

of clear water at different levels. In late summer, the flow is low, but the constant gurgle announces that water is slowly flowing over rocks from the higher to the lower pools. Elevation here is 6700 feet.

After you have enjoyed the deep shade and the serenity of the remote spring, return along the same path. Allow some extra time for the return trip, since the trail will gain 1000 feet by the time it delivers you to the trailhead.

23. DUTCH JOHN TRAIL

Distance ▪ 1.9 miles round trip
Difficulty ▪ Moderate
Features ▪ A shady walk through the woods to two springs, with a good chance of seeing a lot of birds
Starting elevation ▪ 5070 feet
Highest elevation ▪ 6020 feet
Total climb ▪ 960 feet
Location ▪ Coronado National Forest
Map ▪ USGS Mount Wrightson
Hiking season ▪ Year-round

Getting there: The trail is in the Nogales Ranger District of the Coronado National Forest, in the Madera Canyon Recreation Area, about 30 miles south of Tucson. Take I-19 south from Tucson to exit 63 eastbound for Continental Road. Follow the signs to Madera Canyon, about 12 miles, and to Bog Springs Campground. A modest parking fee is charged. Follow the loop through the campground almost all the way around to a parking area, to where spaces are set aside for hikers. From the parking area, cross the road, ascend the short flight of stone steps, and follow the well-worn path to the sign that marks the trailhead. There are restrooms and drinking water available in the campground. *Note: The road into Madera Canyon is paved, but narrow, winding, and with some steep sections, and not recommended for RVs. It is sometimes icy in winter.*

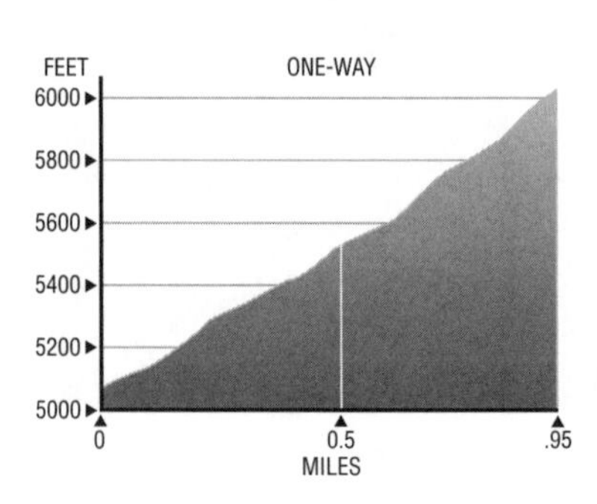

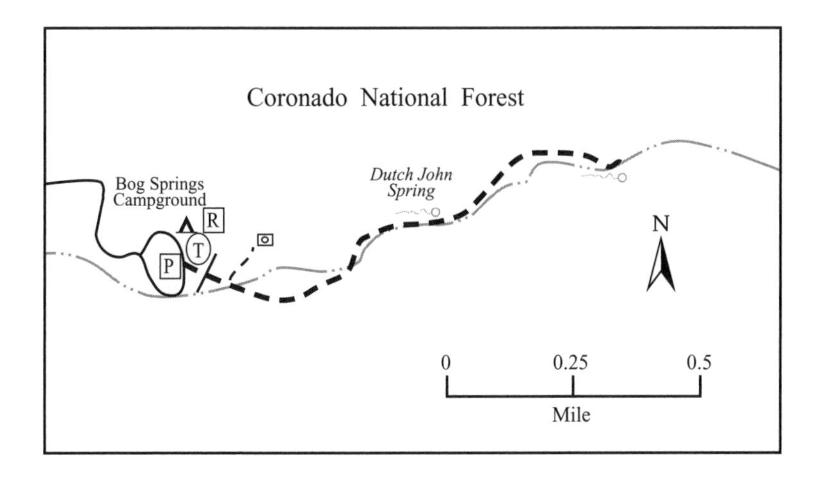

The trees along the Dutch John Trail not only provide shade but they are also sanctuary to hundreds of different types of birds that make Madera Canyon an internationally known birding area. Take a bird identification book and put names to the birds in view—more than a dozen species of hummingbirds have been seen here—and also watch for white-tailed deer. In addition to the wildlife, there are strangely shaped Arizona sycamores, a variety of oak trees, two springs, and red-colored rocks. Leaves from dense oak thickets litter the ground and rustle underfoot. Be on the lookout for beautiful thistles in bloom, yellow wildflowers, and giant alligator junipers. Purify the water from the springs before drinking, or carry all you will need for the hike.

A short 100 feet past the trailhead sign, a gate through the fence limits traffic to pedestrians. Big boulders, some with a dark red hue, lie in a dry creekbed 40 feet below the trail. At the intersection 100 feet past the gate, the left fork leads up a short hill to views of tall mountains and a thick forest of oak trees that cover the valley leading to the springs. The leaves of the Arizona sycamores turn golden in the fall and provide dashes of color along the dry creekbeds. Take the left fork if you wish to see the view, then return to the main trail; to skip the overlook, at the intersection stay to the right.

An odd-looking sycamore grows next to the trail at 0.1 mile, just after the trail crosses the creekbed. Its main trunk grows horizontal to the ground and insects have eaten the internal wood until it looks like lace, yet in spite of the trunk's condition, healthy branches sprout

Spring water storage tank (Photo by Lawrence Letham)

from it and grow skyward. The trees are so thick in areas that moss grows on many of them. The steady climb is broken momentarily at 0.3 mile where a sign marks the Mount Wrightson Wilderness Area boundary. From here the trail gets steeper.

The upward climb continues to an intersection, where the left fork descends to a sign that marks a small metal tank as being Dutch John Spring. The moisture from the spring supports yellow wildflowers and a host of thistles. Mushrooms grow in a hollow stump and a huge log makes a good bench for a short rest.

Leaving the spring, continue up the main trail to where it flattens out as it crosses the wide, dry creek again and then climbs out of the bed past a distinct group of four large sycamores. The trail narrows as it cuts through terrain covered with large clumps of bear grass until it arrives at a false intersection where the trail appears to continue straight into the creekbed, but in reality it turns 270 degrees to the right. Watch for the cairn that marks the path.

Boulders appear among the trees, while occasional golden penstemon flowers add color to the silverleaf oaks that crowd the trail. Acorn caps and thick leaves litter the ground. At just past 0.5 mile, to the right of the trail there is an old oak tree that was burned by fire, yet managed to live. The growth around the burn left it twisted and with a weird shape. A bit farther up, a 4-foot-long stump covers half the trail, which descends again into the creekbed. On the other side, the trail passes a small concrete tank that once collected spring water and ends near a natural pool fed by water from the hill behind it. The water nourishes abundant trees, thick grasses, yucca, moss, and prickly pear cactus.

From here, return to the trailhead along the same route.

Hummingbirds Have Reverse Gear

Often seen along the Dutch John and Madera Canyon Nature Trails, hummingbirds are delightful to watch as they hover over flowers and perform acrobatic mating dances, their little wings a constant blur. They also have a unique quality—hummingbirds are the only type of bird that can fly backwards.

24. MADERA CANYON NATURE TRAIL

Distance ▪ 2.7 miles round trip
Difficulty ▪ Easy
Features ▪ An interpretative nature trail offering panoramic mountain views
Starting elevation ▪ 5000 feet
Highest elevation ▪ 5430 feet
Total climb ▪ 425 feet
Location ▪ Coronado National Forest
Map ▪ USGS Mount Wrightson, Mount Hopkins
Hiking season ▪ Year-round

Getting there: The trail is in the Nogales Ranger District of the Coronado National Forest, in Madera Canyon Recreation Area, about 30 miles south of Tucson. Take I-19 south from Tucson to exit 63 eastbound for Continental Road. Follow the signs to Madera Canyon, about 13 miles, to the signs that mark the amphitheater and nature trail. Turn right into the parking area. A modest parking fee is charged. The trailhead is at the back of the lot. There are no restrooms or water at the trailhead. *Note: The road into Madera Canyon is paved, but narrow, winding, and with some steep sections, and not recommended for RVs. It is sometimes icy in winter.*

The open, mostly level Madera Canyon Nature Trail crosses a creek over a wooden bridge, then climbs slightly to panoramic views of the Santa Rita Mountains and soaring Mount Wrightson. Large outcroppings of weathered granite and rose-colored rocks add texture to the terrain, while tiny, single-sprig ferns hide in the undergrowth. Signs along the way point out mountain muly grass and resurrection plant, and explain geotropism. This is also a good spot to see birds, including more than a dozen species of hummingbirds. Much of the trail is open, providing little shade during the summer.

Follow the paved trail from the parking lot down to a wooden bridge that crosses a stony creekbed. Water flows down the creek in the spring, if winter weather left snow in the crags of the high Santa Rita Mountains, and for about an hour after a rainstorm, but most of the time the bed is dry. However, enough water flows to support sycamore trees like the strangely shaped one at the end of the bridge.

At an intersection just past the bridge, take the left fork where the trail changes from asphalt to dirt and passes behind the small amphitheater. Almost immediately, the trail starts a gentle climb through a rocky section where solid granite rock decomposes into wheat-sized grains. Tiny ferns, between 1 and 2 inches high, grow out of the ground as a single branch instead of a clump of branches, and small oak trees grow near rocks colored red by iron oxide. Four hundred feet from the bridge, resurrection plants grow abundantly on the hillside, helping to hold the topsoil in place.

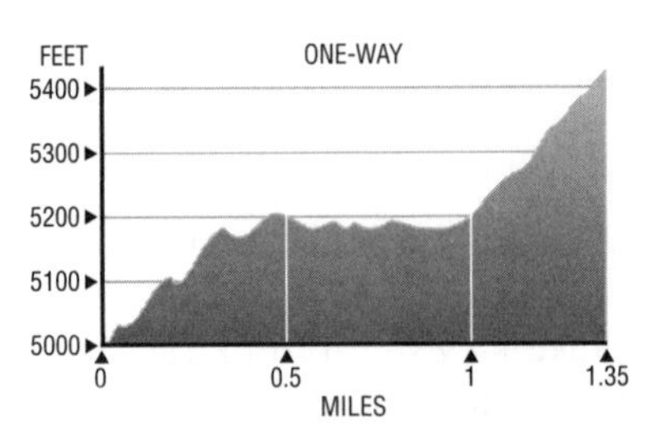

A huge rock overhangs the trail at 0.1 mile where a sign marks the hollow opening at its base as an animal cave. A quick succession of signs identify mountain muly, a grass that likes granitic soils; granite, a volcanic rock; and geotropism, when things grow

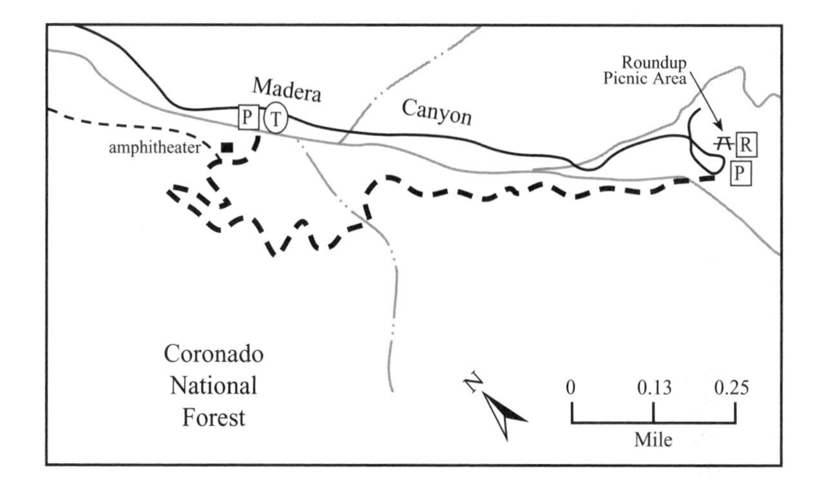

downward toward the force of gravity. Berries from junipers, some up to one-fourth inch in diameter, and decomposing rock from large granite outcroppings, litter the well-maintained trail.

A large sign and picture at 0.4 mile conveniently identify the locations and names of the mountains of the entire Santa Rita range that lies before you. The deep green of the lower altitudes produces an interesting contrast to the dull gray of Mount Wrightson's rocky heights. More pines now appear as the trail cuts across the deep, valley-like drainages that carry water from the hilltops to the valley floors. The water in the drainage at 0.6 mile supports lush grasses and wildflowers, while the same water leaves twisted furrows in the barren hills of predominantly granitic soil. Some granite outcroppings have a rosy hue reminiscent of a beautiful sunset. A huge, dead tree 25 to 30 feet tall stands at the 0.85-mile point. At about the 1-mile point, the undergrowth becomes thicker and Apache pines become more common. You can tell Apache pines by the pom-poms of 6-inch-long needles at the ends of their branches.

At 1.1 miles, the trail turns into a 2-foot-wide strip of concrete that curves through thick oaks splotched with moss, then at 1.2 miles it goes around a fence corner. The trail parallels the creek for about 500 feet, then crosses its dry bed before climbing up to the end at the Roundup Picnic Area. From here you can either turn around and walk back up the trail to where you started, which we recommend, or take a slightly shorter route by walking along the sometimes busy road back to the amphitheater parking lot.

25. HUNTER TRAIL

Distance ■ 4 miles round trip
Difficulty ■ Strenuous
Features ■ A steep, rocky climb to spectacular panoramic views
Starting elevation ■ 2000 feet
Highest elevation ■ 3374 feet
Total climb ■ 1600 feet
Location ■ Picacho Peak State Park
Map ■ USGS Newman Peak
Hiking season ■ Fall through spring

Getting there: Hunter Trail is located in Picacho Peak State Park, about 40 miles north of Tucson via I-10, exit 219. Pay your day-use or camping fees and pick up a park map, which will direct you to the trailhead. Restrooms and drinking water are located near the trailhead. Because you'll need to have both hands free to grasp the cables (gloves are very welcome here), use a backpack or a fanny pack to carry your water and other necessities.

Rising some 1500 feet from its flat surroundings, Picacho Peak provides one of the more popular and challenging hikes in this part of Arizona. The trail is steep and rocky, with steel cables in especially steep places to help provide stability. It might be fair to question whether this is hiking or mountain climbing, but either way it's a rewarding experience, with great views from the top.

Picacho Peak has been a landmark for travelers for possibly a thousand years, from prehistoric Hohokam, Spanish missionaries, and Anglo pioneers. It is along the route of the Mormon Battalion—members of the Church of Jesus Christ of Latter-day Saints that walked past the peak in 1846 when they marched from Iowa to California after being recruited to fight in the Mexican War. This is also the site of Arizona's biggest Civil War battle. Monuments to both the Mormon Battalion and the Civil War Battle are located in the park, and the battle is reenacted each year in mid-March.

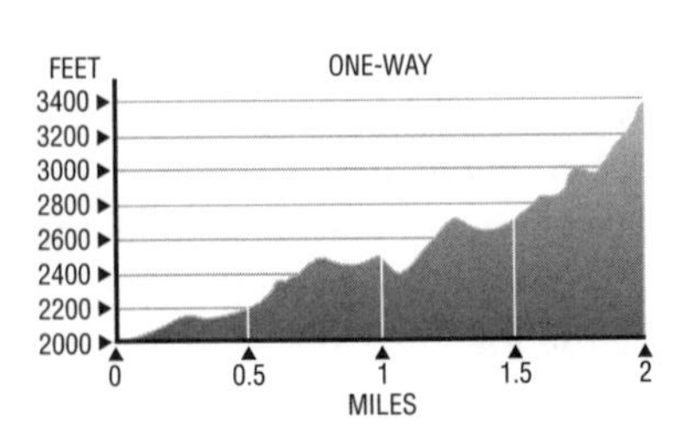

Life seen along Hunter Trail includes swifts and doves that live in holes in the cliffs, plus

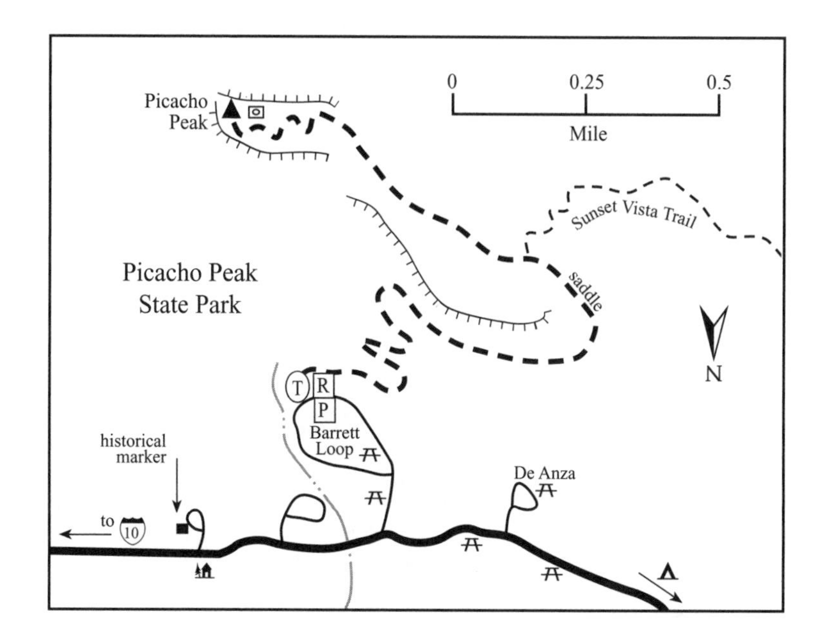

red-tailed hawks, roadrunners, numerous lizards, rattlesnakes, desert cottontail rabbits, and various squirrels. If you are hiking in spring after a wet winter, you'll see an abundance of wildflowers, especially Mexican gold poppies, but also larkspur and brittlebush. Also watch for the flowers of various cacti, including saguaro, hedgehog, fishhook barrel, and both teddybear and Christmas cholla.

From the trailhead, the ground slopes upward to the base of the large, sheer cliffs of the peak. As the trail winds toward the base of the cliff, it passes through a short, steep section that has handrails. At about 0.75 mile, the trail reaches a cliff. Erosion has carved pockets into the cliff base, like round scoops out of ice cream, although none of the holes are very big. Continue along the trail to the hike's halfway point at a saddle, where a bench provides rest. Although not as satisfying as making it all the way to the top, this is a good turnaround point for those not anxious to tackle the really steep sections to follow.

From the saddle, Hunter Trail descends sharply on the other side of the mountain. It is a steep, improved trail with hand cables for safety. The Sunset Vista Trail intersects Hunter Trail on the right about 0.25 mile beyond the saddle; continue straight ahead to stay on Hunter Trail. Where the descent ends, the trail begins a very steep climb—more climbing than hiking—but the handrails give a sense of security.

A saguaro points the way to Picacho Peak.

The steep trail continues with occasional level sections until it reaches a small, semicircular canyon at 1.6 miles. After the level canyon, there is only one more very steep, hard section before the last short walk to the top.

The view from the summit is superb, and on a clear day you can see both Tucson and Phoenix. The closest mountains, the rest of the Picacho Mountain Range, lie to the north, just across I-10. All others are far in the distance across a flat, seemingly endless expanse.

Return to the trailhead by the same route.

26. JUAN BAUTISTA DE ANZA NATIONAL HISTORICAL TRAIL

Distance ▪ 4.5 miles one way
Difficulty ▪ Easy to moderate
Features ▪ An historic route through a riparian area with good birding
Starting elevation ▪ 3262 feet
Highest elevation ▪ 3262 feet
Total climb ▪ 75 feet
Location ▪ Tumacácori National Historical Park
Map ▪ USGS Tubac
Hiking season ▪ Year-round

Getting there: The trail can be accessed from either Tubac Presidio State Historic Park at the north end or from Tumacácori National Historical Park at the south, which is where this description begins. From Tucson head south on I-19 about 45 miles to the exit for Tumacácori National Historical Park (exit 29 at this writing, but that's in kilometers; if the signage reverts to miles, it would be about exit 18). To hike it north to south, take exit 34 for Tubac Presidio State Historic Park (exit 34 in kilometers; about exit 21 in miles). If possible, have a vehicle waiting at the end of the trail; if not, you'll be walking back to your vehicle.

Commonly called the Anza Trail, this is a section of one of the newest of twelve National Historic Trails in the United States, and the first so designated in the Western Region of the National Park Service. Congress gave the trail its blessing on August 15, 1990, and when fully open to the public, the trail will run from Nogales, Arizona, all the way to San Francisco, California. It traces as nearly as possible the route taken in the winter of 1775–76 by Juan Bautista de Anza and some 300 Mexican immigrants.

Of course, the trek actually began in Mexico—Culiacan, Sinaloa, Mexico, to be exact—and there is hope that eventually the 600 miles of Mexico they traversed before arriving at Nogales will also be incorporated, making this the first International Historic Trail in the world. It will take years of planning and negotiating before

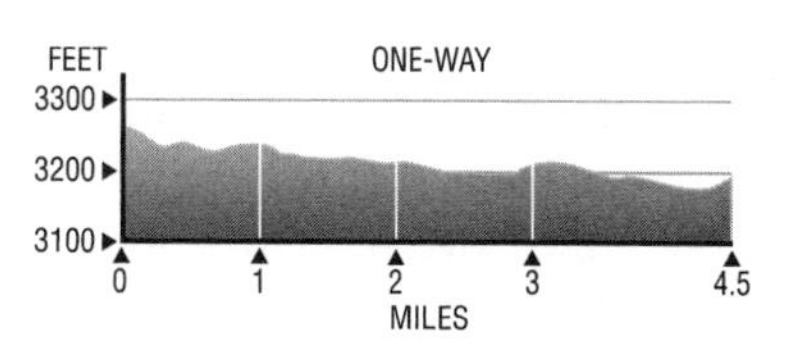

the entire trail will be ready, but there is currently one section open in the Anza-Borrego State Park in California, and this is a description of the first section opened in Arizona.

Each park has a very nice visitor center where you can pick up a trail brochure. Restrooms and drinking water are available at the visitor centers also, but not along the trail. The trail is open to hikers and equestrians, and pets are allowed on leash. Although partially shaded, the trail can be quite hot. Do *not* drink the river water; it is considered unsafe. Watch for rattlesnakes and other desert inhabitants, and stay on the trail. Much of the trail traverses private property, and its continued use is through their courtesy. Please respect it and them.

This is a prime bird-watching area. Birds most frequently seen along the trail year-round include common flicker, Gila woodpecker, vermilion flycatcher, Say's phoebe, raven, roadrunner, American kestrel, red-tailed hawk, turkey vulture, several doves, white-breasted nuthatch, Bewick's wren, loggerhead shrike, cardinal, black-headed grosbeak, house finch, brown towhee, Western meadowlark, red-winged blackbird, bronzed and brown-headed cowbirds, mockingbird, blue-gray gnatcatcher, a variety of hummingbirds, house sparrow, and black-throated gray and yellow-rumped warblers. Great blue herons are seen frequently fall through spring but only occasionally in summer; Gambel's quail are seen most frequently winter through summer.

From the front door of the Tumacácori National Historical Park visitor center, walk north to the clearly marked trailhead. For a while the trail follows the barbed wire fence that marks the park boundary; at about 0.25 mile, stop to read the signs describing the riparian area you are about to traverse, and the importance of the Santa Cruz River to life in the area. From here you can opt to follow a short trail down to the river, which then loops back to the Anza Trail. If you stay on the Anza Trail, it soon makes a left turn (north) and begins to wend its way through mesquite, saltbush, willow, and elder, more or less following the river.

The walk is tranquil and peaceful, punctuated with occasional rustlings from little critters in the brush, and the pleasant call of birds overhead. You can only dimly hear the hum of motor vehicles along the highway to the west. As you approach the first river crossing, at about the 1.25-mile mark, you'll pass through a gate and walk back along the fence a short distance before turning toward the bridge over the river. The trail becomes sandy, and cottonwoods tower overhead. In summer, the atmosphere can be quite close unless a breeze stirs the leaves.

Just short of 1.5 miles there's a fork in the trail with a marker in the middle; stay to the right. You'll sometimes find yourself walking among mesquite and other short scrubby trees, making for a closed-in feeling, and at other times the taller elder and cottonwoods are scattered about in a more open setting. Some large trees have fallen and are rotting away along the trail, and at almost the 2-mile point, there are at least four abandoned and rusting cars!

At about 2.5 miles, you'll come to a falling down, fairly large adobe building, but unfortunately there's no clue to its history. You're over halfway to Tubac now, and the trail continues among changing foliage, occasionally passing through a gate, past a cow pasture, and at 3.5 miles you'll cross back to the west side of the river over a somewhat narrow plank footbridge. As you climb away from the river, the trail

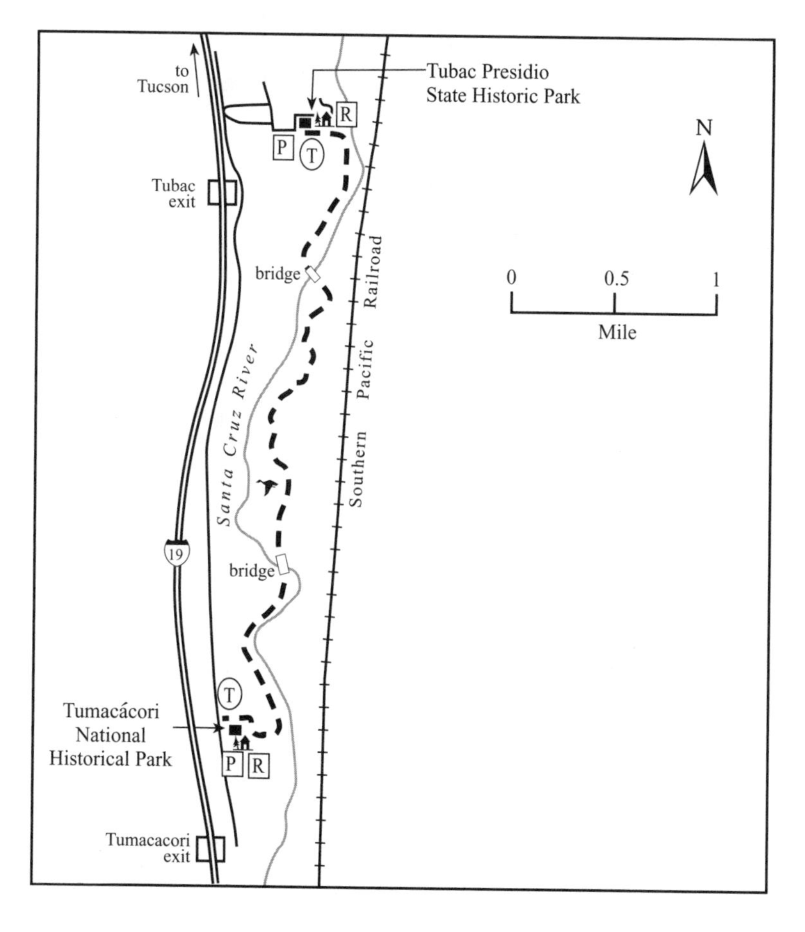

Trail follows a riparian area along the Santa Cruz River.

becomes sandier and a little harder to traverse, and cacti begin reappearing. Another mile brings you to the Tubac Presidio trailhead, the end of this part of the Anza Trail. Now you can head to your waiting vehicle, or start the walk back 4.5 miles to Tumacácori National Historical Park.

97. CREEK AND RAILROAD TRAILS LOOP

Distance	1.75-mile loop
Difficulty	Easy
Features	Excellent birding and riparian habitat
Starting elevation	3969 feet
Highest elevation	4015 feet
Total climb	92 feet
Location	Patagonia-Sonoita Creek Preserve
Map	USGS Patagonia, Nature Conservancy handout
Hiking season	Year-round

Getting there: These trails are located in the Nature Conservancy's Patagonia-Sonoita Creek Preserve in Patagonia, which is about 60 miles southeast of Tucson. From Tucson, take I-10 east to exit 281 for AZ 83, which you follow south for about 25 miles to Sonoita, where it junctions with AZ 82. Turn west on AZ 82 for about 11 miles to Patagonia. In Patagonia turn west onto 4th Avenue, south on Pennsylvania, cross the creek, and go about 1 mile to the Patagonia-Sonoita Creek Preserve entrance. An alternative route is to follow the directions to Patagonia Lake State Park (Hike 28) and continue about 7 miles northeast from the park entrance road turnoff on AZ 82 to Patagonia.

Combining the Creek and Railroad Trails takes hikers along the Sonoita Creek and then back by way of an abandoned railroad bed, dating from the late nineteenth century. There's a small visitor center (with restrooms and water) where you can learn about (and join) the Nature Conservancy and pick up a bird list and trail map. Trail use fees are charged, with discounts for Nature Conservancy members. The trailhead is located a short distance behind, or south of, the visitor center, and the first part of the trail follows the handicap-accessible nature trail as far as post number 7, which is about 1500 feet of trail.

Birds to watch for year-round include the American kestrel, mourning dove, and song sparrow. Fall through spring boasts a wider variety of sparrows—chipping, savannah, Lincoln's, Brewer's, and white-crowned—plus American goldfinch and northern harrier. The warmer months bring out the vermilion flycatcher, blue grosbeak, and indigo buntings.

The Creek Trail starts out in an open meadow scattered with tall sacaton grasses (especially around post number 1), but soon enters a shady riparian woodland leading to the creekbed. Turning right onto the nature trail takes you to post number 2, which marks a groundwater monitoring well, number 3 is where you first step upon the old railroad bed, and number 4 gives the first view of Sonoita Creek, one of the few year-round surface flows in the region. The narrow flow of water between verdant banks below overhanging trees is a peaceful sight. The trail leaves the railroad bed by way of a few stone steps, and post number 5 is streamside.

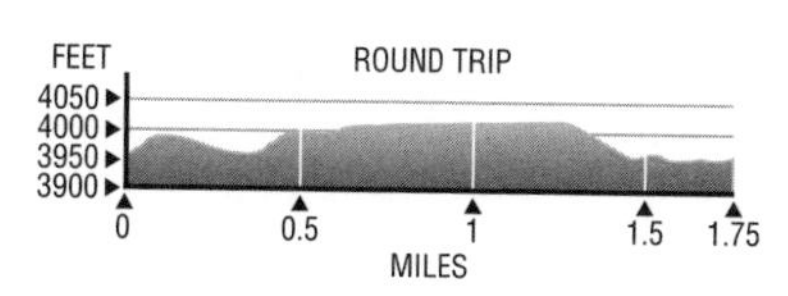

Post number 6 is farther along the creek, about 0.25 mile from the trailhead, and marks one of the oldest and largest Fremont cottonwoods you're likely to see

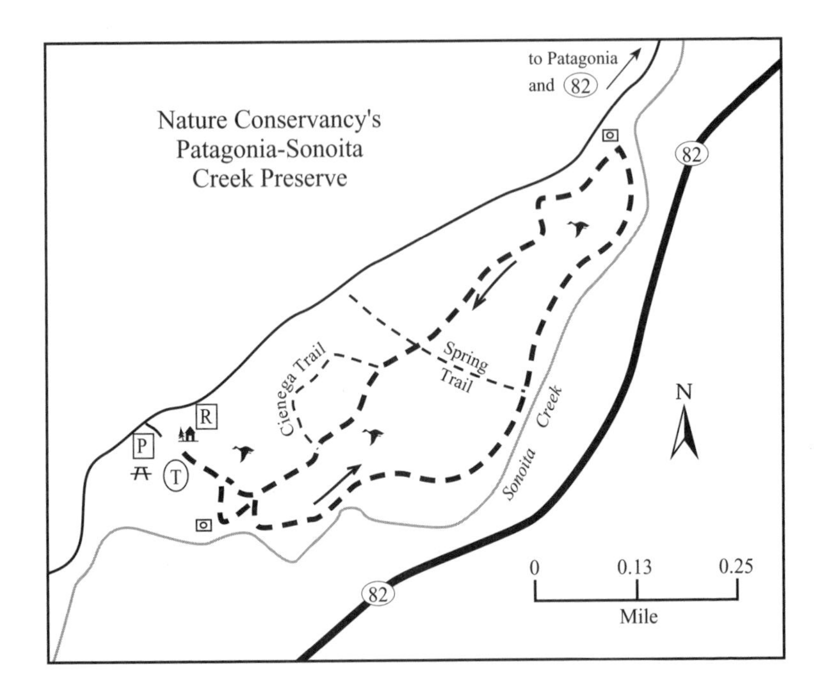

in the region. Cottonwoods are said to be the most productive nesting habitat in North America, and this one has been providing homes for nesting birds for some 140 years.

Raptor sightings (post number 7) in the preserve number about twenty-two, and breeding species include the American kestrel plus red-tailed, Cooper's, and gray hawks. The gray hawk, a tropical species, is seen only as far north as the southernmost parts of Arizona, New Mexico, and western Texas, and mostly in summer; whereas the other raptors live in the preserve year-round.

Now rejoin the Creek Trail (the nature trail turns left) as it meanders easterly along the waterway through a forest of willows and old cottonwoods. These occasionally form a canopy of gnarled branches overhead, which in winter appear black against the blue sky. Numerous dead and down trees lay where they've fallen, becoming slowly hidden in masses of low-growing bushes, vines, and grasses. Unusual in the desert southwest, this phenomenon is only possible because Sonoita Creek runs year-round, supplying the necessary water for a wetland habitat.

As you walk the stream, watch for hummingbirds and butterflies in summer, and keep your eyes peeled for wildflowers peeking out from among the grasses along the water's edge.

At about 0.6 mile the trail crosses a fire break, and a bit farther it cuts through—literally—a huge downed cottonwood. At about 0.9 mile is what's left of an old railroad bridge abutment, where the trail leaves the creek, climbs up onto the abandoned rail bed, and turns southwest on its loop back to the trailhead. You've now left the Creek Trail and are following the Railroad Trail.

In the late 1800s, this berm supported the last link of an international rail line, which ran from St. Louis, Missouri, to the port at Guaymas, Mexico, on the Sea of Cortes. But in 1929 disaster struck: a flood washed out more than 4000 feet of track west of here, after which 15 miles of the line in this area was abandoned. Over the years more sections of track were vacated and service reduced until finally, in 1962, all service between Calabasas (just north of present day Nogales) and Benson, Arizona, was ended.

The hike along the railway bed is through smaller and less water-dependent trees than the cottonwood, including Mexican elderberry,

A pleasant walk through a riparian area

Arizona ash and walnut, and mesquite. In spring look for the brilliant Mexican gold poppy. At about 1.5 miles, shortly after the trail recrosses the fire break, the Cienega Trail branches off to the right, leading through an almost swamplike area, fed by a spring that's part of the same ground waters that feed Sonoita Creek. The term *cienega* comes from two Spanish words: *cien* (hundred) and *agua* (water), and it is used in the Southwest to refer to marshy or swampy areas. The Cienega Trail loops back to the Railroad Trail, so you have your choice of which way to go.

After the Cienega rejoins the Railroad Trail, it's about 0.2 mile to the trailhead.

28. SONOITA CREEK TRAIL

Distance ■ 2 miles round trip
Difficulty ■ Easy
Features ■ A shady hike through a riparian area with an abundance of birds
Starting elevation ■ 3775 feet
Highest elevation ■ 3800 feet
Total climb ■ 100 feet
Location ■ Patagonia Lake State Park
Map ■ USGS Cumero Canyon
Hiking season ■ Year-round

Getting there: Patagonia Lake State Park is located 12 miles northeast of Nogales (which is about 63 miles south of Tucson) on AZ 82 and then 4 miles north on the park access road. Once inside the park, to get to the trail continue on the entrance road to a T, turn right (east), go into the campground, and follow this road east to where it makes a short loop. A small parking area and the trailhead are at the east side of the loop. An alternative route is to follow the directions to Patagonia-Sonoita Creek Preserve (Hike 27), and when you get to the community of Patagonia, continue southwest on AZ 82 for about 7 miles to the state park access road.

Although most people come to Patagonia Lake State Park for fishing or boating, it is also a wonderful bird-watching destination with a shady trail through both desert and riparian habitats, with views of the lake and marsh, and a good chance of seeing birds and other wildlife.

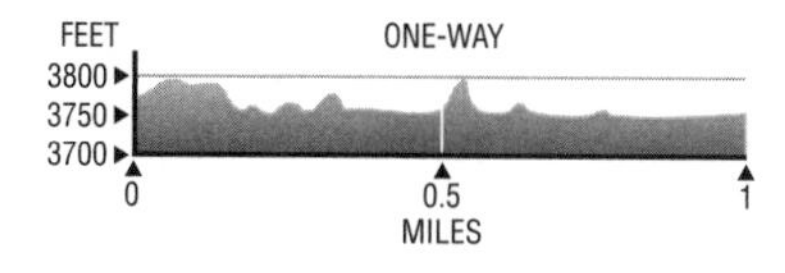

There are park day-use and camping fees; restrooms and drinking water are available in the campground. Day-use hours are 8:00 AM to 10:00 PM daily. The trail is open to hikers and mountain bikers and leashed pets. Because of the trail's proximity to grazing land, you might also encounter a cow or two.

The Sonoita Creek Trail meanders along the shore of Patagonia Lake, moving through changing scenery. From desert terrain of cactus, ocotillo, mesquite, and junipers, it crosses grassy fields into a wetland of marsh grasses and cattails, and to a particularly scenic spot where Sonoita Creek enters the lake. Although mostly easy to follow, some low sections can be a bit mucky after a rain or when the lake level is high, and a few too many social trails can sometimes lead you astray. But you can't go too far wrong; just follow the lakeshore back to the trailhead. A few interpretative signs describe the plants and wildlife that might be seen along the trail.

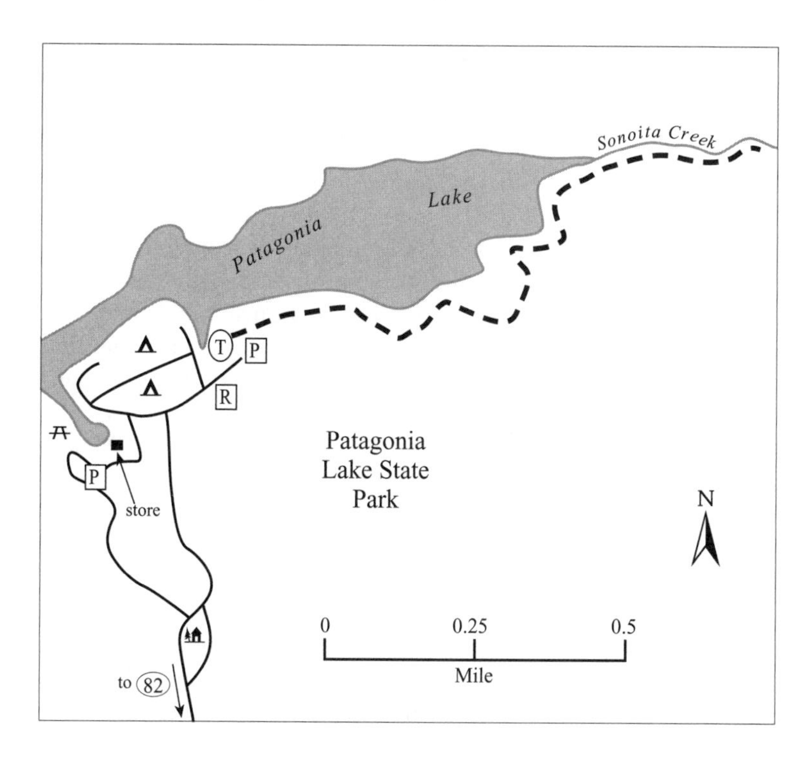

You will often see sailboats and other watercraft at Patagonia Lake.

The trail is an excellent place to see numerous species of birds. Watch for great blue herons walking the shoreline in search of dinner and numerous types of ducks and other shorebirds in the marshes. Among other birds you might spot are Gambel's quail, American coots, mourning doves, Gila woodpeckers, rock wrens, black-tailed gnatcatchers, mountain bluebirds, northern mockingbirds, black-throated sparrows, and white-crowned sparrows. Bird-watching is particularly good in March, April, and early May. Also watch for white-tailed deer, black-tailed jackrabbits, desert cottontails, cliff chipmunks, rock squirrels, and the white-nosed coati—a gregarious and curious member of the raccoon family.

The trail begins as a packed dirt path through a desert environment of prickly pear cactus, mesquite, and various grasses, wandering for about 450 feet along a ridge with views out over the lake. Wooden steps drop down to the riparian area along the lakeshore—here the trail can get muddy—and at about 0.4 mile the trail crosses a large, grassy meadow. A lot of side trails wander around here, and if you head over to the shore of the now swampy lake, you'll likely see a duck or two.

The Sonoita Creek enters the lake as the meadow ends, at about 0.6 mile, and now the trail follows the creek through an open forest of old cottonwoods. Terrain gets a bit hilly and the trail becomes somewhat rocky as it continues to follow the creek, and you'll need to watch out for low branches. The trail now becomes more rugged and increasingly difficult to follow, so we suggest that by about the 1-mile point you turn around, and follow as best as possible the same route back to the trailhead.

29. CORONADO CAVE TRAIL

Distance	1.5-miles round trip hike plus about 0.5 mile of caving
Difficulty	Moderate
Features	A desert hike to a limestone cave
Starting elevation	5230 feet
Highest elevation	5700 feet
Total climb	700 feet
Location	Coronado National Memorial
Map	USGS Montezuma Pass, Coronado National Memorial brochure
Hiking season	Year-round

Getting there: The trail and cave are located in Coronado National Memorial. From Tucson, travel east on I-10 for 45 miles to AZ 90, then south for 30 miles to the town of Sierra Vista and the junction with AZ 92. Follow AZ 92 south about 16 miles to Coronado Memorial Road, which you follow for about 5 miles to the national memorial visitor center parking lot. Restrooms and drinking water are available at the visitor center, and the trailhead is just west of the parking lot.

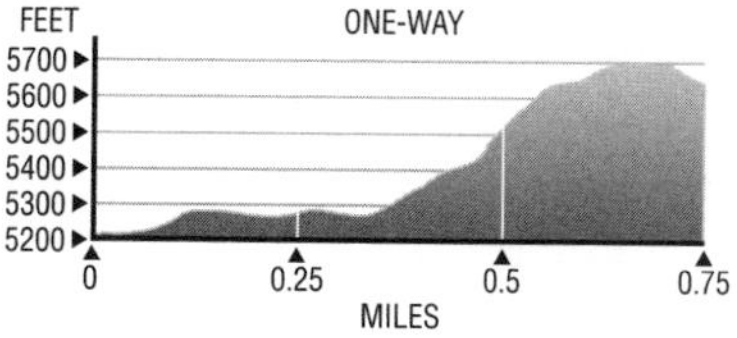

This fine short hike not only takes you through interesting desert terrain but also provides a unique opportunity to explore

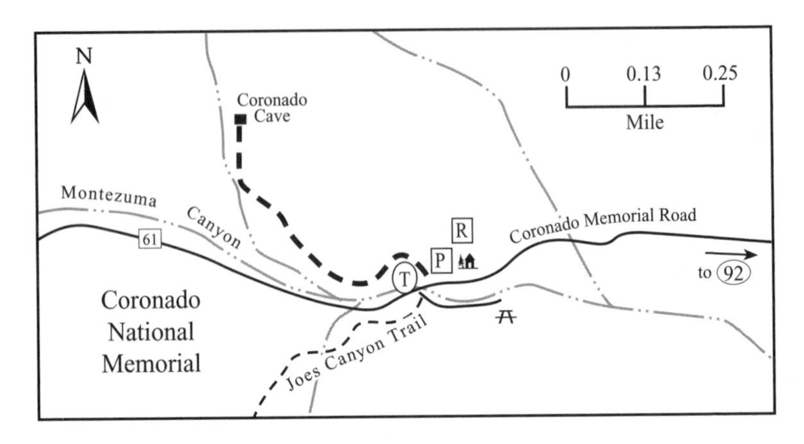

a natural cave. Coronado Cave is undeveloped—no lighting or paved pathways—and well preserved, with beautiful stalactites, stalagmites, columns, scallops, and curtains.

Those planning to enter the cave should obtain the required free permits available at the visitor center. You'll also need a powerful flashlight; rangers say each person should carry two, just in case one stops working. And once you get inside, be careful to not touch any of the formations—the oils and acids on your fingers will discolor the formations and may stop them from growing.

Among the more than one hundred species of birds to watch for here are Mexican jays, acorn woodpeckers, ruby-crowned kinglets, and white-winged doves. You might also see desert cottontail rabbits, white-tailed deer, javelina, lizards, and several varieties of poisonous snakes, including western diamondback rattlers.

The trail starts as an easy walk down through a wash, then up the other side, through manzanita, cane cholla, oaks, and sycamores. It then begins a moderate, continuous climb, with switchbacks and some shaded sections, rising steadily for 0.5 mile. It ends at the cave, where you climb over some boulders and down the sloping cave entrance to the level floor inside. The light flooding in from the entrance reveals a large chamber, but there is not enough light to make out any details.

With two connected rooms, the limestone cave is about 600 feet long, some 20 feet high, and about 70 feet wide. Inside you'll see a variety of cave formations, ranging from the draperies just inside the entrance to stalagmites, stalactites, helictites, cave coral, and rimstone

Opposite: *The Coronado Cave Trail*

dams, which are ridges of calcite that sometimes hold pools of water.

Legend has it that Apache leader Geronimo used the cave as a hideout during the Indian Wars of the late 1800s, and he supposedly used a narrow shaft in the cave as an escape route. Graffiti on the cave ceiling was left by miners in the late nineteenth century, and you may also see light-colored cave crickets and several species of bats. Cave visitors should not disturb any wildlife, and especially hibernating bats, which may die if they're awakened.

After exploring the cave, return back down the path to the trailhead. Before leaving the memorial, you'll want to examine the exhibits in the visitor center that tell the story of the 1540 expedition that passed by here in which Francisco Vásquez de Coronado led a group of soldiers and priests from Spain in search of the fabled Seven Cities of Gold.

ORGAN PIPE CACTUS NATIONAL MONUMENT

Our favorite national monument in Arizona, Organ Pipe boasts excellent hiking trails, scenic drives, a very pleasant campground, a rugged Sonoran Desert landscape, and an abundance of birds and other wildlife. Operated by the National Park Service, the monument is named for the organ pipe cactus, a large cactus of multiple stalks that is common in the hot areas of Mexico, but rare in the mostly cooler United States. In fact, Organ Pipe Cactus National Monument contains the bulk of the species in the United States. However, the monument is more than one particular plant, and is an ideal spot to experience a

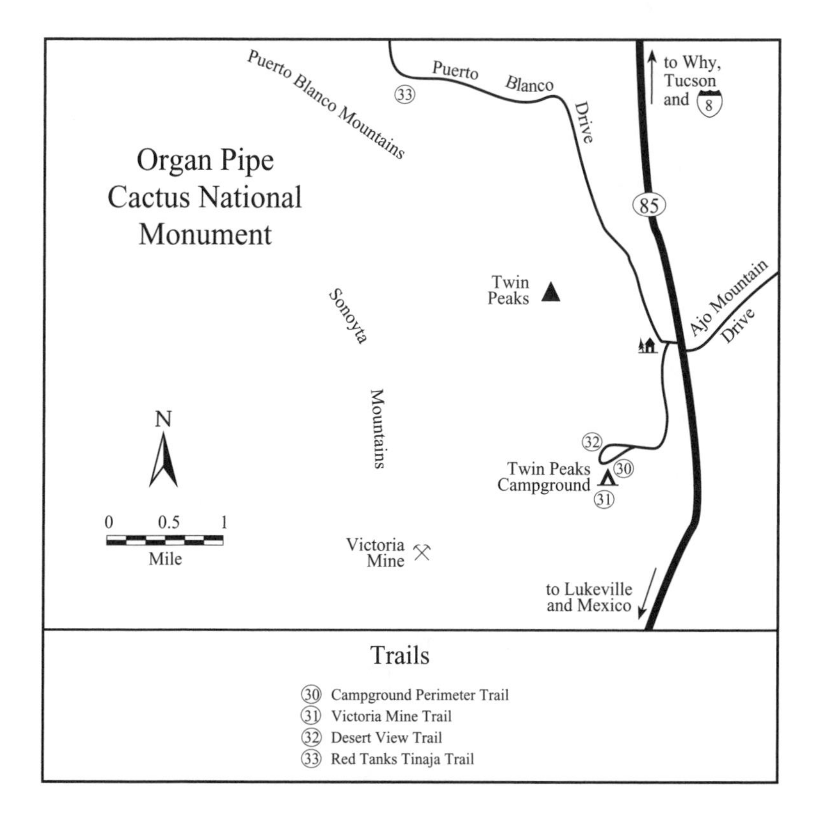

Organ Pipe Cactus National Monument's namesake cactus

classic Sonoran Desert terrain, with more than two dozen species of cacti alone, plus numerous other plants and animals that have adapted to this extreme climate of hot sun and little rain.

Organ pipe and saguaro cactus dominate the views here, as they tower over the other desert plants. At first they appear similar, especially the younger plants, but the two are actually fairly easy to distinguish. Organ pipe branches, or arms, are generally smaller in diameter, and the multiple arms all grow from the base. On the other hand, saguaros have one tall, fairly thick trunk from which its arms emerge at varying heights.

The monument has more than a dozen established hiking trails plus opportunities for backcountry hiking. Because of the extreme heat in the summer, the best times for hiking are from October through April, and even then hikers should avoid overexertion and overexposure to the sun, and carry a gallon of water per person per day. In addition, rangers warn hikers to watch out for cactus spines and poisonous desert creatures such as rattlesnakes, Gila monsters, and scorpions. Those hiking or even walking around the campground after dark should use flashlights to avoid stepping on rattlesnakes, which are generally nocturnal.

Throughout the monument are a wide variety of plants, and many of them put on an annual wildflower display if the weather has cooperated and sent the right amount of rain at the right time. The best time to see wildflowers is usually from March through July, with annuals such as lupine and the Ajo lily first, then perennials such as paloverde, fairy duster, and ocotillo, and finally the colorful cacti, including hedgehogs, cholla, saguaros, and organ pipes.

About 275 species of birds have been seen in the monument, and more than 60 species are known to breed here. The monument's mammals include desert bighorn sheep, mule and white-tailed deer, pronghorns, bobcats, javelina, and numerous smaller species. There are also more than a dozen species of lizards, including the poisonous Gila monster, which can grow up to 2 feet long, and six species of rattlesnakes. Bird and wildlife checklists are available at the visitor center.

The visitor center has a bookstore and a variety of exhibits on the Sonoran Desert, and from mid-December through March rangers offer guided walks and talks.

Organ Pipe Cactus National Monument is located along the U.S.-Mexico border, 22 miles south of Why via Arizona Highway 85 (AZ 85). For additional information, contact the monument office. You'll find complete contact information in the appendix at the back of this book.

The Truth About Turkey Vultures and Coyotes

Bird-watchers at Organ Pipe Cactus National Monument often see turkey vultures, also known as buzzards, soaring through the skies, and may sometimes mistake them for golden eagles, which are about the same size and from the ground look quite similar. The easiest way to tell the two birds apart is that unlike the golden eagle, the turkey vulture has the ability to glide practically forever without flapping its wings, riding on columns of warm air.

Also seen, and frequently heard here, are coyotes. They hunt rabbits, rodents, and other small animals, and can run at over 25 miles per hour, sometimes reaching 40 miles per hour. Usually colored tan or yellow-gray, with bushy tails, coyotes are sometimes mistaken for domestic dogs, especially from a distance. The way to easily tell them apart is by watching the animals run—coyotes run with their tails down, while dogs run with their tails up.

CAMPGROUNDS

The nearest commercial campgrounds, with RV hookups and other amenities, are in the small communities of Lukeville, along the

Mexican border about 5 miles south of the park entrance; Why, 22 miles north of Organ Pipe; and Ajo, about another 10 miles to the northwest. Contact the national monument office for additional information.

Twin Peaks Campground. This spacious campground has sites separated by typical desert vegetation, such as paloverde and creosote bush, and an abundance of cacti. It offers panoramic views, especially photogenic at sunset, and easy access to several hiking trails. It is open year-round and has 208 campsites, restrooms with flush toilets, but no showers or RV hookups. There is an RV dump station. RVs over 35 feet are prohibited. Reservations are not accepted and a modest fee is charged.

30. CAMPGROUND PERIMETER TRAIL

Distance	■	1-mile loop
Difficulty	■	Easy
Features	■	A scenic walk through the Sonoran Desert
Starting elevation	■	1690 feet
Highest elevation	■	1720 feet
Total climb	■	50 feet
Location	■	Organ Pipe Cactus National Monument
Map	■	USGS Lukeville
Hiking season	■	Year-round

Getting there: Organ Pipe Cactus National Monument is located along the U.S.-Mexico border, 22 miles south of Why via AZ 85. Not surprisingly, the Campground Perimeter Loop circles the campground, which is located about 1.4 miles southwest of the visitor center. Leashed pets are permitted on the trail, but owners are asked to clean up after them. There are restrooms and drinking water in the campground.

Especially convenient for those camping at Twin Peaks Campground—the national monument's main campground—this fairly flat and easy walk is an excellent introduction to the plants and general terrain of the Sonoran Desert. It's also scenic, with organ pipe cactus, several types of cholla, and ocotillo

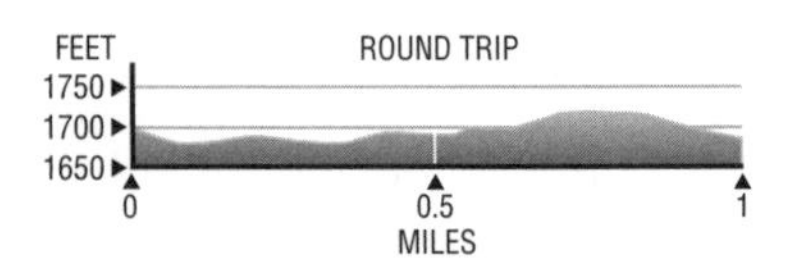

standing tall in front of distant peaks. It is especially scenic just after sunrise or before sunset.

This trail has an abundance of chain-fruit and teddybear cholla, some of it very close to the path, and hikers should watch young children and

Ocotillo in bloom

pets carefully to avoid an unpleasant encounter (see the sidebar "Beware the Attack Cholla!").

Because this loop circles the campground, you can start and end it practically anywhere. For this description, though, start near the entrance station, where you'll find a kiosk with a bulletin board and free book exchange (a nice touch, we think). From here head to the right (west). The trail crosses the road several times before getting away from the campsites and into the desert, and even though the campground remains in sight, there is a feeling of being out in the wilds. Turning south, the trail passes some attractive ocotillo—especially pretty in spring when they're in bloom—and then passes a turnoff for the campground amphitheater.

After 0.4 mile the trail turns east and passes a path to the Victoria Mine Trail, which is discussed below. Continuing east, the trail maneuvers around the RV dump station and meanders through a wash, which is loaded with tall ocotillo, paloverde, and some mesquite. The trail bends to the left, heading north, and passes the Palo Verde Trail, a 1.3-mile path that connects the campground with the visitor center (leashed pets allowed). The trail continues north, passes another connection to the Palo Verde Trail, and gradually bends to the west to return to the starting point.

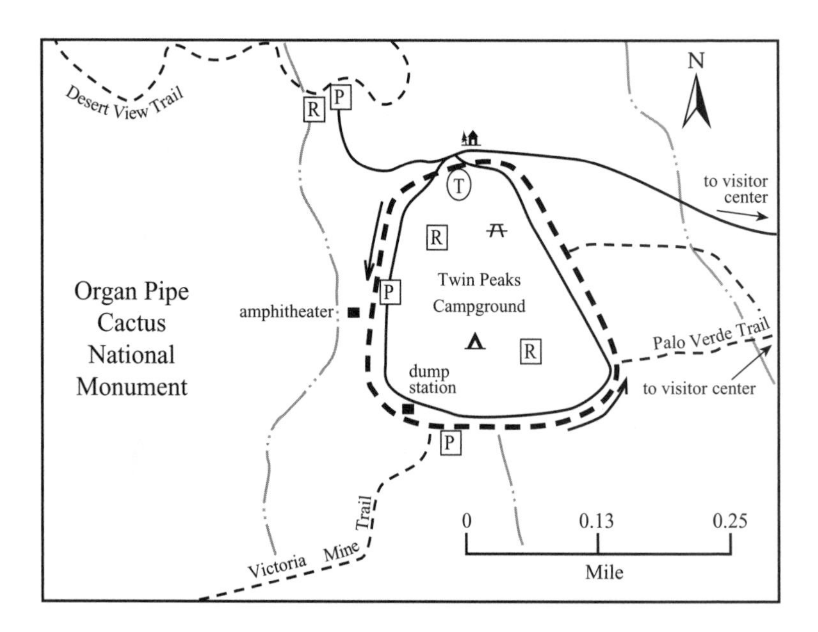

Beware of Attack Cholla!

At least ten different species of cholla cactus grow at Organ Pipe Cactus National Monument, and although they are very pretty to look at, especially when the sun makes their spines sparkle, give them a wide berth if you value your skin. Two types in particular—chain-fruit (also called jumping) and teddybear (for its soft, almost cuddly appearance)—have a nasty habit of attaching themselves to anyone who brushes against them, even lightly. Both species have short branches, attached by joints, that detach easily and seem to jump out at passersby, digging in for a free ride to some other spot to put down roots. Their spines are painful, and the experience is especially terrifying for young children and pets. They're found throughout the park and are a bit too close for comfort along some sections of the Campground Perimeter Trail.

31. VICTORIA MINE TRAIL

Distance	5 miles round trip
Difficulty	Moderate
Features	An historic mine reached through rolling desert
Starting elevation	1683 feet
Highest elevation	1692 feet
Total climb	65 feet
Location	Organ Pipe Cactus National Monument
Map	USGS Lukeville, Organ Pipe Cactus National Monument brochure
Hiking season	Late fall through early spring

Getting there: Organ Pipe Cactus National Monument is located along the U.S.-Mexico border, 22 miles south of Why via AZ 85. The trailhead is at the south edge of the national monument's campground, about 1.5 miles southwest of the visitor center. Both the campground and visitor center have restrooms and drinking water available. Although easy to moderate in

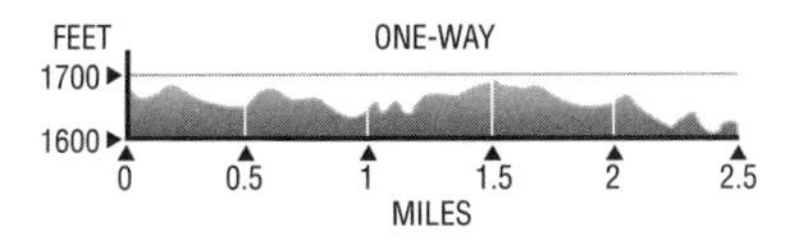

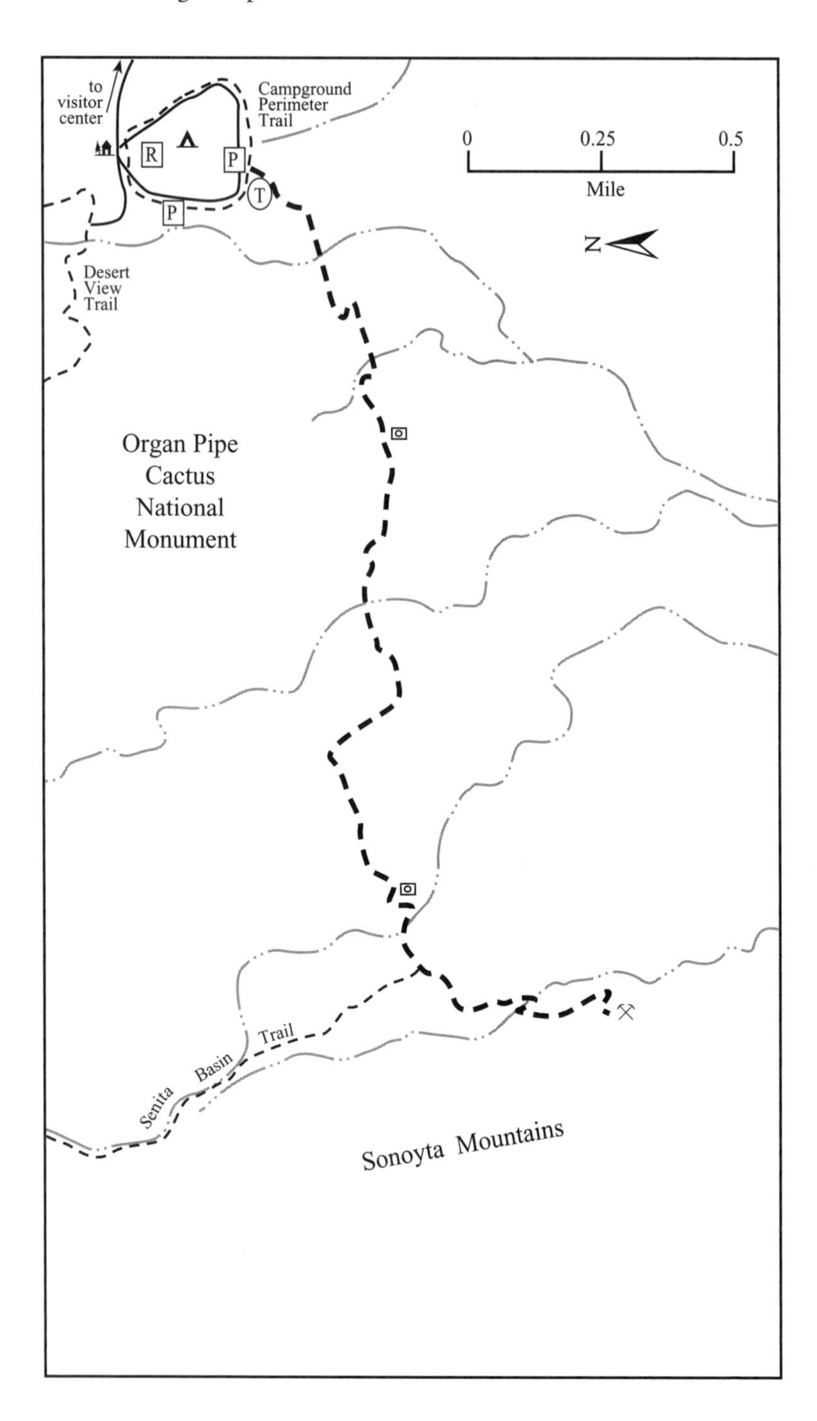
to
visitor
center
Campground
Perimeter
Trail
0
0.25
0.5
Mile
N
R
P
P
T
Desert
View
Trail
Organ Pipe
Cactus
National
Monument
Senita Basin Trail
Sonoyta Mountains

Remains of a stone store

cool weather, the rocky trail offers little shade and no drinking water and can be strenuous on hot days.

With abundant views of surrounding mountains, this pleasant hike through rolling desert terrain leads to the site of an historic silver mine. You won't be able to enter the mineshafts, but there is plenty to see, including the stone ruins of a building and various leftovers from mining days.

Beginning as a walk through the desert, among greasewood, creosote, and cactus, the trail soon passes through several sandy washes. The washes, which offer at least a bit of water for desert flora, are home to paloverde, with its unmistakable smooth green bark, mesquite, and occasional wildflowers in spring. Just past the 0.5-mile point, the trail climbs to a hilltop, with panoramic views in all directions. It then continues through another series of washes and ascends a few low hills, where you'll see an abundance of organ pipe cacti.

A hilltop at about the 2-mile point offers spectacular views south-southeast into Mexico, and here the variety and amount of vegetation increases, with cholla, saguaros, and a lot of ocotillo and paloverde. Just beyond this hilltop the trail comes to a junction, where signs indicate the way to Victoria Mine and several other destinations. Here the trail begins to follow an old wagon track, which is said to predate the 1853 Gadsden Purchase, in which this area became part of the United States. Going south the trail crosses a large wash before arriving at Victoria Mine.

Originally called *La Americana* by its Mexican owner Cipriano Ortega, the mine had been worked since the 1880s, producing mostly silver plus some gold, copper, and lead. In 1899 the mine became the property of shopkeeper Mikul Levy, who renamed it after Victoria Leon, the young wife of a clerk in Levy's store.

The most impressive ruin here is the old stone store, which is believed to have been built in the late 1800s or early 1900s, and at one time the area near the mine included several adobe buildings plus a bunkhouse, a boarding house, a blacksmith shop, and other structures. There are also remains of an old bathtub and a variety of rusting pieces of machinery used for smelting. The mine shafts can be seen, but for safety have been covered with metal grates to prevent entry.

After perusing the ruins, most hikers will head back the way they came. An option for those who want to double the round-trip length of this hike is to continue to Lost Cabin Mine. Ask for directions at the monument's visitor center.

What Is That, a Crown?

Some saguaro cacti sport some very odd-looking growths. Botanists call the abnormalities cristates, or crested development: curling, fan-shaped phenomenon. They have the appearance of an upsweep of curls, reminiscent of the extreme hairstyles of the French Revolution or Regency England, and occasionally seen on prom night in the 1950s.

32. DESERT VIEW TRAIL

Distance ■ 1.2-mile loop
Difficulty ■ Easy to moderate
Features ■ Desert terrain with signed plants and panoramic views
Starting elevation ■ 1700 feet
Highest elevation ■ 1857 feet
Total climb ■ 285 feet
Location ■ Organ Pipe Cactus National Monument
Map ■ USGS Lukeville
Hiking season ■ Year-round (very hot in summer)

Getting there: Organ Pipe Cactus National Monument is located along the U.S.-Mexico border, 22 miles south of Why via AZ 85. The trail leaves from and returns to the parking area for the group campground, northwest of Twin Peaks Campground, and there's a connecting trail from the entrance station at the entrance to Twin Peaks Campground. Restrooms and drinking water are available at Twin Peaks Campground. To hike the trail counterclockwise, as we suggest, start at the eastern side of the parking area.

This delightful loop trail can be hiked in either direction, but the easier, more gradual ascent is counterclockwise. The well-marked trail is gravel, and frequent signs identify the numerous cacti and other desert plants that flourish in this hot arid clime. Many of the signs also offer suggestions of how native peoples used parts or all of the plants for food, medicine, clothing, or materials for baskets or tools. There's no real shade on the trail, so on hot days be sure to take the hike in early morning or late in the day when the heat is not so intense.

As you begin, the trail leads gently along the eastern hillside in a northerly direction. You are immediately among a wide variety of cactus and other desert plants, many of which have identifying signs. The surrounding terrain is rocky, although the path itself is mostly gravel. At about 0.25 mile you'll cross an old roadbed, and just before the trail turns toward the west, look up and straight ahead for a good first view of the Twin Peaks, then turn and descend into a shallow wash (about 0.35 mile). After the wash, the trail begins climbing to the top of a ridge.

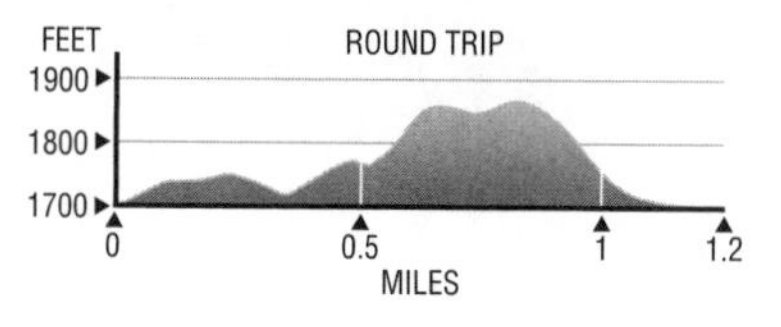

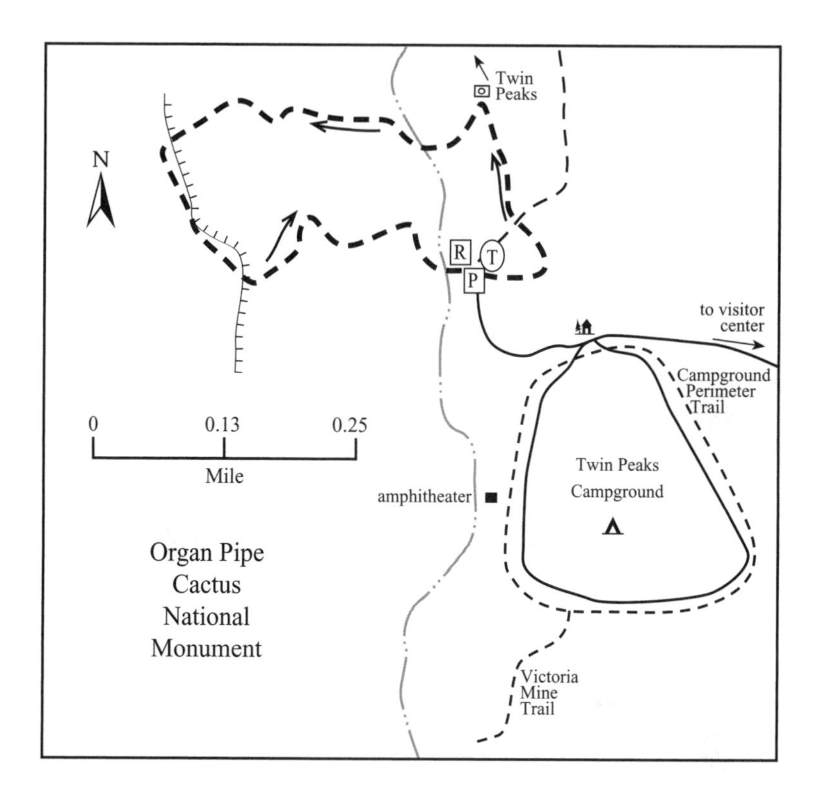

Once on top, the views in all directions are grand. Also, there are a few benches placed up here where you can rest and catch your breath. The Twin Peaks lie to the north (behind you), and the Sonoyta Mountains are off to the west, running north-south all the way into Mexico. You also have a view of the entire Twin Peaks Campground spread out below to the southeast.

On the trail down, watch for the compass barrel cactus: it leans south as it grows. The wash you crossed before climbing the ridge continues along its base and you will cross it once more shortly before you reach the parking area. A few more steps bring you to restrooms and the end of the trail.

By now you should be able to identify several varieties of cactus: chain-fruit—sometimes called jumping—cholla, prickly pear, several different barrel cacti, of course the awe-inspiring saguaro, and the monument's namesake organ pipe; plus ocotillo, mesquite, and paloverde trees.

Opposite: *Organ pipe, saguaro, and teddy bear cholla are seen along the trail.*

Park's Namesake a Fascinating Giant

The organ pipe cactus looks a lot like its name. From a single root, a multitude of slender branches shoot straight into the air and can withstand the abuse of 118° Fahrenheit heat with very little water. Like most other cacti, they are susceptible to freezing during the winter, so they wisely grow mostly on the south side of slopes, where the winter sun warms them. The lavender-white flowers bloom sometime between May and July, but their blossoms open only during the cooler temperatures of nighttime. Organ pipe can grow to about 15 feet tall.

33. RED TANKS TINAJA TRAIL

Distance ■ 1.2 miles round trip
Difficulty ■ Easy to moderate
Features ■ A walk through the desert to a natural water catch-basin that attracts wildlife
Starting elevation ■ 1850 feet
Highest elevation ■ 1880 feet
Total climb ■ 50 feet
Location ■ Organ Pipe Cactus National Monument
Map ■ USGS Lukeville
Hiking season ■ Year-round (very hot in summer)

Getting there: Organ Pipe Cactus National Monument is located along the U.S.-Mexico border, 22 miles south of Why via AZ 85. The marked trailhead is on Puerto Blanco Drive, about 5 miles from the beginning, about 0.2 mile before pullout #3, which is a marked, wide spot in the road where you can park your vehicle. There are no restrooms or drinking water at the trailhead, and any water in the tinaja is not considered potable. Anyway, any water there should be left for wildlife.

A step into the past, the short hike to Red Tanks Tinaja is a reminder of the importance of water in the desert. Through a landscape of cholla, saguaro, ocotillo, creosote, and organ pipe cactus, the trail leads to a stone depression in a wash, called a *tinaja*. The word is Spanish for a

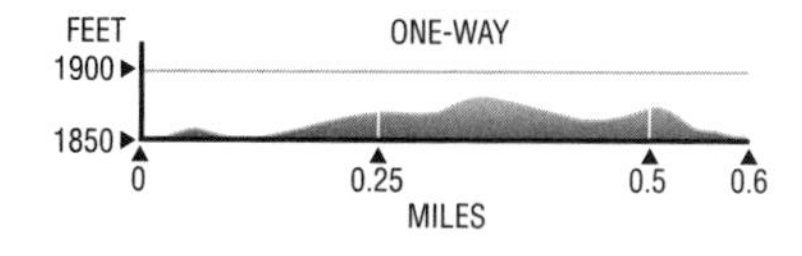

large jar or bowl, but here refers to a natural basin carved into rock by erosion that catches rainfall. Today, as in ancient times, the tinaja holds water long after the rush from a rainstorm is gone. Unlike today, water in the tinaja preserved the lives of early desert travelers whose routes followed the series of tinajas that lie in the washes winding through the desert.

The trail begins as a narrow dirt path, but soon widens as it joins an old wagon road. Along the trail, notice the silver-colored cholla, some as tall as a human. The sun reflecting from their silver needles produces a bright halo around their branches. At 0.25 mile, the trail passes through a sandy wash where piles of debris, snagged on bushes, accumulate. As the trail rises out of the wash, look at the nearby 40-foot saguaro. Step back for a more distant perspective that reveals its strange proportions. Its arms sprout from its body at a height of only 12 feet, giving it a strange, stunted look. Just above the arms, facing the trail, is a hole drilled by a Gila woodpecker; there are several others on the other side of the cactus.

At 0.3 mile, 200 feet to the right of the trail a square fence surrounds an abandoned mine shaft, whose entrance is blocked by a metal grate. Small piles of greenish rock near the opening are the waste products of the old malachite mining operation. The trail continues past sagebrush, organ pipe cactus, prickly pear cactus, and Mormon tea as it goes through a series of shallow washes, and you'll notice that the plants are bunched together in the low spots.

Rough, brown rock lies embedded in the trail at just past the

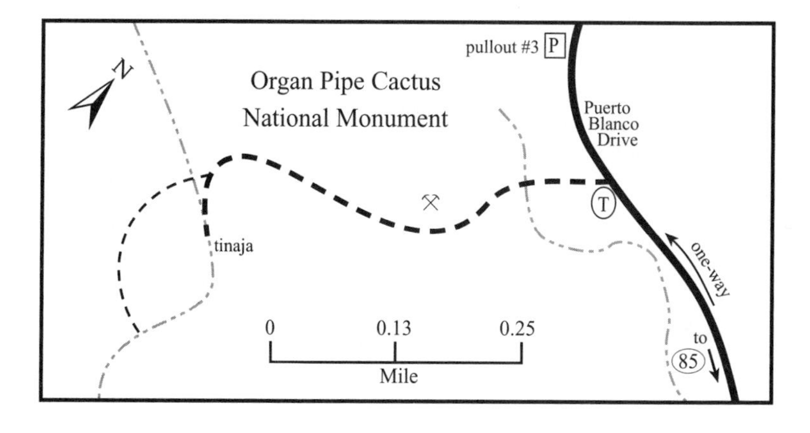

0.5-mile point, and its colors and texture make it look more like wood than stone. About 250 feet later the trail appears to cross a wide, sandy wash, but a cairn leads to the left, down the wash a few hundred feet to the reddish, solid stone that forms the tinaja. If water has collected in the tinaja, birds and other wildlife may be in the area; even if it's dry, you're likely to see feathers and other signs of wildlife.

Birds that may be seen here include Gambel's quail, rock doves, mourning doves, greater roadrunners, Gila woodpeckers, cactus wrens, rock wrens, red-tailed hawks, turkey vultures, American kestrels, and ravens. Mammals to watch for include desert bighorn sheep, mule and white-tailed deer, pronghorns, coyotes, rock and roundtail ground squirrels, antelope and black-tailed jackrabbits, and desert cottontails. Javelina—also known as collared peccaries—are sometimes seen here, and you're almost sure to see the mouth-shaped cutouts left in the pads of prickly pear cacti from the javelina's bite.

The dramatic mountain you see to the north is Pinkley Peak, 3145 feet elevation. After exploring the tinaja, return to the trailhead along the same path.

Organ Pipe National Monument (Photo by Lawrence Letham)

CHIRICAHUA NATIONAL MONUMENT

Spectacular scenery of rugged and often surreal stone towers, scattered among tall pines, and streams bubbling over piles of fallen rocks make this out-of-the-way national monument one of Arizona's hidden gems. Named for the Chiricahua Apaches who lived in these mountains, this National Park Service property is 86 percent designated wilderness, making it a wonderful destination for hikers. It also has a scenic drive with a half-dozen pullouts, an historic ranch house, and excellent bird-watching and wildlife viewing opportunities.

The striking rock formations here owe their creation largely to a volcanic eruption that struck the region some 27 million years ago. The

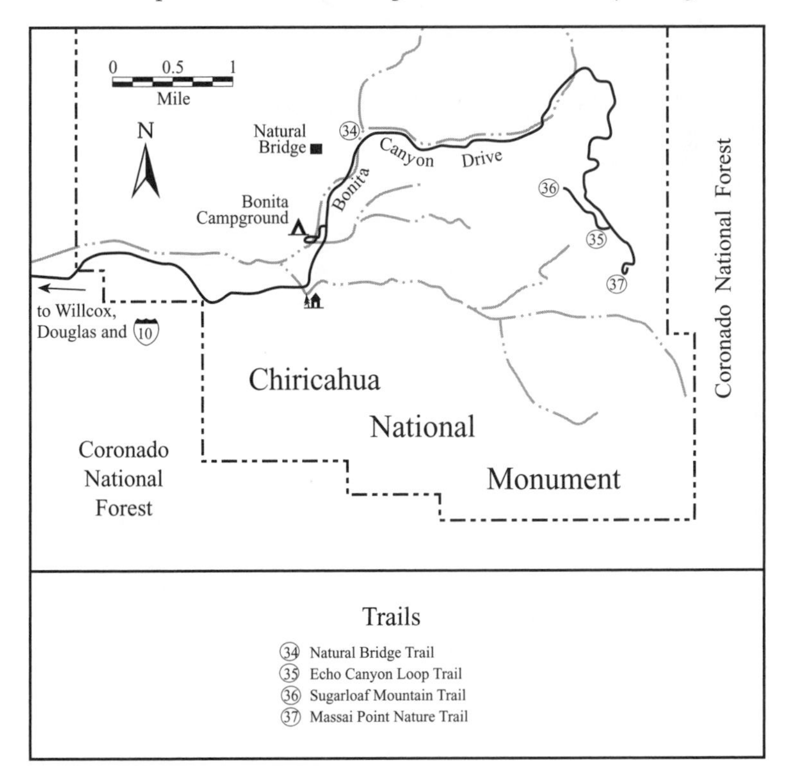

Rock formations along Echo Canyon Loop Trail

eruption spit tons of hot ash into the air, which fell to earth, cooled, and formed a layer of dark volcanic rock almost 2000 feet thick. This rock, called rhyolite tuff, formed the basis of the Chiricahua Mountains, which were then sculpted by the forces of water, ice, and wind over millions of years into the fascinating towers, columns, walls, and balanced rocks that led the Apaches to call this spot "the land of standing-up rocks."

The monument has about 17 miles of maintained day-use hiking trails, ranging from less than 0.25 mile to about 8.5 miles round-trip, and from flat and easy to steep and rocky. No overnight hiking or backcountry camping is permitted. Most trails are also open to horseback riders, but all trails are closed to mountain bikes. This is a prime wildlife viewing and bird-watching area, where you might see animals and birds more common to the mountains of Mexico than those of the United States. Surrounded by desert, but with the largest forested areas in the region, the Chiricahua Mountains provide a cool, moist oasis, where a wide variety of species prosper.

Birds are usually seen near Bonita Creek and other water sources. Year-round residents include Gambel's quail, mourning doves, acorn woodpeckers, Mexican jays, white-breasted nuthatches, and black-throated sparrows. In summer watch for black-throated, magnificent, and black-chinned hummingbirds, along with solitary vireos, Cassin's and western kingbirds, Scott's orioles, red-faced warblers, hepatic tanagers, and western wood-peewees. Winter residents include dark-eyed juncos and ruby-crowned kinglets. Prairie falcons sometimes nest in the cliffs along Bonita Canyon Drive, and red-tailed hawks and golden eagles have been seen above the meadows near the monument entrance. Mammals seen here include white-tailed deer, the piglike javelina (also called collared peccaries), hog-nosed and hooded skunks, and Chiricahua fox squirrels.

These mountains were home to the Chiricahua Apaches for about 400 years, and they fiercely resisted the invasion of white settlers that began in the mid-1800s. Although their more than 30 years of raids on the settlers may have slowed the so-called civilization of the region, the Apaches were eventually defeated, and the Indian Wars officially ended with the surrender of Geronimo in 1886.

The monument is located 36 miles southeast of Willcox via AZ Highways 186 and 181. Willcox is about 75 miles east of Tucson via I-10. A small per-person entry fee is charged. For additional information, contact the monument office and the Willcox Chamber of Commerce & Agriculture. You'll find complete contact information in the appendix at the back of this book.

That's a Funny-Looking Raccoon

While hiking or camping at Chiricahua National Monument, keep an eye out for the coatimundi, also called the white-nosed coati. A relative of the raccoon, the coatimundi has a long, pointed nose with a white facial mask, white ears, a mostly brown body, and a long, thin tail. Females and young often travel in groups of several dozen, and the playful young are sometimes seen chasing each other up and down trees.

CAMPGROUNDS

In addition to the national monument campground discussed below, there are several commercial RV parks, with hookups and other amenities, in Willcox, located 36 miles to the northwest. There is also camping nearby in the **Coronado National Forest.** Facilities are limited and only small trailers and motor homes are allowed. A map and other information can be obtained at the monument's visitor center and from the national forest's Douglas Ranger District office.

Bonita Campground. The national monument's campground certainly lives up to its name—*bonita* is Spanish for pretty—with a lot of trees, mostly well-spaced sites, and an easy walk to the visitor center. The campground is located just off Bonita Canyon Drive north of the visitor center. It has 22 sites for tents and RVs 29 feet and shorter. There are restrooms but no showers or RV hookups. It is open year-round and a modest fee is charged. Reservations are not accepted.

34. NATURAL BRIDGE TRAIL

Distance ▪ 4.8 miles round trip
Difficulty ▪ Moderate to strenuous
Features ▪ A climb through woodlands to an overlook of a natural stone bridge
Starting elevation ▪ 5550 feet
Highest elevation ▪ 6065 feet
Total climb ▪ 700 feet
Location ▪ Chiricahua National Monument
Map ▪ USGS Cochise Head
Hiking season ▪ Spring through fall

Getting there: The monument is located 36 miles southeast of Willcox via AZ Highways 186 and 181. Willcox is about 75 miles east of Tucson via I-10. A small per-person entry fee is charged. From the monument's visitor center, follow Bonita Canyon Drive for a short distance to the marked trailhead parking area on the left side of the road. Restrooms and drinking water are not available at the trailhead, but are at the visitor center and campground.

The Natural Bridge Trail is a good choice for bird-watchers, as it climbs through groves of oak, juniper, and pine to an overlook of a

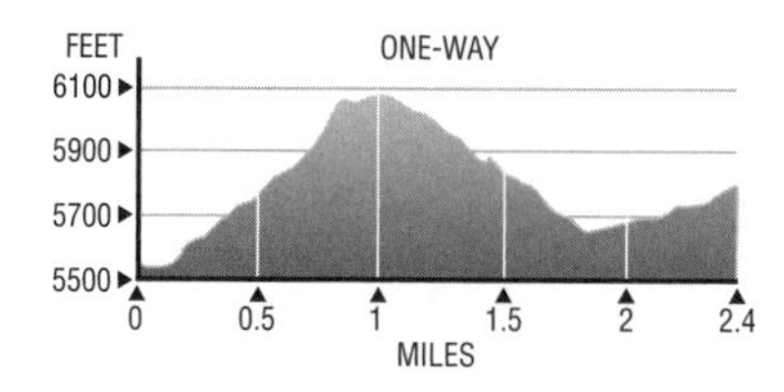

small natural rock bridge. Along the way it has some steep, rocky sections, but also a very pretty forest with a type of pine seen in very few places in the United States. Birds to watch for include Gambel's quail, mourning doves, acorn woodpeckers, Mexican jays, white-breasted nuthatches, and black-throated sparrows; plus black-throated, magnificent, and black-chinned hummingbirds in summer.

The trail begins heading north, away from the natural bridge that is its destination, first crossing a wash and then climbing steeply up the side of a canyon through woodlands of juniper and oak. As the trail rises, good views of stone pillars appear. The trail climbs through manzanita and bear grass, with a few cacti, and makes its way to a plateau, where piñon and alligator juniper dominate, and of course more views of tall rock spires.

After about 0.75 mile going north, the trail turns northeast, then west. It has some ups and downs—mostly ups—and then drops rapidly down into Picket Park at about 1.75 miles. Picket Park is a good spot for bird-watching, and has a delightful forest of Apache pine, which is easily recognized by its very long needles—up to a foot long. This pine species, which can grow to 70 feet high, is more at home in northern Mexico, and in the United States is found primarily in southeastern Arizona and southwestern New Mexico.

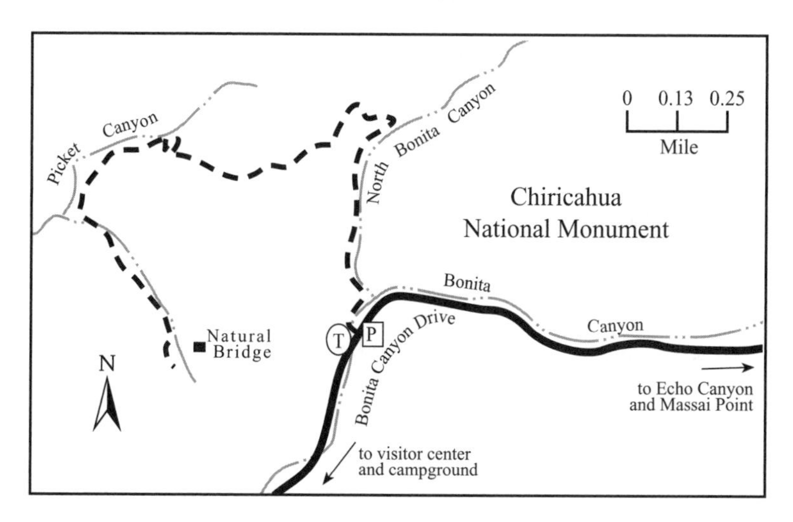

Leaving Picket Park the trail starts climbing again, although not as steeply as at the beginning, until it reaches its conclusion at an overlook for the natural rock bridge about 25 to 30 feet long. The bridge, which spans a narrow canyon, is composed of bedrock that has been carved out by the force of water. From the overlook, head back along the trail the way you came.

A Bridge or an Arch?

They might look pretty much the same to most of us, these natural stone bridges and arches we see throughout the rugged backcountry of Arizona and neighboring Utah, but to those in the know there is a world of difference. According to geologists, natural bridges such as the one seen on the Natural Bridge Trail in Chiricahua National Monument are formed when a river literally cuts a hole through a rock. The more common arches, on the other hand, are the result of erosion from rain and snow, often driven by wind, plus the freezing and thawing of moisture that gets into tiny cracks, slowly chipping away at the stone.

35. ECHO CANYON LOOP TRAIL

Distance ▪ 3.3-mile loop
Difficulty ▪ Moderate to strenuous
Features ▪ Fascinating rock formations on a trip through desert and forest
Starting elevation ▪ 6780 feet
Highest elevation ▪ 6780 feet
Total climb ▪ 1100 feet
Location ▪ Chiricahua National Monument
Map ▪ USGS Cochise Head
Hiking season ▪ Spring through fall

Getting there: The monument is located 36 miles southeast of Willcox via AZ Highways 186 and 181. Willcox is about 75 miles east of Tucson via I-10. A small per-person entry fee is charged. From the monument's visitor center, follow Bonita Canyon Drive almost to its end to a turnoff marked with signs for Echo Canyon

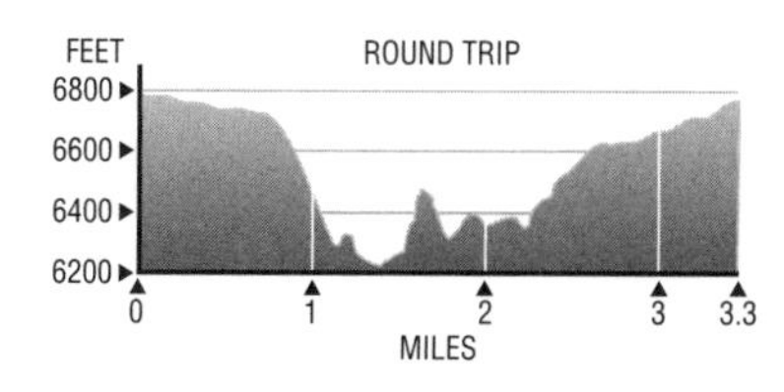

and Sugarloaf parking. Turn right onto this road and travel approximately 0.25 mile to the Echo Canyon parking lot turn-off on the left. The trailhead is at the end of the lot. Restrooms are available at the trailhead, and water is available at the visitor center and campground. This loop can be hiked in either direction, but we prefer doing it counterclockwise so the shadiest part is near the end.

Our favorite hike in Chiricahua National Monument, this especially scenic loop combines the Echo Canyon, Hailstone, and Ed Riggs Trails on a trek among spectacular rock formations and into a densely wooded area. You'll see the tall, flat walls of stone that form Wall Street and massive boulders perched on tall stone columns, plus flora that ranges from scrubby bushes and stunted, windblown trees to magnificent pine giants.

The wide, well-defined path of the Echo Canyon Trail starts in surroundings of bear grass, manzanita, small scrub bushes, and stunted trees and proceeds to the first of many balancing rocks, 150

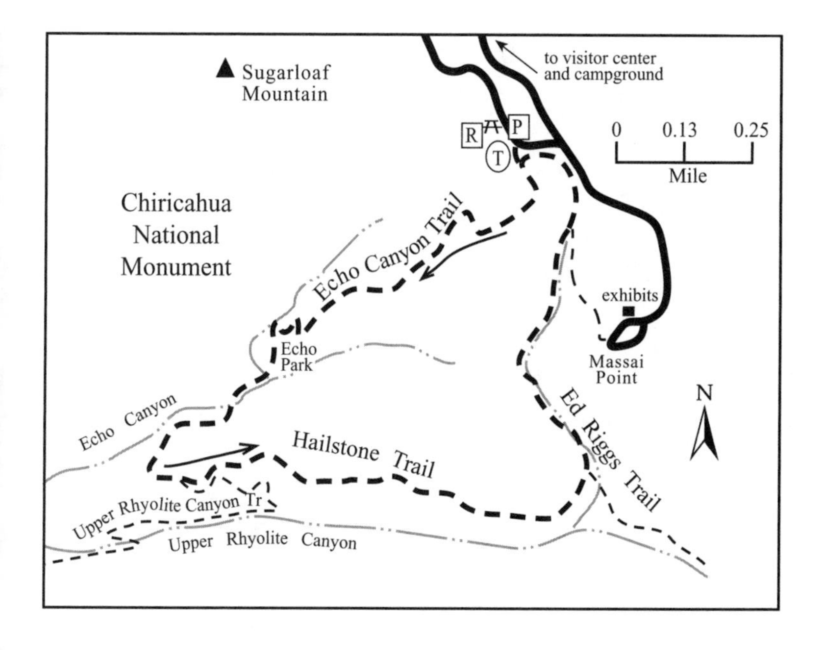

feet from the trailhead. This formation looks like a bird perched on a pillar with its head pointing to the right. At the intersection 150 feet past this formation, stay to the right to head down into Echo Canyon. At 0.2 mile, the trail narrows and descends past a pile of boulders that look like they were stacked on top of each other, but in reality the entire pile was once a single stone that eroded unevenly to leave what looks like separate boulders. To the left of the trail, the rocks stacked against each other look like toy blocks, while another rock balances about 15 feet over the trail. Other balancing rocks stand near the trail, and the distant valley below is covered with narrow-looking, greenish pillars.

At 0.3 mile, the trail passes between two 25-foot pillars to a turn-off to the right of the trail that leads to a massive balancing rock. As the trail begins to drop, there are more columns, with diameters of

Hiking the Echo Loop Canyon Trail

between 20 and 40 feet, but even more intriguing are the nooks and passages between the closely spaced spires that wind and twist before disappearing out of sight.

Just under 0.5 mile, stones fallen from their pedestals above form a mixed-up pile. One rock crashed into a pine tree, which survived and grows around the boulder's jagged edge. Where the trail makes a sharp 270-degree turn to the left, at about 0.6 mile, look for two columns, one of which has fallen over and leans against the other. The trail now drops around and between columns until it is flanked on both sides by the tall, very flat walls that form the corridor known as Wall Street. These flat walls seem out of place in an area dominated by rounded pillars and highly eroded, rough rocks. Turn around at the end of Wall Street to see a balancing rock perfectly framed by the wall's straight lines.

The trees grow taller as the trail descends into the thick forest of Echo Park at about 1.2 miles, where columns can be seen only through breaks in the trees. A mostly dry creekbed, with occasional pools of water, cuts through the park, and big stones—the remnants of pillars—lie between the trees. Soon the lush forest ends and the trail starts to climb over rocky slopes where the trees are once again stunted. A sign at 1.6 miles marks the intersection of Echo Canyon Trail with Hailstone Trail and Upper Rhyolite Canyon Trail. Take the left fork to proceed along the Hailstone Trail.

The dry terrain here supports desert plants, including alligator juniper, prickly pear cactus, and numerous agaves. Also watch for small, white, spherical stones, called spherulites, which are often found in clumps, with many stuck together. Once the volcanic ash landed on the ground, the spherulites formed in place through a process that is similar to crystallization. The trail now climbs along a deep canyon studded with columns and occasionally shaded by trees until an intersection at 2.4 miles with the Ed Riggs Trail. Take the left fork for the shady Ed Riggs Trail.

Big boulders abound, but the tall columns are less frequent as the trail continues among tall pines and wavyleaf oak undergrowth. The trail makes a right turn across a dry drainage that parallels the trail and is the resting place of many massive boulders. At the intersection at 3.1 miles, bear to the left (the right fork leads to Massai Point) and continue 0.2 mile back to the trailhead. Near the end, plants are once again stunted and windblown, while the massive columns, strange formations, and tall pines are obscured.

36. SUGARLOAF MOUNTAIN TRAIL

Distance ▪ 1.8 miles round trip
Difficulty ▪ Moderate
Features ▪ Hike to the top of a mountain for panoramic views
Starting elevation ▪ 6810 feet
Highest elevation ▪ 7260 feet
Total climb ▪ 570 feet
Location ▪ Chiricahua National Monument
Map ▪ USGS Cochise Head
Hiking season ▪ Spring through fall

Getting there: The monument is located 36 miles southeast of Willcox via AZ Highways 186 and 181. Willcox is about 75 miles east of Tucson via I-10. A small per-person entry fee is charged. From the monument's visitor center, follow Bonita Canyon Drive to a turnoff marked with signs for Echo Canyon and Sugarloaf parking. Turn right on the road and travel to its terminus, which is marked as the parking lot for Sugarloaf Mountain. The trailhead is at the end of the lot. Restrooms are located at the trailhead, and drinking water can be obtained at the visitor center and campground.

What appears at first to be an average trail climbs to uncommon views, but not before passing among piñon and juniper trees, going through a tunnel, stopping at a picnic table made of stone slabs, and passing by walls of thick manzanita. The highlight of this hike, though, is the varying views of the rock formations that fill the canyons. At the summit, hikers are rewarded with spectacular views in all directions, as the tall stone pillars stand as silent sentinels in the canyons below.

This well-maintained dirt trail, cut into the side of Sugarloaf Mountain, begins by immediately climbing past piñon pine, manzanita, and alligator junipers scattered between brown and rust-colored rocks. A 5-foot-tall stone escarpment flanks the left side of the trail, while the right opens to views of distant stone columns in Bonita Canyon. Grasses cover the hillside, along with pretty purple wildflowers. At 0.15 mile the trail passes through a tunnel, cut through solid stone

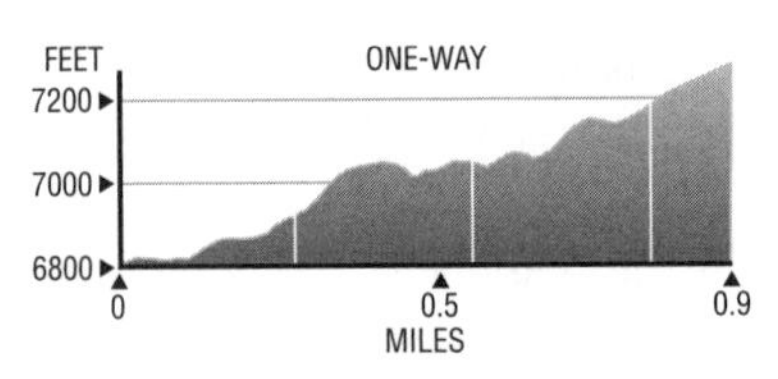

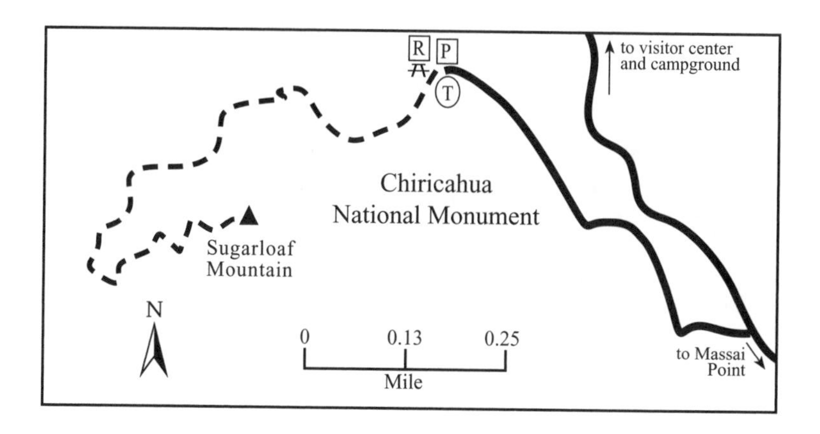

by the Civilian Conservation Corps when the trail was built in 1935, and then the route becomes steeper. Just 250 feet past the tunnel, a cavity eroded in a natural stone column has two pieces of rock hanging from the top, like teeth in an open mouth. More of the canyon is seen below, along with a broad plain beyond the mountains in the distance.

Near the 0.3-mile mark, a cliff of white rock capped by rust-colored stone begins to appear. The white rock is soft, volcanic tuff, while the red is the hard lava layer that protected the hill from erosion. Over millions of years, erosion cut away at the tuff but could not get through the hard cap, thereby leaving Sugarloaf Mountain as the highest point in the area. As the trail continues uphill, the white cliff to the side gets taller, but it is always capped with the red lava. At 0.35 mile, part of the lava broke from the top and left a jumble of large rocks behind some bushes. Near the 0.4-mile point, sections of the white rock show black, exposed lines that give the stone the appearance of marble. As the cliffs continue, the trail becomes covered with a white dust from the stone.

At 0.5 mile, by the side of the cliff a small picnic table made from slabs of natural stone invites passersby to rest and possibly eat lunch. The elevation provides views of a long canyon filled with narrow columns that rise above their surroundings, dotting the landscape. The trail bends around to the south side of the mountain and reveals a vast canyon filled with tall pillars of rock, much of it with a greenish tint. Manzanita grows more abundantly along the trail, along with junipers and small piñons, and by 0.7 mile the manzanita chokes out all other plants. Like a 4-foot-tall hedge, the branches of separate bushes intertwine into a red thicket so dense it is impossible to see through it.

A short break at a picnic table of natural stone (Photo by Lawrence Letham)

The trail reaches the summit and a fire lookout station, with spectacular sweeping views across this unique land of stone columns. Off to the northeast in the Chiricahua Mountains look for Cochise Head, which some say looks like the profile of the Apache chief's head, lying on his back. It's fairly easy to see a forehead, prominent nose, thin lips, and chin.

From the summit, head back down along the same route to the trailhead.

37. MASSAI POINT NATURE TRAIL

Distance ■ 0.5-mile loop
Difficulty ■ Easy
Features ■ A walk among rock formations and plants to a scenic viewpoint
Starting elevation ■ 6875 feet
Highest elevation ■ 6875 feet
Total climb ■ 100 feet
Location ■ Chiricahua National Monument
Map ■ USGS Cochise Head
Hiking season ■ Spring through fall

Getting there: The monument is located 36 miles southeast of Willcox via AZ Highways 186 and 181. Willcox is about 75 miles east of Tucson via I-10. A small per-person entry fee is charged. From the monument's visitor center, follow Bonita Canyon Drive all the way to where it ends in a short loop. The marked trailhead

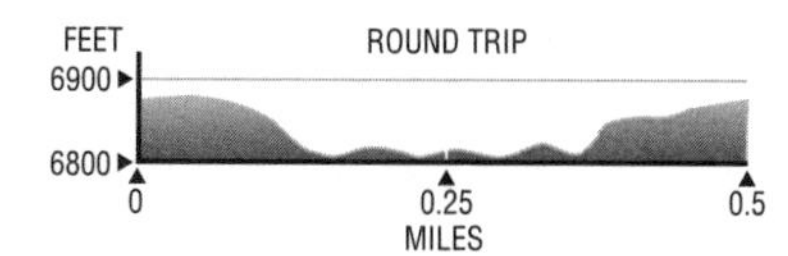

is on the right side of the road near the entrance to the loop. Restrooms are available at the trailhead, and drinking water can be obtained at the visitor center and campground.

The short, easy Massai Point Nature Trail provides an excellent introduction to this land of strange rock formations and unusual plants and animals. Signs discuss the area's geology and the trail offers panoramic views of distant mountains and closer stone columns, plus a look at a large balanced rock. There is a variety of plant life, from bear grass and manzanita to stunted piñon pines, gnarled alligator juniper, and yucca.

Although the trail is easy, it involves climbing some steps and has uneven footing in some spots.

Just after beginning the trail, in about 50 feet, stay to the right to make a detour up a short rise to the Exhibition Building. Built of volcanic tuff from the area, it houses a variety of exhibits, including one on spherulites—round stones formed from volcanic ash through a form of crystallization.

Back on the mostly dirt trail, continue as it passes over sections of solid stone, past windblown, twisted trees and nature signs, to a stone pillar at 0.2 mile. The 12-foot column is an up-close, miniature version of the huge spires that tower in the valley below, complete with green and black lichens. The green lichens are the most prolific and give the rocks in the area a greenish color. Continuing, balanced

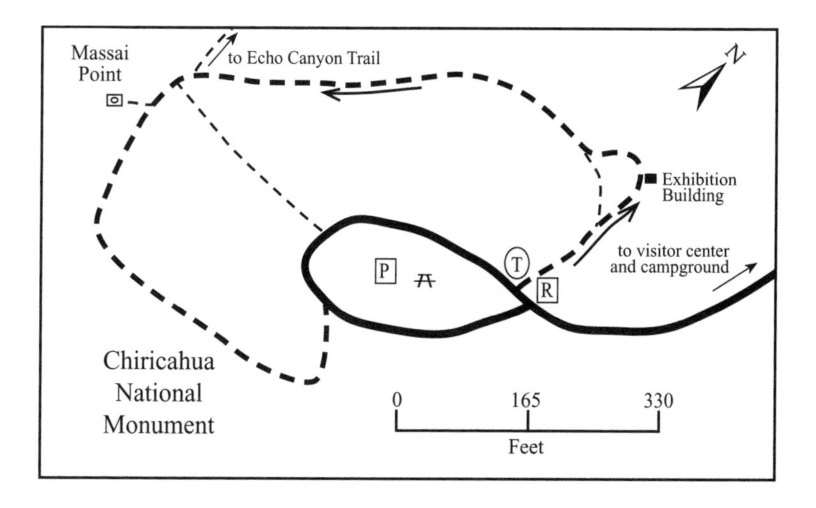

rocks come into view, and explanatory displays of their formation stand close to the trail.

Look for rocks where erosion narrowed the base more than the upper portions. A balancing rock—which usually isn't really balancing but remains barely attached to its pillar—forms when the wind removes the soft tuff between two sections of hard tuff. The rock stays on its narrow base until the base erodes too much and gravity topples the rock from its perch to the ground. Scattered among the rock formations are yucca, manzanita, bear grass, piñon, and alligator juniper.

The formation at 0.25 mile is an excellent example of a balancing rock. Just past the rock is an intersection where the nature trail goes to the left to more balancing rocks. Just after these rocks is another intersection, where the left fork is a shortcut back to the parking area. However, take the right fork as it leads down a set of stairs, and then a short spur trail to the right takes you to Massai Point—a round, fortresslike lookout that provides a fascinating view of the hundreds of columns in the deep valley below.

Descend from the lookout and go to the right to regain the nature trail. At 0.35 mile, the trail passes between two boulders about 12 feet apart, and the next formation is a dramatic balancing rock where the diameter of the base is much smaller than the rock perched on top. The trail ends about 150 feet later as it emerges onto the loop road. You could return immediately to your car, but good views and explanatory signs are posted along the loop, so stay to the left and follow the edge of the asphalt. Soon a sign on the left shows the short path from the parking lot down to the Massai Point lookout. The trailhead is just ahead.

View from Massai Point Nature Trail

GRAND CANYON NATIONAL PARK

Carved through solid rock by the tremendous power of water over six million years, the Grand Canyon is one of the best-known of America's national parks, and at the top of their must-see list for many visitors to Arizona. The main lure of this awe-inspiring work of nature is the spectacular scenery—a dramatic and immense canyon cut through colorful layers of rock, with a variety of buttes, plateaus, pinnacles, and other formations—but this natural wonder also offers splendid opportunities for hiking, mule rides, and rafting. The park is also an excellent location for seeing wildlife, including mule deer, elk, desert cottontails, cliff chipmunks, tassel-eared and Kaibab squirrels, golden eagles, red-tailed hawks, great horned owls, violet-green swallows, mountain chickadees, and even some California condors.

Most visitors go to the easily accessible South Rim, although those with more time are well-rewarded by a trip to the North Rim. The distance from rim to rim averages only 10 miles across, but the North Rim, which can be easily seen from the South Rim, is over 200 miles away by car or 21 miles by foot on a very strenuous hike. The park contains 277 miles of the Colorado River, which is about 5000 feet below the South Rim and 6000 feet below the higher North Rim. The South Rim is open all year but the North Rim is closed during snow season. Facilities at the North Rim usually close in mid-October, although the road is often open until mid-November or mid-December. The road and facilities are usually open by mid-May.

On the South Rim, you can get excellent views of the canyon from a number of overlooks along the 26-mile (one-way) Desert View Drive. Nine-mile (one-way) Hermit Road (open to shuttle buses only from March through November) also provides access to some splendid overlooks. There are a number of overlooks along the North Rim's 23-mile (one-way) Cape Royal Drive. There are hiking trails along both rims and into the canyon, and hiking into the canyon at least a little way is an excellent way to experience the park. Mule rides are

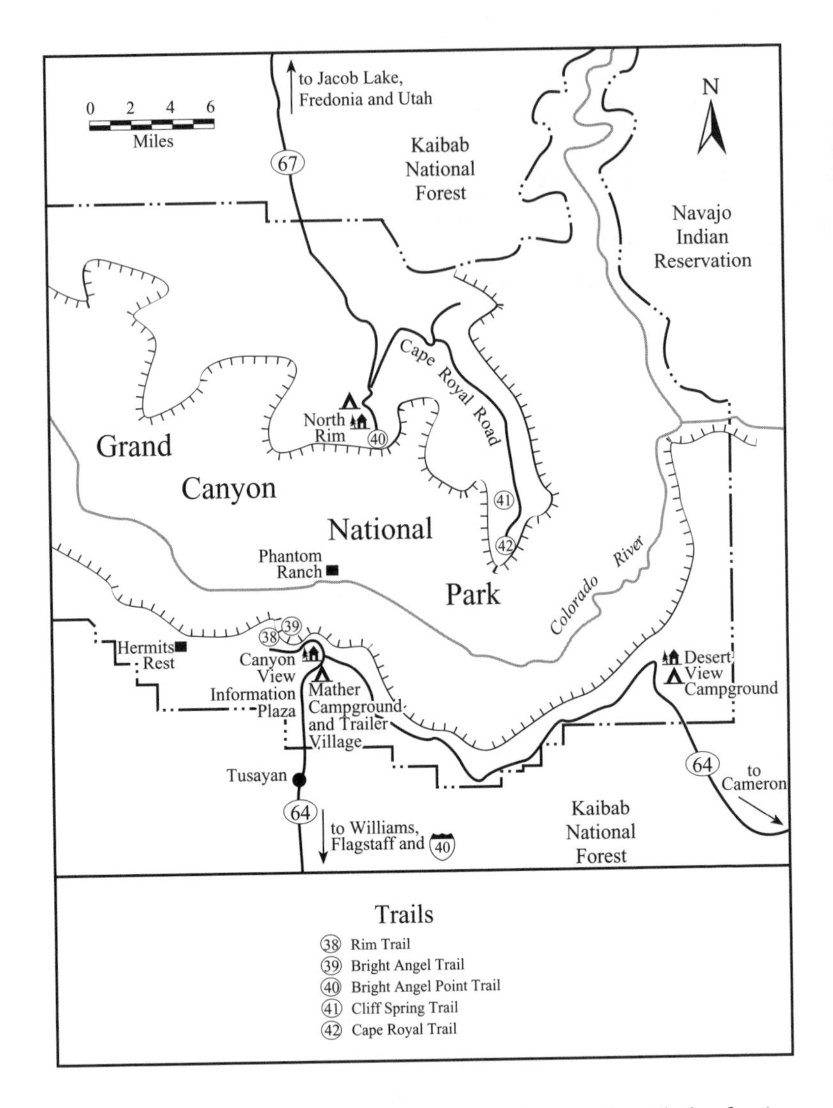

offered from both rims by park concessionaires, and guided raft trips down the Colorado River through the canyon are also available.

Visitor centers and campgrounds are located on both rims, and the park also offers a variety of ranger programs. Shuttle buses, included in the park entrance fee, are the best way to get around on the busy South Rim. Parking lots are usually crowded, especially in summer, and parking for large vehicles such as motor homes is very limited. Pets are not permitted on the shuttle buses.

The South Rim's Grand Canyon Village, what we might call the heart of the South Rim, is located 60 miles north of Williams (along I-40) via AZ 64 or on the more scenic but mountainous route from Flagstaff (also along I-40), which is 80 miles northwest via US 180 and AZ 64. The North Rim is 44 miles south of Jacob Lake via AZ 67, also called the North Rim Parkway. To get to the North Rim from Flagstaff, take US 89 north for about 112 miles, then exit onto Alternate US 89, which eventually travels west to Jacob Lake, a distance of 55 miles. From Jacob Lake, follow AZ 67 south to the parking lots

View from Grand Canyon's North Rim

at the North Rim visitor center. Those driving directly from rim to rim can save some time and miles by following AZ 64 between the South Rim and the trading post community of Cameron, which sits along US 89 southeast of the park.

For additional information, contact the National Park Service and the Grand Canyon Chamber of Commerce. You'll find complete contact information in the appendix at the back of this book.

CAMPGROUNDS

In addition to the campgrounds inside the national park that are discussed here, there are commercial campgrounds, with RV hookups and other amenities, in Tusayan just outside the South Rim entrance station and at Jacob Lake, about 44 miles north of the North Rim. There are also campgrounds and campsites in the park below the rim, which are available with reservations to those on overnight backpacking trips. All of the national park campgrounds charge moderate fees.

Those who want a forest camping experience but don't want to be in the park should consider the Kaibab National Forest, which has campgrounds near the South Rim in the Tusayan Ranger District and near the North Rim in the North Kaibab Ranger District. Campgrounds are primitive—vault toilets and little else—but the deep forest offers a spectacular place to set up your tent or park your RV, and the forest service campgrounds are slightly less expensive and sometimes less crowded than the national park campgrounds.

The forest service also permits what it calls dispersed camping. By this, they mean that you just go find a spot you like off the road and set up camp. No established campground, no toilets, and no fee. There are restrictions, however, and dispersed camping may be prohibited during dry periods because of fire danger. For information on both the established forest service campgrounds and dispersed camping in the national forest, contact the Kaibab National Forest.

South Rim

Mather Campground. This large, partly shaded national park campground is our personal favorite at the South Rim. It has well-spaced tent and RV sites set among ponderosa pine, piñon, and juniper trees, but no RV hookups, and motor homes and trailers must be no longer than 30 feet. You can walk to restrooms, the store, showers, laundry, visitor center, and rim, but you'll need to use the shuttle or a personal vehicle to get to some trailheads and restaurants. It's located in Grand

Canyon Village, south of the commercial area off Market Plaza Road. There are about 320 sites and restrooms with flush toilets. Open year-round; reservations recommended during the summer.

Trailer Village. This concessionaire-operated campground, in an open piñon-juniper forest, is almost as nice as nearby Mather Campground, plus it offers RV hookups (electricity, water, and sewer). There are 84 RV sites and showers and laundry are nearby. Open year-round. Reservations are strongly recommended, especially from March through October, by contacting the concessionaire, Xanterra Parks & Resorts.

Desert View Campground. Located 26 miles east of Grand Canyon Village, the Desert View Campground lives up to its name with open desert terrain. Because it is away from the main part of the park, the campground is quieter and really quite delightful. However, you have to keep in mind that most of the major South Rim trailheads are at least a 45-minute drive away. There are 50 RV and tent sites, restrooms, but no RV hookups or showers. The campground, which is open from mid-May through mid-October only, is along AZ 64 at the east entrance to the park. Reservations are not accepted, and during the summer it's best to arrive before noon to claim a site.

North Rim

North Rim Campground. The only National Park Service campground on the North Rim, and with an abundance of trees and a true forest camping atmosphere, it is the perfect spot to camp here, especially if you can get one of the higher-priced sites along the rim. The campground is near the store and gas station, and within walking distance of most of the trails. Showers and laundry are nearby. Located on AZ 67 at the North Rim developed area, it has 82 tent and RV sites. Open mid-May to mid-October; reservations are recommended.

Chipmunk Identification 101

Chipmunks and their cousins the squirrels are often seen in Grand Canyon National Park, frequently begging along trails or in campgrounds. But just what is that little creature scurrying by? It may be a challenge to determine the exact species of chipmunk or squirrel, but it's easy to tell chipmunks from squirrels—chipmunks have black-and-white stripes on the sides of their faces, but squirrels do not.

38. RIM TRAIL

Distance ▪ Up to 11.75 miles one way
Difficulty ▪ Easy
Features ▪ Splendid views down into the magnificent Grand Canyon
Starting elevation ▪ 6820 feet
Highest elevation ▪ 7052 feet
Total climb ▪ 200 feet
Location ▪ Grand Canyon National Park (South Rim)
Map ▪ USGS Grand Canyon, Phantom Ranch
Hiking season ▪ Year-round

Getting there: The South Rim's Grand Canyon Village, what we might call the heart of the South Rim, is located 60 miles north of Williams (along I-40) via AZ 64 or on the more scenic but mountainous route from Flagstaff (also along I-40), which is 80 miles northwest via US 180 and AZ 64. You can get to some parts of the trail by personal motor vehicle or by foot from nearby parking areas, lodges, and campgrounds. But the best way to get to and from the trail, or portions of it, is via the park's shuttle bus system, which pretty much parallels the Rim Trail. When you arrive at the park and pay the entrance fee, you will receive information on the shuttle bus schedule and route, as well as current restrictions on the use of private motor vehicles. Use of the shuttle bus is included in the park entrance fee.

So you don't think that a trail of almost 12 miles one way is a short hike? Neither do we, and we're not suggesting that most Grand Canyon visitors will want to walk the entire Rim Trail (although you certainly can if you want to). Instead, this trail, which winds along the South Rim of the Grand Canyon, is ideal for park visitors who want a choice of short walks between viewpoints. Using the park's shuttle bus system, you can cover as much or as little of this trail as you want, and get easy access to a variety of wonderful views into the enormous Grand Canyon. This practically flat trail is also a good hike for snowy and icy winter days, when venturing down a steep trail into the canyon can be hazardous. A 5-mile section of the Rim Trail from Pipe Creek

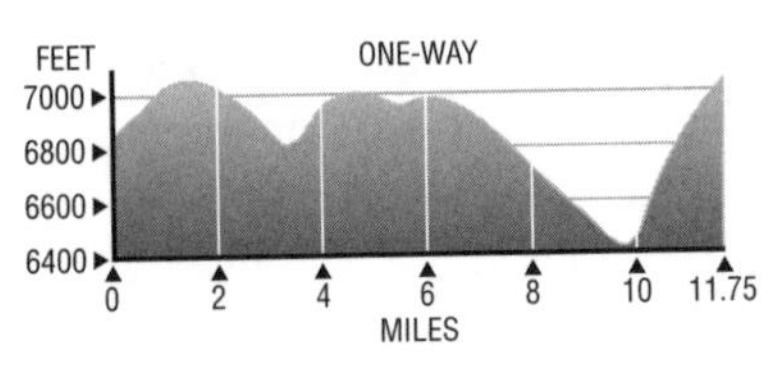

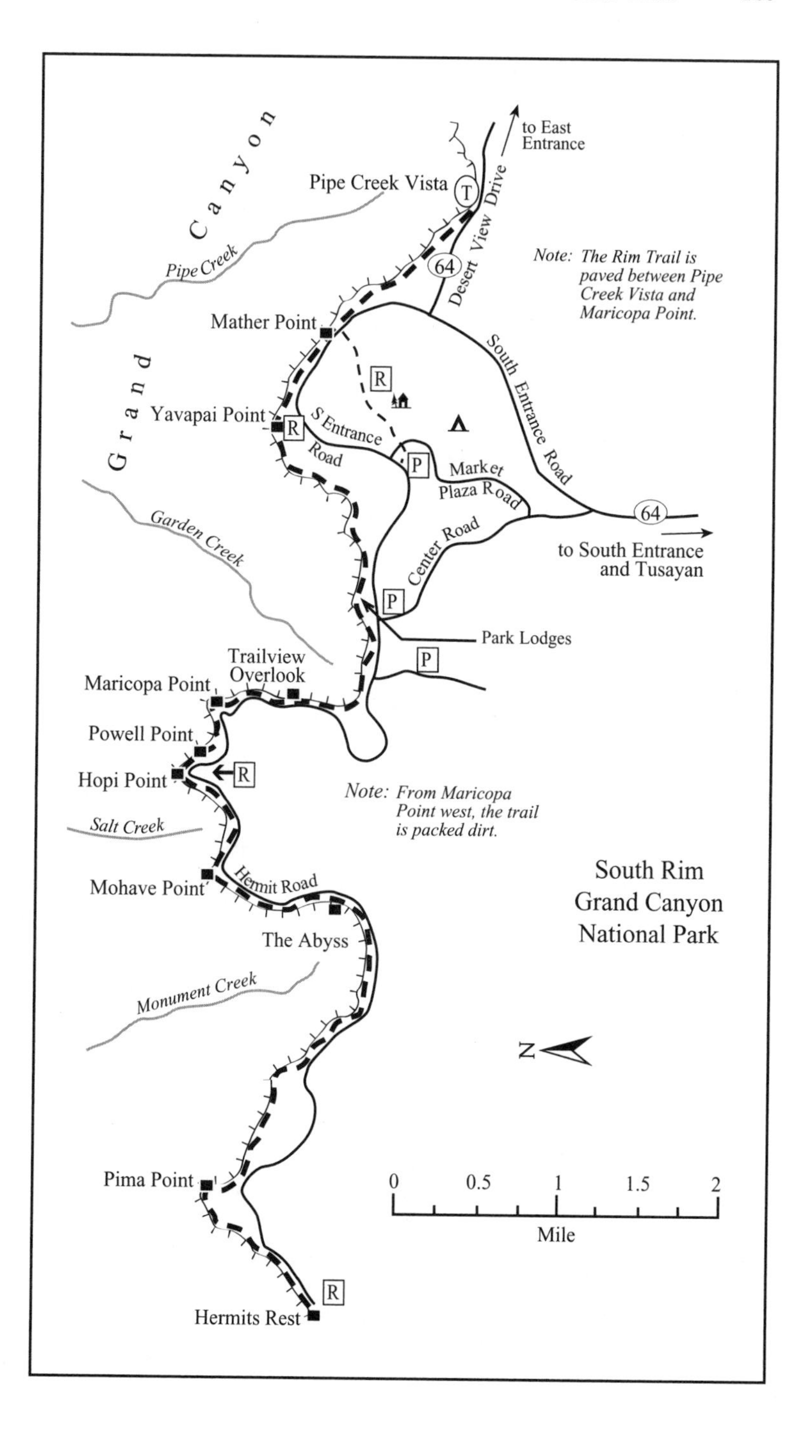
Grand Canyon
to East Entrance
Pipe Creek Vista
Desert View Drive
Pipe Creek
64
Note: The Rim Trail is paved between Pipe Creek Vista and Maricopa Point.
Mather Point
South Entrance Road
R
Yavapai Point
R
S Entrance Road
P
Market Plaza Road
Garden Creek
64
Center Road
to South Entrance and Tusayan
P
Park Lodges
P
Trailview Overlook
Maricopa Point
Powell Point
Hopi Point
R
Note: From Maricopa Point west, the trail is packed dirt.
Salt Creek
Mohave Point
Hermit Road
South Rim Grand Canyon National Park
The Abyss
Monument Creek
N
Pima Point
0
0.5
1
1.5
2
Mile
R
Hermits Rest

Vista west to Maricopa Point is paved and accessible to wheelchairs and strollers; from there to Hermits Rest it is dirt and rougher, but fairly level. The entire trail is also open to leashed dogs.

We'll discuss the trail in its entirety from east to west, but keep in mind that most people just walk a few sections. We do, however, strongly recommend that you walk at least one or two sections and not get your views of the Grand Canyon only from the established viewpoints—even on this very busy trail, you'll find that the crowds thin out considerably just a few hundred yards from a viewpoint.

Beginning at its eastern edge, the 5-mile paved section of the Rim Trail starts at Pipe Creek Vista, which is also a shuttle bus stop. From here you walk west about 1.3 miles to Mather Point, an excellent (and often crowded) overlook. This is just across the road from a large visitor information center where you'll find restrooms and drinking water. Continuing west for 0.6 mile, the next stop is Yavapai Point, where there is a glass observation area with information about the canyon. There are also restrooms here and a shuttle bus stop.

After another 0.75 mile the trail intersects with a path to the park headquarters offices, and this route will also eventually lead to Mather Campground and Trailer Village. Continuing on the Rim Trail takes you past several historic buildings, more restrooms, and drinking water, and after 1 mile, another shuttle bus stop at Village Route Transfer. Following the canyon rim, the trail goes for 0.7 mile, bending to the right (north), to the Trailview Overlook, where there are good views down to Bright Angel Trail (see Hike 39), and another shuttle bus stop. From here it is another 0.7 mile to Maricopa Point, where there is another shuttle bus stop and where the paved section of the trail ends.

From Maricopa Point the trail—which is now packed dirt—turns west again. There's another shuttle bus stop 0.5 mile ahead at Powell Point. Continuing along the rim for another 0.3 mile brings you to Hopi Point, which offers especially good views to the west—a good but often crowded choice at sunset—and where there is yet another shuttle bus stop. There are also restrooms here. The trail continues, first southwest and then due west, with shuttle bus stops in 0.8 mile at Mohave Point, then 1.1 miles at The Abyss, and then in another 2.9 miles at Pima Point. From Pima Point it is 1.1 miles to Hermits Rest, the western end of the Rim Trail, where there are restrooms,

Opposite: *View into Grand Canyon from trail*

drinking water, a small gift shop and snack bar, and the last shuttle bus stop. History buffs will be interested to know that some of the sections of trail near its western end follow the original alignment of the park road, built in 1912.

39. BRIGHT ANGEL TRAIL

Distance	3 miles round trip
Difficulty	Moderate to strenuous
Features	Dramatic views from within the Grand Canyon and a steep hike up
Starting elevation	6785 feet
Highest elevation	6785 feet
Total climb	1065 feet
Location	Grand Canyon National Park (South Rim)
Map	USGS Grand Canyon
Hiking season	Year-round (hazardous if snowy or icy)

Getting there: The South Rim's Grand Canyon Village, what we might call the heart of the South Rim, is located 60 miles north of Williams (along I-40) via AZ 64 or on the more scenic but mountainous route from Flagstaff (also along I-40), which is 80 miles northwest via US 180 and AZ 64. Bright Angel Trail branches off the Rim Trail (see Hike 38) near the mule corral, between Bright Angel Lodge and the Village Loop Transfer shuttle bus stop. It is well marked, so finding the trailhead is not a problem, but parking is, especially in summer. If you can leave your vehicle at your lodging and take the shuttle bus, you won't waste a lot of time trying to find a parking space. Restrooms and drinking water are near the trailhead.

All visitors to the South Rim of the Grand Canyon who are physically able to do so should hike at least a little way down this trail. Not only does it offer incredible views—yes, the views are different inside the canyon than they are from the top—but hiking this trail even a little way gives a sense of the Grand Canyon's immensity, as well as a feeling of accomplishment. This

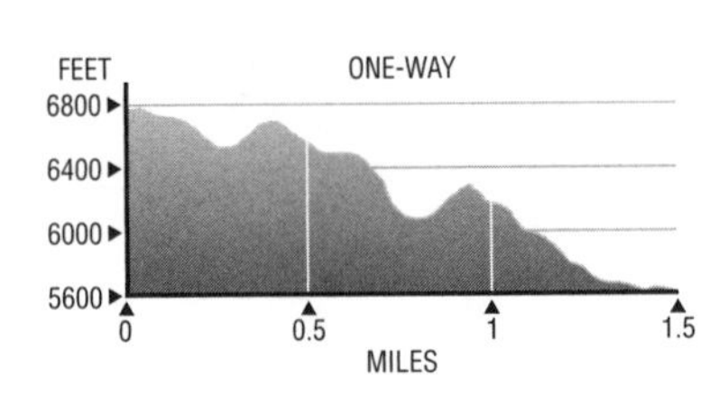

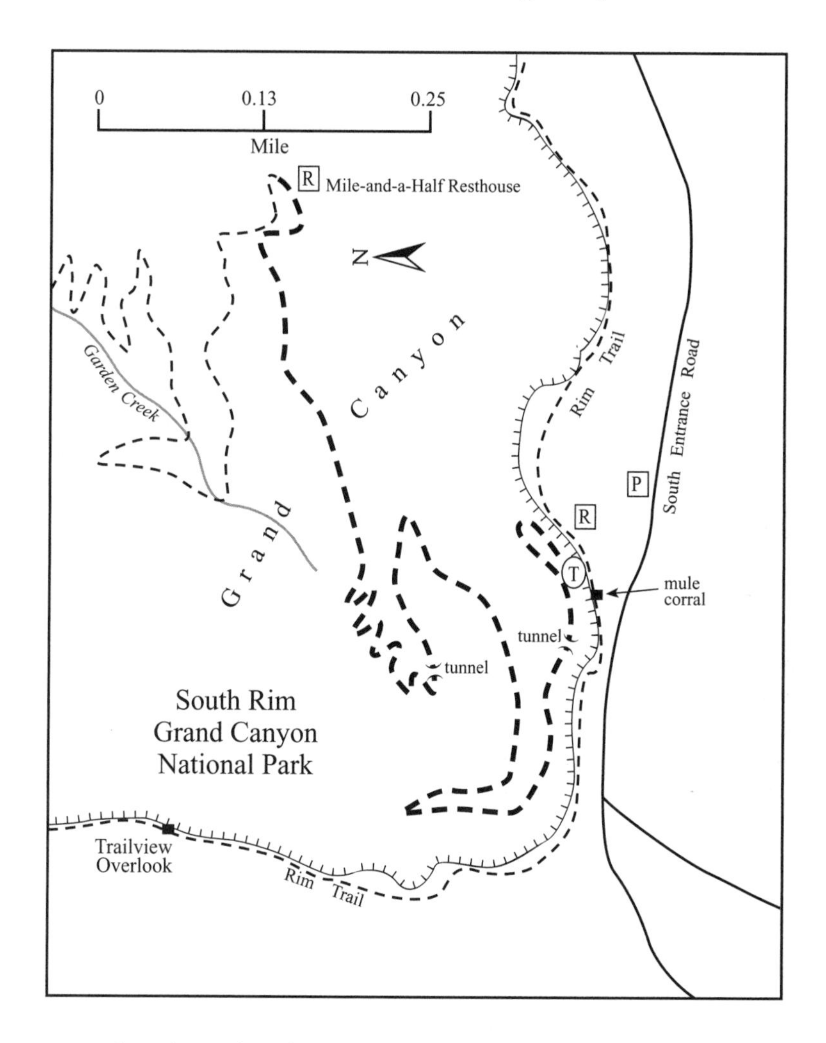

entry describes a short but very rewarding section of the trail.

Of course, let's not be stupid. This is definitely not an easy trail, and if you go down you have to get back up to the rim, either under your own power or with the help of rescuers. No one wants to be one of the more than 250 people rescued from the canyon each year, and going down this steep trail is a whole lot easier than going up. So before you attempt this hike, realistically assess your physical condition and determine whether it is right for you. You can turn back at any time; a lot of people do. It's also worth mentioning that in winter the upper part of the trail can be extremely icy, and instep crampons, which attach

A hiker descends Bright Angel Trail.

to your boots for extra traction, are recommended. These are available at park stores.

Park rangers recommend that everyone going on this hike, even for a short distance, carry plenty of water and some snacks. Also, during the summer, they recommend not hiking during the hottest time of day—between 10:00 AM and 4:00 PM. Keep in mind that it gets hotter—sometimes much hotter—as you drop down into the canyon. Also keep in mind that you'll be sharing the trail with mules, which always have the right of way.

The trail is old—it is believed to have begun as a path used by American Indians, and then was improved in the late 1800s to provide access to mining claims. It then became a toll trail for tourists, and was acquired by the National Park Service in the late 1920s. The entire Bright Angel Trail goes from the canyon rim all the way down to the Colorado River and Phantom Ranch, which makes for a round-trip hike of over 19 miles, obviously not a "short" hike, which is the theme of this book. We suggest going to the Mile-and-a-Half Resthouse, where you'll find restrooms and drinking water (water during the summer only), for a 3-mile round-trip hike.

From the trailhead, at an elevation of 6785 feet, the well-worn gravel path starts heading downhill almost immediately, although the beginning is not really too steep. As you descend there will be plenty of photo opportunities—we especially like the views with gnarled trees framing the canyon—and you'll notice that the reddish brown sandstone wall to the left (west) becomes increasingly more prominent as you drop into the canyon.

The first tunnel—blasted through solid Kaibab limestone—is reached at 0.18 mile at an elevation of 6708 feet, and the first switchback is at 0.45 mile, after which the trail gets a bit steeper. The second tunnel is at 0.9 mile, at 6240 feet elevation, and from here on down to the Resthouse there are a number of steep switchbacks.

You'll reach the Mile-and-a-half Resthouse at (surprise!) the 1.5-mile mark, at an elevation of 5720 feet. This is a good spot for a break and to appreciate the views, which are spectacular. The trail continues, of course—there is another Resthouse at 3 miles—but we suggest turning back at the 1.5-mile point. As you climb the more than 1000 feet up to the rim, take the time to pause to look at the views again. As the sun moves across the sky and clouds appear and disappear, the lighting changes, sometimes dramatically, and the view might be even more impressive than on the way down.

40. BRIGHT ANGEL POINT TRAIL

Distance ■ 1-mile round trip
Difficulty ■ Easy
Features ■ A shady walk to an awe-inspiring view of the Grand Canyon
Starting elevation ■ 8240 feet
Highest elevation ■ 8240 feet
Total climb ■ 350 feet
Location ■ Grand Canyon National Park (North Rim)
Map ■ USGS Bright Angel Point
Hiking season ■ Spring through early fall

Getting there: The North Rim is 44 miles south of Jacob Lake via AZ 67, also called the North Rim Parkway. To get to the North Rim from Flagstaff, take US 89 north for about 112 miles, then exit onto Alternate US 89, which eventually travels west to Jacob Lake, a distance of 55 miles. From Jacob Lake, follow AZ 67

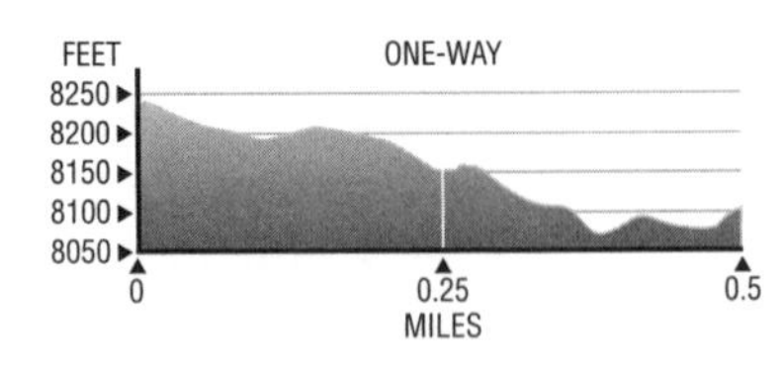

south to the parking lots at the North Rim visitor center. This trail begins at a small log shelter display near the parking area for the Grand Canyon Lodge, located at the end of AZ 67. There are restrooms, drinking water, and a visitor center nearby. Trail guides are available at a box along the trail.

The Grand Canyon is so big that it is difficult to comprehend and even harder to describe, but this paved, smooth path not only provides an incredible view but also lets us see dwarf trees, fossils in Kaibab limestone, and a statue of the famous burro Brighty. Along the narrow ridge that leads to Bright Angel Point, you'll hear the roar of the wind and feel its buffeting as it sweeps from the bottom of the canyon up over the edge. The trail ends at a fenced point with unsurpassed scenery on an enormous scale. Portions of the trail are not fenced, so although this is an especially good trail for children, they should be watched carefully.

Before starting down the asphalt path, stop behind the wooden building to look over a stone wall at the deep gorge called Roaring Springs Canyon. When the wind is just right, you can hear the spring flowing deep down inside the canyon. As you make your way along the trail, watch for juniper with its rough bark, Gambel oak, and clumps of grass. An opening between the trees, at about 0.1 mile, reveals a distant mesa with a crown of green plants perched on alternating

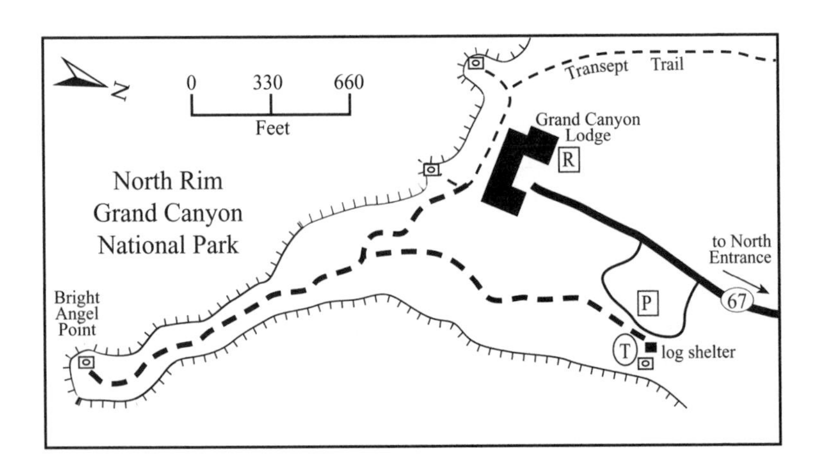

layers of white limestone and red shale. This is often a good spot to watch for chipmunks.

At the intersection at 0.15 mile, stay to the left and you'll see the immense canyon come into full view. As you descend the hill, stay left at the next intersection and walk onto the ridge that leads to Bright Angel Point. The trail is flanked by limestone, which is the solidified remains of ancient shelled animals. Mixed in the dull white stone are

Sunrise silhouettes a dead tree. (Photo by Lawrence Letham)

shining minerals and round fossils shaped like miniature vertebrae. Both sides of the narrow ridge are easily seen from a small bridge at 0.3 mile, where the force of the buffeting wind is often felt.

Bright Angel Point, at 0.5 mile, provides stunning views on all sides and also straight down, deep into the Grand Canyon with views of the Colorado River far below. There is also a log bench to sit on and enjoy the serenity if, by chance, you have the popular point to yourself. Then return along the path. At the first intersection on the return trip, at about 0.75 mile, the path to the right leads uphill to return to the parking lot along the trail you came in on. But stay to the left to go to the back entrance to Grand Canyon Lodge, taking the several spur trails along the way for additional canyon views.

Entering the lodge and looking out the windows, you'll have a higher vantage point than from the trail and you can see other parts of the canyon. Also while in the lodge be sure to find the statue of Brighty and rub his nose (see the sidebar below). Exit the front of the lodge and stay to the right on the road that leads back to the parking lot.

Brighty—The North Rim's Most Famous Resident

Named Bright Angel for the creek that flows from the North Rim down into the canyon, this small, friendly burro lived at the Grand Canyon from about 1892 until 1922. Called Brighty for short, it is believed that he was discovered by a prospector who taught the animal to carry mining equipment. After the prospector died, Brighty roamed the canyon, spending winters in the warm lower elevations and summers on the cool North Rim, where he carried water from a spring to tourist accommodations and agreeably let children ride on his back. The popular burro was the first to cross a new bridge at the bottom of the canyon, and assisted former President Theodore Roosevelt on a hunting trip. In 1953, Brighty was immortalized in the book *Brighty of the Grand Canyon* by Marguerite Henry, and in 1967 the book was made into a film of the same name. Sitting quietly in a corner of the North Rim's Grand Canyon Lodge is a bronze statue of Brighty by sculptor Peter Jepson. It is said that rubbing the statue's nose brings good luck.

41. CLIFF SPRING TRAIL

Distance ■ 2 miles round trip
Difficulty ■ Moderate
Features ■ A pleasant hike from open forest past limestone cliffs to cooling springs
Starting elevation ■ 7740 feet
Highest elevation ■ 7740 feet
Total climb ■ 310 feet
Location ■ Grand Canyon National Park (North Rim)
Map ■ USGS Walhalla Plateau, Cape Royal
Hiking season ■ Spring through early fall

Getting there: The North Rim is 44 miles south of Jacob Lake via AZ 67, also called the North Rim Parkway. To get to the North Rim from Flagstaff, take US 89 north for about 112 miles, then exit onto Alternate US 89, which eventually travels west to Jacob Lake, a distance of 55 miles. From Jacob Lake, follow AZ 67 south to the parking lots at the North Rim visitor center. The trailhead is directly across the Cape Royal Road from a small pullout, on a curve 0.3 mile north of Cape Royal (the end of the road). This trail is on the North Rim, just under 20 miles from the intersection of Cape Royal Road and AZ 67. There are no restrooms or drinking water at the trailhead.

What starts as a hike through a pine forest turns into a trek into a rocky side canyon, with sheer cliffs and limestone overhangs that were formed as spring water dissolved the stone. Here you can see up close the distinct dividing line between white limestone and the thin red layer of sandstone that often sits on top of a layer of buff-colored Coconino sandstone. The thick pines in the narrow canyon and the beds of large thistles under the tall limestone ledges are a stark contrast to the barren, windswept cliffs near the end of the trail. There is also a small Ancestral Puebloan ruin along the way.

From its beginning, the hard-packed dirt trail descends a short slope into a wide, flat stand of ponderosa pines, where the lack of thick undergrowth increases the sense of openness, and red and white rocks line the trail. A small ruin of an Ancestral Puebloan

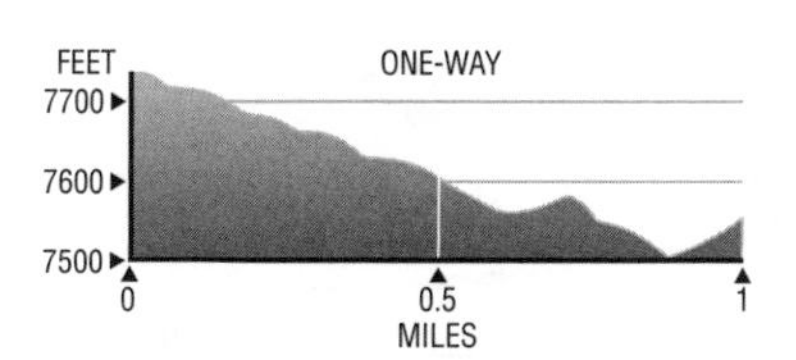

granary, built about AD 1050, is on the right just 400 feet down the trail. From here the trail drops, and twice crosses a drainage, before rising above the valley and passing between two 5-foot-tall boulders at 0.3 mile. Just ahead, a rock wall slightly overhangs the path. It appears fractured, with a wide, vertical crack filled with a dark brown stone.

As the trail curves around a corner, an even longer wall with deeper overhangs stretches ahead. Flowers grow from the overhang's ceiling, and by 0.4 mile the drainage along the trail has become a small canyon whose true depth is revealed by the height of the tall trees stretching up from its bottom. The sheer limestone walls across the canyon make the area feel like a miniature version of the entire Grand Canyon. As the trail turns a corner, you'll see a panorama of buttes, pinnacles, and other formations. Although they are at a distance, they are close enough that their large size is made comprehensible by comparing them to the depth of the small canyon along the trail.

Water dripping from the limestone overhangs forms pools that support thick patches of thistles, and wildflowers and moss also thrive in the oasis around the pools. Under one overhang, the spring water gushes from the rock. By 0.6 mile, the overhangs end while the near-level trail provides views of additional formations in the Grand Canyon. At 0.7 mile, a piñon tree takes root on the right side of the trail, grows horizontally across the trail, then turns up to grow skyward on the left side. The trail continues up and down past yucca, piñon pine, juniper, and small purple flowers until it reaches the side of a tall, white, limestone cliff at 0.85 mile.

The trail now turns around the cliff edge, hugging the side, and within 400 feet takes a distinct step down, just as the rock abruptly

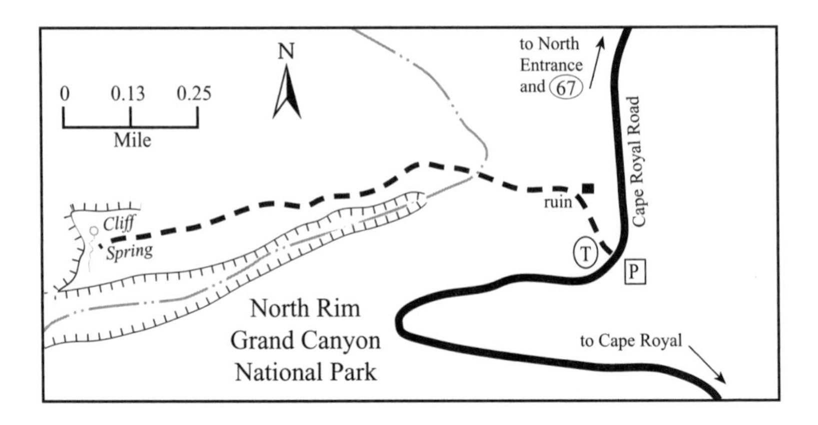

Limestone overhangs (Photo by Lawrence Letham)

changes from white limestone on top to a red-colored stone on the bottom. The trail ends where a chest-high boulder sits under a large overhang, with the spring on the cliff side of the boulder. Don't drink the water as it is not considered potable. From here you return to the trailhead over the same route.

42. CAPE ROYAL TRAIL

Distance ▪ 1 mile round trip
Difficulty ▪ Easy
Features ▪ A pleasant, sunny walk to a splendid view into the Grand Canyon
Starting elevation ▪ 7900 feet
Highest elevation ▪ 7900 feet
Total climb ▪ 70 feet
Location ▪ Grand Canyon National Park
Map ▪ USGS Cape Royal
Hiking season ▪ Spring through early fall

Getting there: The North Rim is 44 miles south of Jacob Lake via AZ 67, also called the North Rim Parkway. To get to the North Rim from Flagstaff, take US 89 north for about 112 miles, then exit onto Alternate US 89, which eventually travels west to Jacob Lake, a distance of 55 miles. From Jacob Lake, follow AZ 67 south to the parking lots at the North Rim visitor center. The trailhead is located on the

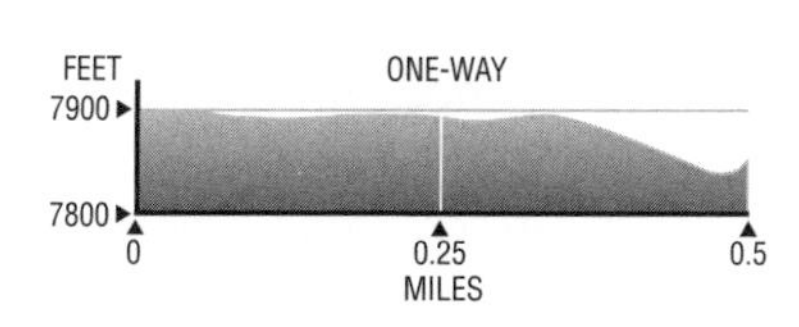

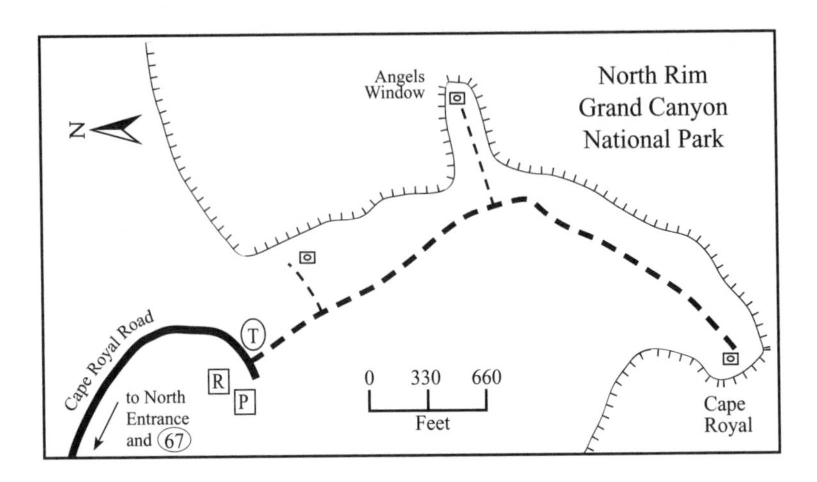

southeast side of the parking area at the very end of Cape Royal Road, about 20 miles from the intersection with AZ 67. There are restrooms, but no drinking water, at the trailhead.

This meandering, wheelchair-accessible asphalt trail on the North Rim leads through Upper Sonoran piñon pine, Utah juniper, and sagebrush to a magnificent view of the Colorado River, which carved the Grand Canyon. The expansive views of Angels Window and colored, distant buttes are a backdrop to fern bushes with their delicate leaves, holes drilled into the rough juniper bark by sapsuckers, and trees that seem to be miraculously growing out of solid stone. The overlook above Angels Window is a cliff with sheer 200- to 300-foot drops that would be scary if not for the fence. The distance from the trailhead directly to the overlook at Cape Royal is a short 0.3-mile walk on a nearly level trail, but be sure to explore the side trails to see the wonderful views.

Signs along the trail provide information about the plants, animals, and geology. Along the trail you'll see high desert vegetation, including juniper, sagebrush, cliff rose, and the tough, drought-resistant piñon pine. A small turnout with wooden benches, about 250 feet from the trailhead, offers a good view of Angels Window—a large, rectangular hole in an even larger limestone ridge—and in the canyon below you can see colored bands of red and white rock all the way down to the Colorado River.

The turnoff to the left at 0.25 mile leads to a fenced overlook above

Opposite: *A lone man ponders the imponderable: the Grand Canyon.* (Photo by Lawrence Letham)

Angels Window. In the middle of the solid stone overlook, two small trees grow where no topsoil is visible. The secret to plants appearing to grow out of solid stone is a crack or indentation where wind has deposited finer soils and water has collected. The first seed to germinate grows quickly, then often dies for lack of nourishment. Its remains, however, improve the soil in the crack, giving the next seed a greater chance of survival. After hundreds, possibly thousands of years, the microclimate in the crack has developed enough to support long-term plant life. Along the fenced edges, the sheer cliff of the overlook falls 200 to 300 feet before a ledge blocks the view. Look from the drop-off at other cliffs across the expanse to get a better perspective on the Grand Canyon's enormous depth.

Once back on the Cape Royal Trail, look for two plants in particular: the fern bush and the juniper. The fern bush is easily identified by its red bark, its fine, tiny leaves that look just like a fern, and white blossoms. Ferns are delicate plants that require shade, but not so the fern bush, which can withstand the searing heat of the Upper Sonoran Desert. The attraction of the juniper is not the plant itself, but the tiny holes made in its bark by a bird called a sapsucker. Similar to a woodpecker, the bird clutches the trunk with its feet and drills holes in the bark to drink the sap and eat insects that become trapped in the sap.

At a little over 0.7 mile the trail ends at Cape Royal, where a wide, fenced overlook has endless views of eroded limestone rocks that look like columns, and narrow stone ridges dividing deep canyons. From here, return about 0.3 mile along the Cape Royal Trail directly to the trailhead.

FLAGSTAFF AND NORTHERN ARIZONA

Although this part of Arizona is best known for the spectacular Grand Canyon (discussed in its own chapter above), this region has a lot to offer outside its world-famous national park. Here you'll find the state's tallest mountain, lakes and rivers, and the stark mesas and buttes of Indian country—home of the prehistoric ancestors of today's Hopi and other Pueblo tribes, as well as the vast Navajo Nation. Elevation in Flagstaff is about 6900 feet. The state's highest point—Humphreys Peak, at 12,633 feet—is located just north of Flagstaff in the Kachina Peaks Wilderness Area in the San Francisco Mountains.

There are abundant hiking opportunities in the region's national forests and several national monuments, and you'll discover that while trails in Grand Canyon National Park and other big-name outdoor

Grizzly bear prickly pear cactus in bloom along Sandal Trail

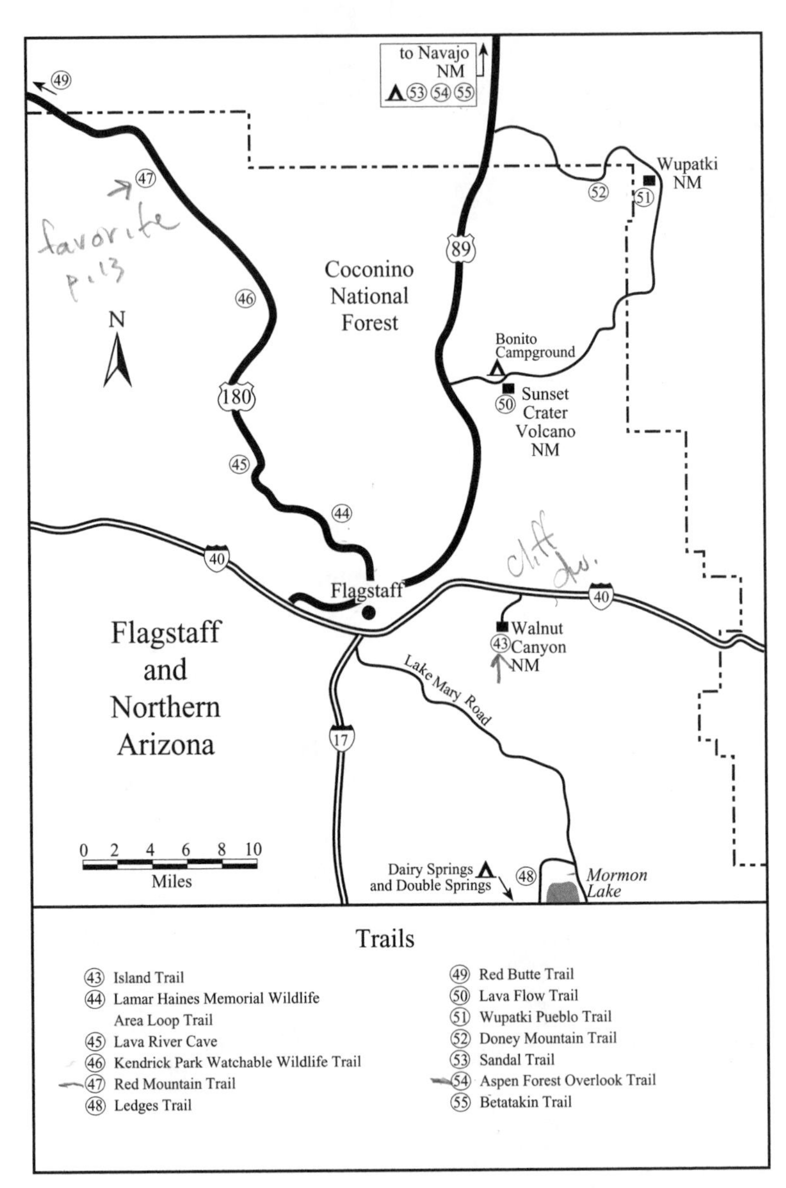

attractions are often crowded, especially in summer, there will be far fewer people exploring the national monuments and even fewer on many of the trails in the national forests. Among the highlights of the trails discussed here are hiking through a lava tube, walking into a volcanic crater, exploring well-preserved prehistoric Indian cliff dwellings, and seeing a variety of birds and animals.

Another plus here is the cost, or maybe we should say the lack of cost. Fees at national monuments are much less than at national parks, and the national forests in this chapter charge no fees at all (as of this writing, anyway). On the downside, parking is often limited at these National Forest Service trailheads and there is no security at all, so be sure to lock any valuables out of sight before leaving your vehicle.

For additional information, contact the various government agencies mentioned below, as well as the Flagstaff Convention and Visitors Bureau. Those planning to visit the vast Navajo Nation, which covers much of northeastern Arizona and where the last three trails in the section are located, may also want to get additional travel information from the Navajo Nation Tourism Department. You'll find complete contact information in the appendix at the back of this book.

CAMPGROUNDS

There are commercial campgrounds, with RV hookups, hot showers, and all the usual amenities in Flagstaff. In addition, there are several campgrounds on public lands.

Coconino National Forest. There are several rustic campgrounds in the national forest, including **Bonito Campground,** located in the Peaks Ranger District across the road from the Sunset Crater Volcano National Monument's visitor center, just outside the monument entrance. It offers a delightful forest camping experience. There are 44 campsites, vault toilets but no showers or RV hookups, and it is usually open from mid-April through mid-October. Reservations are not accepted, and the campground often fills by mid-afternoon from June through August. A fee is charged.

Also in the forest are the **Dairy Springs Campground** and nearby **Double Springs Campground,** in the Coconino's Mormon Lake Ranger District. From Flagstaff, take Lake Mary Road southeast about 20 miles to Mormon Lake Road (Forest Road 90), turn right (west) and go 3.5 miles to the entrance to Dairy Springs Campground. Double Springs Campground is a bit farther down Mormon Lake Road. Set among white firs and ponderosa pines, they are above pretty Mormon Lake and close to the Ledges Trail (Hike 48). Together the campgrounds have 27 sites as well as restrooms, but no showers or RV hookups. They are usually open from early May through mid-October. There is a moderate fee, and reservations are available.

Navajo National Monument. This national monument, which

is far from practically everything, has two free campgrounds, both with nicely spaced sites in an open piñon-juniper forest. **Sunset View Campground** is open year-round with 31 small sites (no RVs over 28 feet), flush toilets, and running water. **Canyon View Campground,** open from April through September, has 16 sites, vault toilets, and no water. Neither campground has RV hookups and neither accepts reservations (except for several group sites at Canyon View).

43. ISLAND TRAIL

Distance	0.9-mile loop
Difficulty	Moderate
Features	A walk around and among prehistoric cliff dwellings
Starting elevation	6690 feet
Highest elevation	6690 feet
Total climb	185 feet
Location	Walnut Canyon National Monument
Map	USGS Flagstaff East, Walnut Canyon National Monument brochure
Hiking season	Year-round

Getting there: The trail is located in Walnut Canyon National Monument. From Flagstaff, drive east on I-40 for 10 miles to the Walnut Canyon Road exit, then south on Walnut Canyon Road 4 miles to the national monument parking lot. A modest fee is charged to enter the monument, and restrooms and drinking water are available in the monument's visitor center. Although generally open year-round, the trail may be closed at times during the winter because of snow and ice.

The deep Walnut Canyon makes the small mountain it surrounds look like an island, and thus the name of this trail that loops around the mountain past broken chunks of limestone, tall pine trees, and a series of 800-year-old cliff dwellings built by a group of people known as the Sinagua.

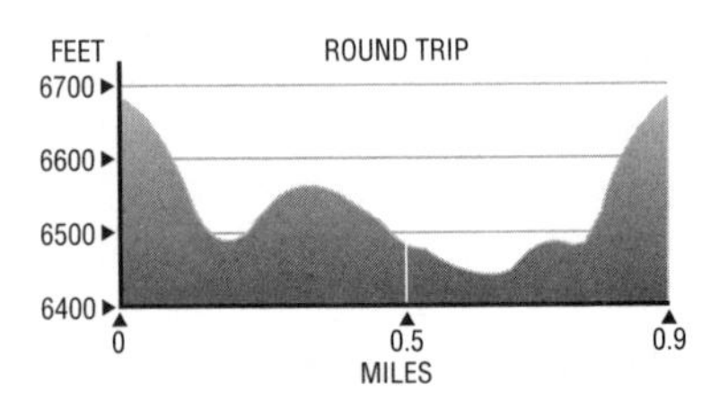

Start your visit in the visitor center to examine the exhibits

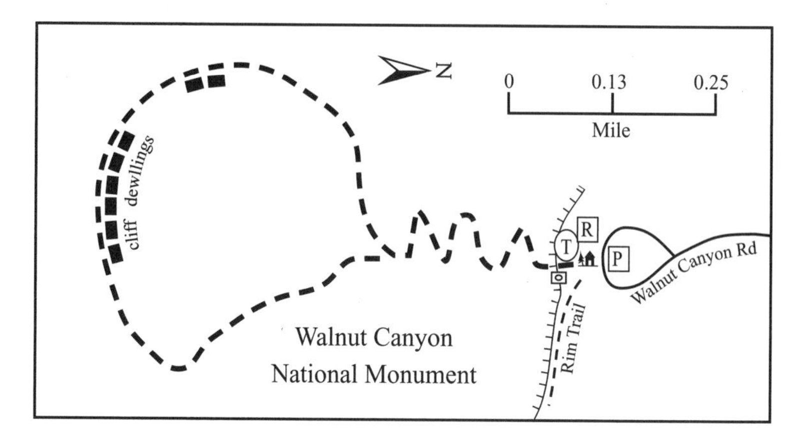

that tell the story of the Sinagua—Spanish for "without water"—before heading out to see the ruins firsthand.

The trail begins behind the visitor center at a patio, which offers a bird's-eye view of Walnut Canyon as it writhes like a snake across the plateau. The upper limestone layers have eroded to form the ledges that shelter the ruins, while the lower sandstone layer, left by ancient sand dunes, has weathered to look like twisted taffy. From the high patio, 240 steps descend 185 feet to the asphalt trail, which circles the island of cliff dwellings.

From the very start, florae of all varieties crowd the edges of the trails. Salt brush, mountain mahogany, prickly pear cactus, claret cup cactus, red penstemon, and tiny daisies are among the plants that grow on the sunny southern slopes. The cooler northern slopes boast ponderosa pine and Douglas fir.

After descending the stairs, turn right, as the trail slopes down slightly under a limestone ledge past Gambel oak and ponderosa pine. Cliff dwellings are visible across the canyon, while the first ruins near the trail are a few incomplete walls that you'll encounter under a ledge after about 0.25 mile. The larger, completely enclosed rooms at about 0.4 mile give a better picture of life in a cliff dwelling, and you're welcome to squeeze through the small door into the dark interior and ponder the lives of the people who lived here.

As the trail curves around the mountain, the tall conifers are slowly replaced by juniper, yucca, and piñon pine. The 0.5-mile point marks the best preserved and largest dwellings. Long rows of rooms stretch under ledges, accessed by narrow, short, T-shaped doors crowned with smoke holes. Enter the rooms to see the blackened ceilings, touch the stone used to construct the walls, and find fingerprints in the mud mortar left by the original builders.

By about 0.65 mile all that remains is a few walls, but it is evident that these rooms must have been warm in the winter because they're on the fully exposed south side, which gets full benefit of the low winter sun. You'll notice that only desert plants can survive here, while on the opposite side of the canyon, on the north side of the adjacent cliff, tall pines grow. Even on the south side of the mountain, golden penstemon and lizards greet passing hikers. The white limestone cliffs that line the trail also offer opportunities to search for embedded fossils from ancient oceans. Here you'll also see Utah junipers.

Shortly after the junipers are the stairs that begin the return trip to the top—strategically placed benches with scenic overlooks provide welcome rest stops along the climb.

Cliff dwelling ruins along the trail

44. LAMAR HAINES MEMORIAL WILDLIFE AREA LOOP TRAIL

Distance	1.8 miles round trip
Difficulty	Easy
Features	A pleasant mountain meadow offering bird-watching and historic buildings
Starting elevation	8590 feet
Highest elevation	8625 feet
Total climb	220 feet
Location	Coconino National Forest
Map	USGS Humphreys Peak
Hiking season	Spring through early fall

Getting there: To get to the trailhead, which is in the Coconino National Forest's Peaks Ranger District, go northwest out of Flagstaff on US 180 for about 7 miles, turn right on Snowbowl Road (Forest Road 516), and continue north for 4.5 miles to a parking area, at the far end of which is a gate that leads to the trailhead. Restrooms and drinking water are not available. Just inside the gate are large signs showing a map of the trail and explaining that Lamar Haines (1927–1986), for whom the area is named, was a local teacher and outdoorsman, and a leader in the conservation movement.

Quaking aspens, lush grasses, several springs, and towering ponderosa pines are the hallmarks of this shady walk in the woods that also offers a look at some large volcanic boulders and the remains of an historic homestead. Singing birds and wildflowers along the trail make the hike especially nice in summer, and it is a popular hike for families with young children.

The trail, which is sometimes also called the Veit Springs Trail, consists of a well-defined dirt path that begins by meandering among lichen-covered boulders and dead trees moldering on the ground. Quaking aspens—especially colorful in fall—grow among the tall pines that shade the trail. You're likely to see Abert's and red squirrels, as well as birds such as mountain chickadees, red-breasted nuthatches, western flycatchers, and various species of woodpeckers.

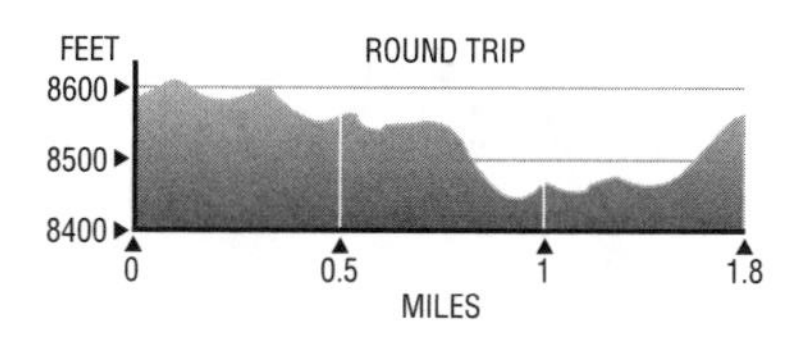

After about 0.1 mile the trail takes a sharp left turn and begins a mild descent down a hill through more quaking aspen. Soon a large, interesting boulder rises to the left of the trail. Its rounded appearance, divided into three sections, makes it look like a volcanic version of a snowman, and at the top a small pine tree juts from the stone like a locket of hair. The trail continues to descend as it continues past purple wildflowers (in summer) and scattered boulders, until it arrives in a picturesque meadow thick with the white trunks and delicate green leaves of quaking aspen.

A small trail peels off the main trail at about 0.3 mile; this is the return leg of the loop. For now, stay straight and continue through increasingly thicker stands of aspen. As the trail continues, it rises above the meadow and pines are seen more frequently. At about 0.5 mile, the roots of a big, long-dead tree surround a 3-foot boulder, and large pinecones, some up to 6 inches long, lie scattered on the ground. Alternating patches of pines and quaking aspen accompany the trail to an earthen dam, built to catch spring waters, at about 0.8 mile.

At about the 1-mile point there is a plaque memorializing Lamar Haines and nearby the well-preserved remains of a small, low, log cabin. Beyond the cabin are a small stone building, a spring, and a pond. This was the site of the 1890s homestead of Ludwig Veit. The stones of the building are natural, uncut, and put together with concrete. Cliffs rise 70 to 100 feet in a long escarpment of volcanic boulders, and if you

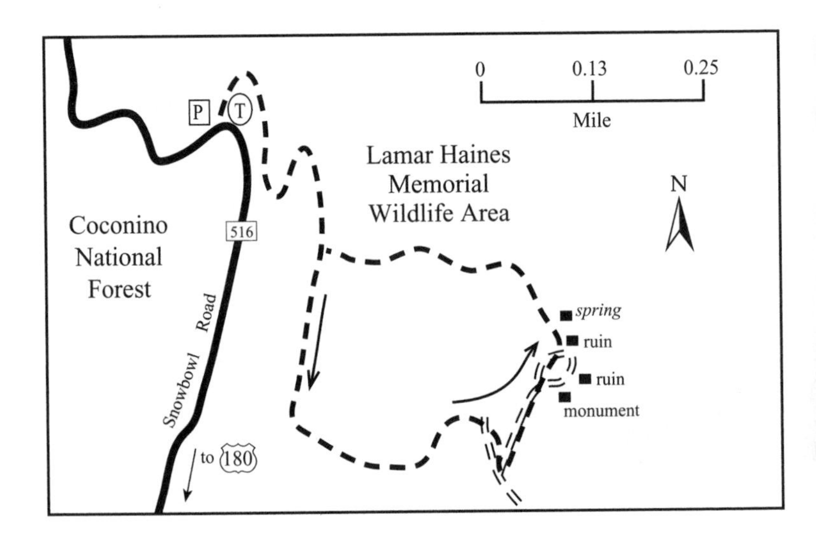

look carefully you will find some American Indian rock art.
The trail continues to an open area, through more aspen groves, and loops back to the trailhead.

The Nose Knows

Ponderosa pines, which are seen along the Lamar Haines Memorial Wildlife Area Loop Trail as well as near Sedona and in many other higher-elevation areas in northern Arizona, are tall, straight, impressive trees that are recognized by their long needles—up to 10 inches—that usually grow in bundles of three. The mature trees have orange-tinted bark, but their most distinctive feature is that if you stick your nose up to the bark you will smell a fragrance that is very definitely like vanilla.

Remains of an old cabin

45. LAVA RIVER CAVE TRAIL

Distance	2 miles round trip
Difficulty	Easy
Features	Exploration of an underground lava tube
Starting elevation	7680 feet
Highest elevation	7680 feet
Total climb	120 feet
Location	Coconino National Forest
Map	USGS Wing Mountain
Hiking season	Spring through fall

Getting there: The lava tube is located in the Peaks Ranger District of the Coconino National Forest. From Flagstaff, take US 180 northwest for about 15 miles to mile marker 230. Turn left onto unpaved Forest Road 245 and drive approximately 3 miles to a T intersection. Turn left onto Forest Road 171, continue about 0.7 mile, then turn left on Forest Road 171B, which you follow about 0.25 mile to the Lava River Cave parking area. There are no restrooms or drinking water, and the Forest Service asks all hikers to pack out everything they carry into the cave. From here it is a 0.25-mile walk on a dirt road to the cave entrance.

A lava tube winding under the surface of the earth sounds a lot like Jules Verne's story *Journey to the Center of the Earth*. A gaping hole in the forest floor leads to an underground adventure of volcanic tunnels, loose rocks, and brilliant silver- and rust-colored streaks on the walls. It's also dark—pitch black dark—so at least two powerful flashlights per person are strongly recommended, just in case one fails. Some hikers like to use a propane or battery-operated lantern, which illuminates the rock formations better than flashlights. The tunnel is chilly, usually in the low forties, so take a jacket or sweater too. And because the cave ceiling is low, a helmet or hat is also a good idea.

The cave, discovered in the early 1900s by lumberjacks working in the area, was formed by volcanic activity some 700,000 years ago. Molten rock erupted from a nearby volcano and as it flowed out, the top, sides, and bottom cooled and solidified, but the lava continued to flow through

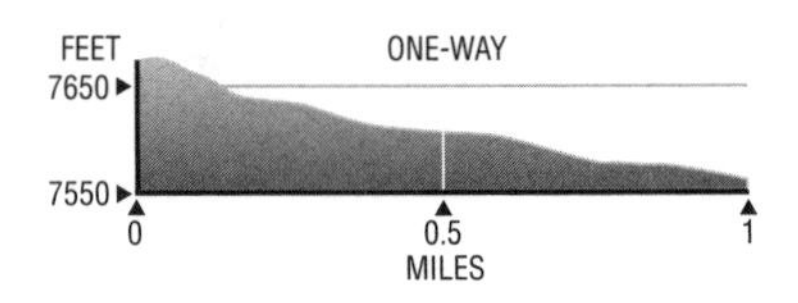

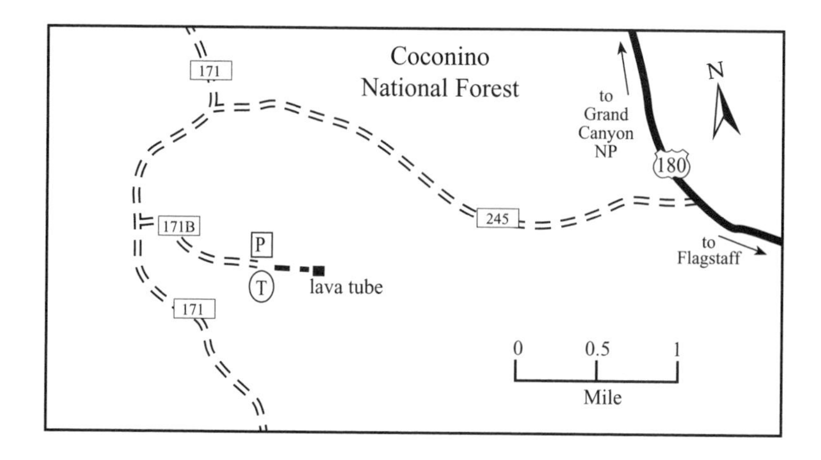

the middle. When the lava finally stopped flowing, it left the tunnel. Ripples in the floor show where the last bits of lava began to solidify, and icicle-shaped rock formations hanging from the ceiling are evidence that some last-minute heat caused a bit of melting of the solidified stone.

The cave entrance is a dark hole surrounded by a circular, 4-foot-high wall of stacked lava rocks. Pass through the opening to begin the steep but short descent, moving past and over large lava boulders, to the first cavern about 200 feet into the tunnel. The beginning of the cave is the coldest part, and there may be ice in spring.

Enough light filters into this first cavern to see a floor strewn with broken rocks under a rough, arching ceiling. The light from the opening fails after only a few more steps into the tunnel, but your flashlight reveals broad silver streaks on the dark rock of the ceiling and walls. A closer look reveals myriad closely and uniformly spaced individual water droplets that glisten like silver jewels in the light. After a short section of low ceilings, the tunnel opens up at about 0.25 mile to the nearly semicircular shape of a railway tunnel that curves through the underground darkness.

Flat rock slabs that have fallen from the ceiling cover the tunnel floor unevenly. The wide, tall winding tunnel continues to where it splits into two tunnels at just under 0.5 mile. They merge back together after about 250 feet, but we suggest that now you take the right tunnel, which has a few sections only about 3 feet high, so you'll need to crawl on your hands and knees. Just after the lowest section, the other branch appears on the left, but keep to the right after this junction and prepare to duck a few more times. Just after 0.5 mile, the tunnel, once more tall and wide, displays rust-red streaks on the walls. Water has deposited iron oxide as it seeps down from the forest floor above. The floor here is clear of fallen rock, with a long 3-inch-wide, 2-foot-deep crack exposed.

Several other short sections have low ceilings, but the floor is flat and mostly free of obstacles, so passage is easy. Deeper into the tunnel, the air is a bit warmer, with less moisture, so there are fewer silver bands of water droplets on the walls. The tunnel continues past occasional piles of boulders that have flaked off from the ceiling, until the cave suddenly ends at about 1 mile.

On the return trip, take the right fork where the tunnel splits to see the other side. At the cave entrance, follow the road back to the parking area.

46. KENDRICK PARK WATCHABLE WILDLIFE TRAIL

Distance ■ 1.5 miles round trip (0.25-mile wheelchair-accessible loop)
Difficulty ■ Easy
Features ■ A shady walk offering a good chance of seeing wildlife
Starting elevation ■ 7890 feet
Highest elevation ■ 7940 feet
Total climb ■ 160 feet
Location ■ Coconino National Forest
Map ■ USGS Kendrick Park, US Forest Service brochure
Hiking season ■ Late spring through fall

Getting there: The trailhead is in the Peaks Ranger District of the Coconino National Forest. From Flagstaff, go northwest on US 180 about 20 miles to the well-marked Kendrick Park Watchable Wildlife Area, which is along the highway. The trail is open to foot and wheelchair travel only. A 0.25-mile paved loop is wheelchair accessible; the rest is packed dirt. There are restrooms and drinking water at the trailhead. The trail as we describe it here begins near the restrooms at the northwest corner of the parking lot; you can also walk the trail in the opposite direction, beginning at the other end of the parking lot.

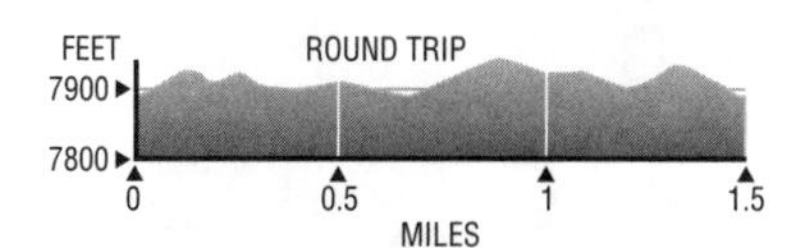

This pleasant walk through woods and grassy areas, especially good for families with children, bridges two habitats and thus offers possibilities of seeing birds and animals of both grasslands and forests. A series of interpretative signs helps explain the plants and animals—including human animals—that make or have made this area their home.

The trail begins with a paved section, suitable for wheelchairs, and at about 0.15 mile passes the remains of an old corral, which was used by potato farmers in the early to mid-1900s to pen their horses. From here you can continue on the paving for a pleasant 0.25-mile paved loop or branch off on a well-packed dirt path for the 1.5-mile walk. From either one you get good views of Kendrick Mountain, off to the west. This 10,418-foot broad-topped mountain is named for Major Henry Kendrick, who escorted a government exploration of the area in the 1850s.

Both options also give you a taste of woodlands and grasslands, and at least a chance of seeing birds and other wildlife. Watch for Steller's jays, northern flickers, red-tailed hawks, and hairy woodpeckers, plus

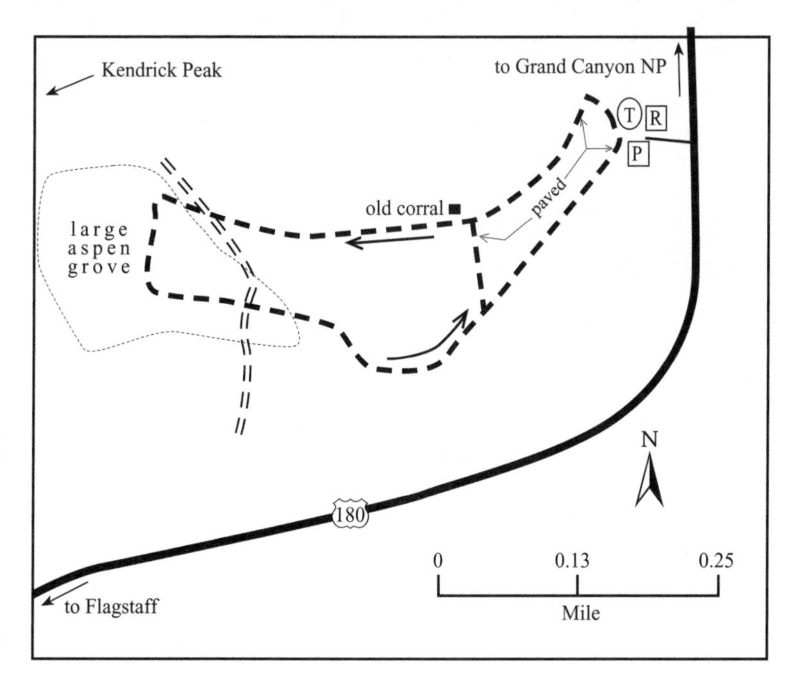

Lots of aspen along the trail

Abert's squirrels, badgers, long-tailed weasels, porcupines, coyotes, mule deer, and even pronghorn and elk. The best chances for seeing the larger mammals are early morning and early evening.

Staying on the main (dirt) trail will take you past the skeleton of an old car, and then after about 0.5 mile you enter a crowded grove of tall, mostly thin aspen, where the white bark of many of the trees have prominent black scars. The trees here are especially pretty when the leaves turn golden yellow in the fall. The trail meanders back toward the parking lot, passing among ponderosa pine, spruce, and fir, and joins the final leg of the paved trail. A large pile of trash from an old campsite lies deliberately undisturbed because future archeologists might want to check it out!

The trail ends at the opposite end of the parking area from where you started.

Scarred for Life

When you see ugly black scars marring the pure white bark of aspen trees in Kendrick Park and other areas in northern Arizona, your first thought is that some despicable humans have been busy with their knives. And although you will find a bit of that (Does Bill still love Mary? We wonder . . .), most of the scarring is really the work of elk, who clean off their antlers by rubbing them on the aspen bark.

47. RED MOUNTAIN TRAIL

Distance ■ 2.4 miles round trip
Difficulty ■ Easy to moderate
Features ■ Bizarre rock formations in an eroded volcanic cinder cone
Starting elevation ■ 6750 feet
Highest elevation ■ 7045 feet
Total climb ■ 350 feet
Location ■ Coconino National Forest
Map ■ USGS Chapel Mountain
Hiking season ■ Spring through early fall

Getting there: To get to the trailhead, located in the Peaks Ranger District of the Coconino National Forest, drive northwest from Flagstaff on US 180 about 25 miles to mile marker 247, and just past a sign for Red Mountain Trail turn left (southwest) onto Forest Road 9023V, which you follow about 0.25 mile to the marked trailhead. Drinking water and restrooms are not available. The gravel trail is easy to follow, with signs in

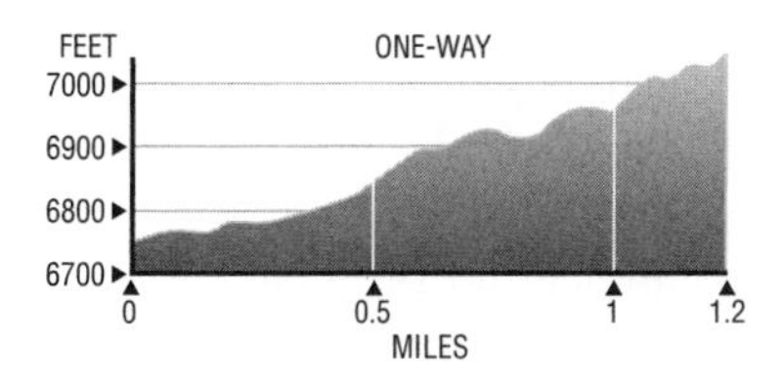

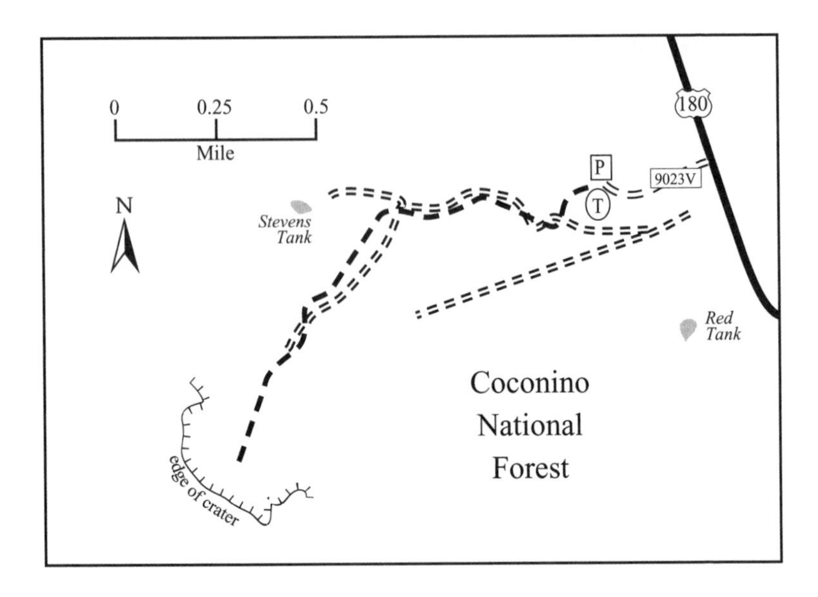

the few places where hikers might go wrong. You'll see the aptly named Red Mountain straight ahead.

One of the lesser-known gems among northern Arizona hikes, the Red Mountain Trail provides an easy walk up into the eroded cinder cone of an extinct volcano, formed about 740,000 years ago, with an amphitheater composed of numerous fascinating hoodoos—eroded pillars of stone.

Like many other volcanoes in the region, lava oozed through a break in the earth's crust to form the steep-sided Red Mountain. Unlike others, however, Red Mountain formed with a huge crater in its middle as though it were cut in half, leaving most of its insides exposed.

The trail starts in common desert surroundings and begins a gentle climb among piñon and juniper toward Red Mountain, which is visible through most of the hike. The striking mountain formed when thick, hot magma forced its way to the surface. Its consistency allowed the lava to build up as a steep cone instead of flowing away over the ground. Red Mountain did not form as a complete cone but, for some reason, as only a partial cone. The red cliffs, seen now only in the distance, are what the other volcanoes in the area look like on the inside.

Prickly pear cactus grows along the trail and a wide variety of colorful wildflowers will be seen in summer and early fall—August usually has the best displays. Watch for golden groundsel, orange globemallow, and pink windmill near the beginning of the trail, and as the elevation increases, be on the lookout for the tiny yellow flowers of four-winged saltbush, bright red cliff rose, pink wild four o'clock, and the yellow blooms of the paperflower.

In addition to piñon pines and Utah junipers, the narrow canyon also has some large ponderosa pines. At just past the 0.5-mile point a juniper and a pine grow twisted together as though they were one plant. After about 0.75 mile, the trail follows a sandy and usually dry

Oddly eroded rock formations give the trail an otherworldly look.

stream bed, and soon you'll begin to see volcanic boulders of various sizes and colors.

After just over 1 mile there is a low wall, which is ascended by climbing up a short, sturdy ladder. Here, tall, pointed, black lava rocks with a greenish hue—caused by lichen—rise on each side of the wall, giving this stone corridor the appearance of some sort of fantasyland. Continue a short distance to where the trail dumps you into the picturesque amphitheater on the northeast flank of the cinder cone. Watch for golden eagles, prairie falcons, and raptors, which sometimes nest in the cliffs.

The rounded, well-weathered rock formations, which are mostly a light reddish brown, are reminiscent of the formations at Bryce Canyon National Park in Utah, and to our way of thinking this is one of the most aesthetically interesting volcanic cinder cones in the West. This appears to be the center of the volcano, where the molten rock erupted, but the amphitheater was formed after the eruption occurred. The actual center is out of sight, back behind the amphitheater's back wall.

When you are done exploring the amphitheater and its weird formations, return to the trailhead by the same route, and here is a pleasant surprise—the walk to the crater was slightly uphill, so the trip back down is even easier.

48. LEDGES TRAIL

Distance ■ 2 miles round trip
Difficulty ■ Easy
Features ■ A scenic view of Mormon Lake and the surrounding mountains
Starting elevation ■ 7150 feet
Highest elevation ■ 7325 feet
Total climb ■ 180 feet
Location ■ Coconino National Forest
Map ■ USGS Mormon Lake
Hiking season ■ Spring through fall

Getting there: The trail is located in the Mormon Lake Ranger District of the Coconino National Forest. From Flagstaff, take Lake Mary Road southeast about 20 miles to Mormon Lake Road (Forest Road 90), turn right (west), and go 3.5 miles to the Montezuma Lodge Road, which you follow a short distance to a large parking area in front of the gate of Dairy Springs Campground. Park here

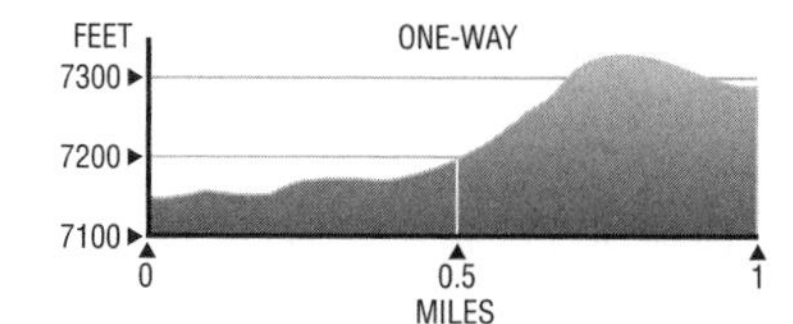

and walk to the marked trailhead. Water and restrooms are available in the campground during the summer.

Mormon Lake, which is the main attraction on this short hike, is a picturesque, natural lake nestled among volcanic hills, that in good water years is a favorite fishing hole of Flagstaff area residents. It was called Mormon Dairy Lake in the 1800s for the Mormon pioneers who operated a dairy nearby. Pine trees and tall junipers shade the winding trail as it gently climbs past occasional rock outcroppings to the huge rocks that form the rocky outcrop—the ledges—for which the trail is named.

The well-defined trail begins in an open forest of ponderosa pine and juniper, and passes some vacation cabins and small meadows, where you might see deer or elk. Some grasses clothe the ground, but almost no dead wood clutters the forest floor due to its proximity to the campground (if you're planning to camp there, please take your own firewood). The trail begins slowly climbing almost immediately, and by about 0.25 mile you should get your first views of Mormon Lake.

By 0.4 mile, small outcroppings of dark, rough boulders begin to appear irregularly and infrequently between the trees. As the trail continues to climb, junipers grow more abundantly. Grasses are replaced by flat, gray rocks, which are at times so thick that no earth is visible. The colorful orange and green lichens on the rocks provide contrast to the gray skin of resting lizards, but the iridescent blue streaks on the lizards' bellies are seen only by those who quietly move close enough without scaring them away.

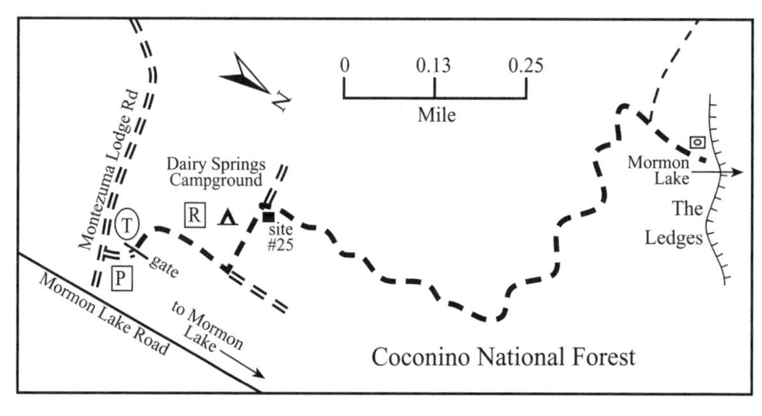

As the trail climbs, the growth under the pines becomes thicker and bushier. Soon, alligator juniper and Gambel oak crowd the trail. Wildflowers are common here during the summer, pushing up through the narrow spaces between the closely packed rocks. Trees conceal, but cannot entirely hide, a view of a wide plain in the distance.

At a bit over 0.75 mile the trail reaches its namesake ledges, which provide an unobstructed view of Mormon Lake and the surrounding mountains. This is also a good spot to watch for bald eagles and hawks, hunting along the shoreline.

Return to the trailhead by the same path.

49. RED BUTTE TRAIL

Distance ■ 2.4 miles round trip
Difficulty ■ Moderate
Features ■ A hike on a unique geological formation to spectacular panoramic views
Starting elevation ■ 6460 feet
Highest elevation ■ 7326 feet
Total climb ■ 885 feet
Location ■ Kaibab National Forest
Map ■ USGS Red Butte
Hiking season ■ Spring through fall

Getting there: The trail is in the Tusayan Ranger District of the Kaibab National Forest. From Flagstaff, take US 180 northwest 31 miles to where it meets AZ 64 near the town of Valle. Go north on AZ 64, toward the Grand Canyon, to Forest Road 320, which intersects the highway at mile marker 224. Turn right onto Forest Road 320 and travel east 1.5 miles to Forest Road 340, where you turn left (north), and go 0.75 mile to a spur road, where you turn right (east) and go 0.25 mile to the trailhead, where the road ends. There are no restrooms or drinking water at the trailhead.

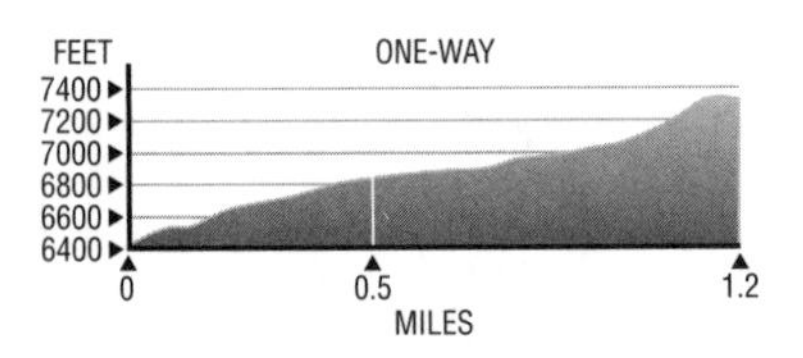

There is little difference between hiking to the top of the world and the top of Red Butte—not because it is an especially difficult trail but because once on top, you can see forever. The trip to the

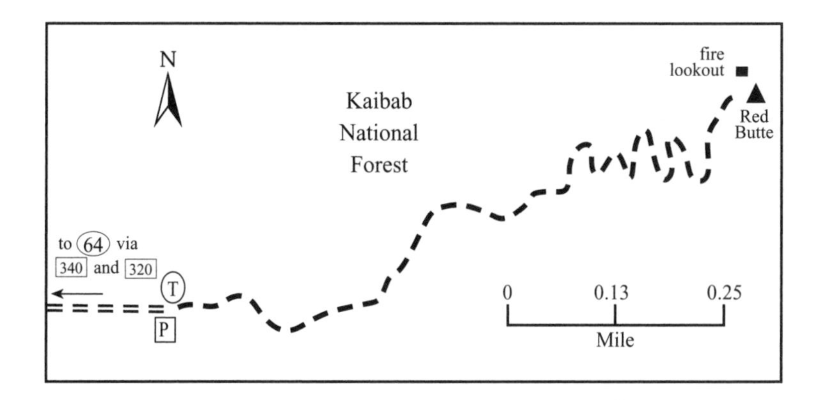

top travels through juniper, yucca, grasses, and wildflowers, past layers of red sandstone, white limestone, conglomerates of sedimentary rock, and finally the thick basaltic cap that preserved the butte while everything around it was eroded away.

A sign at the trailhead describes the three layers of stone that form the butte. The entire formation rests on a foundation of Kaibab limestone, the same limestone that is seen in the upper elevations of the Grand Canyon. The butte's first layer is red Moenkopi sandstone and siltstone deposited by water at the beginning of the Mesozoic era. Shinarump conglomerate—small stones cemented together—form the next layer up, while the top is a splotch of basalt, a tough volcanic rock, from a nearby volcano.

The woodlands near the base provide opportunities to see coyotes, jackrabbits, mule deer, and sometimes elk; and the cliffs provide homes for red-tailed hawks, ravens, and prairie falcons.

The wide, well-defined trail begins in a sparse forest of juniper and some piñon pine. Clumps of grass occasionally push their way up through the small stones that cover the ground. The sparse vegetation provides no interference to clear views of the vast, surrounding plain, and each step upward provides a better vantage point. The first 0.7 mile climbs fairly gradually, with only a few switchbacks, and the last 0.5-mile has steeper grades and more switchbacks.

The rocks along the trail tell the geologic story. The gray, slatelike volcanic rock seen along the entire trail has broken from the protective cap and fallen onto the lower slopes. Solid Moenkopi sandstone appears underfoot at about 0.4 mile, next to a 2-foot-wide, 3-foot-long sandstone boulder. At 0.85 mile, the trail makes one of its rare and short descents as the soil changes from a brown to a red hue, and an

Red Butte rises above a flat, endless plain. (Photo by Lawrence Letham)

opening in the trees provides a distant view of the reds and whites that color the North Rim of the Grand Canyon.

Just beyond the 1-mile mark, the tall, red sandstone layer, seen in the distance from the highway, comes into full, close-up view. Here you'll see broadleaf yucca, Mormon tea, and similar desert plants. The trail continues up until it reaches the top—a small plateau of rich brown volcanic rock, cholla, prickly pear cactus, and a few short trees. The view of the wide plain that surrounds the butte is now complete: a 360-degree vista that includes the majestic San Francisco Peaks to the southeast and the cliffs of the North Rim of the Grand Canyon.

On the far side of the butte stands a lone fire lookout tower. Follow the same route back down to the trailhead.

50. LAVA FLOW TRAIL

Distance	1-mile loop
Difficulty	Easy to moderate
Features	Self-guided interpretative trail to various volcanic formations
Starting elevation	6980 feet
Highest elevation	6990 feet
Total climb	85 feet
Location	Sunset Crater Volcano National Monument
Map	USGS Wupatki SW
Hiking season	Year-round

Getting there: This hike is in Sunset Crater Volcano National Monument. From Flagstaff, take US 89 north 16 miles to Forest Road

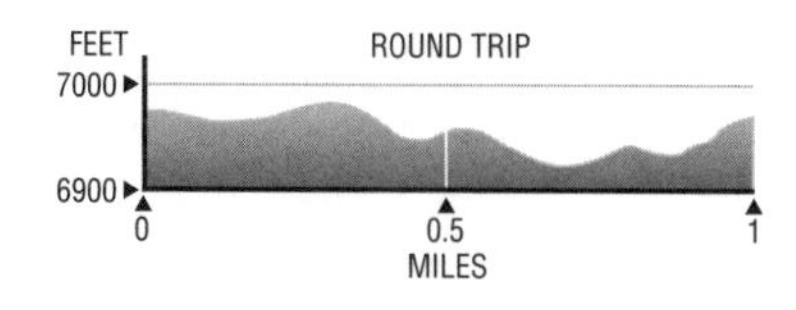

545, turn right, and continue about 5 miles to the national monument. Stop at the visitor center to see the exhibits, and for restrooms and drinking water, and then drive several miles to a parking area and the well-marked trailhead, where there are restrooms but no drinking water. A trail guide is available at the trailhead.

There was a rumble accompanied by fire and clouds of deadly gas. Rocks fell from the air, animals ran for their lives, trees burst into flames. When the eruption was all over, everything lay wasted and smoldering. This trail is a walk through the volcano's destructive path at the base of Sunset Crater Volcano, where you'll see an abundance of lava rock, cinder cones, a miniature volcanic ring, an ice cave, and the Bonito lava flow.

The first section of the trail is paved, providing a 0.25-mile loop that is wheelchair accessible; the rest of the trail is made of rough cinders, so you'll want sturdy shoes.

Looking up from the trailhead, it is hard to believe that the 1000-foot-tall Sunset Crater is not solid stone, but instead is a huge pile of small, loose volcanic particles called cinder. Over 800 square miles were covered with cinder and thick lava by the volcano between the years AD 1164 and 1250, creating what would eventually become this

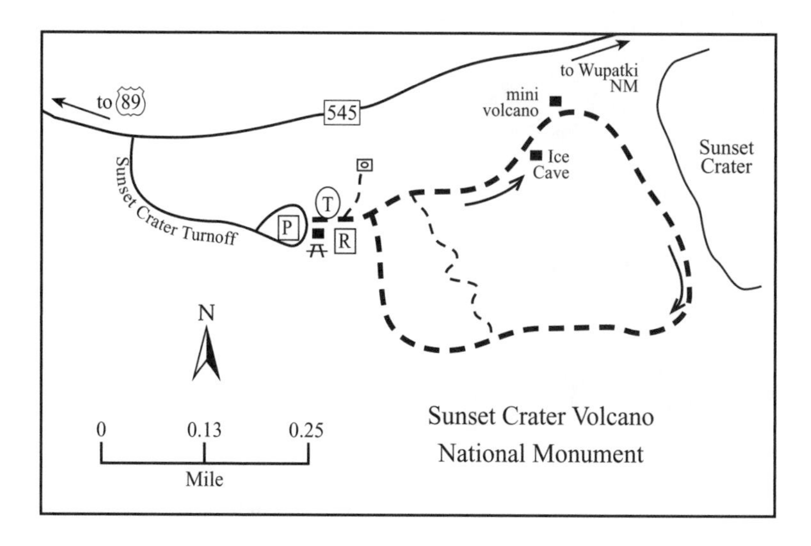

land of strange rock formations, scattered bushes, and tall pines.

Shortly after you begin the trail, about 150 feet from the trailhead, there is a trail intersection, with the left fork going a short way to an overlook. After checking out the overlook, go back to the main trail and take the right fork to a wooden bridge that spans a hardened river of rough lava. Continuing, the trail passes a wide, flat area completely covered with cinders in which almost no plants are growing. A sign announces that deep under the cinders lie homes buried by the eruption. Fortunately, the slow eruption likely afforded the inhabitants plenty of time to escape without harm.

The trail winds past sparse plants growing amid black cinders until it reaches a fork at 0.1 mile. The right path is the return wheelchair-accessible route. Continuing on the main, cinder trail, at about 0.25 mile you will notice that lava formations along the trail are colored black, red, white, and light brown, with a bubbly texture that looks like sponge cake. Shortly the nearly flat trail reaches the entrance of a 225-foot underground tunnel, called Ice Cave, that is actually a lava tube similar to the one you can explore on the Lava River Cave hike (Hike 45), discussed above. Here the water that seeps through the lava freezes and remains frozen most of the year. Although you can feel cold blasts of air from the tunnel, it is closed to exploration.

Green lichen and white snow accent black rocks.

A bit farther down the trail is a 6-foot-high, circular lava wall about 18 feet in diameter. Pass through the broken part of the wall to investigate the insides of a miniature volcano. Along the trail, notice that the roots of every tree are partially exposed because they cannot grow deep into the solid lava, but instead spread wide, just under the surface, to catch any water that might fall.

At about the 0.5-mile point, a 100-foot cliff drops to a bed of hardened lava and looks much like a seaside cliff that overlooks turbulent waters. The trail now descends between Sunset Crater and the end of the cliff into a land of almost no plant life. At 0.75 mile, stairs climb over the lava cliff and past several large lava chunks. Look ahead, along the cliff, to see a lone quaking aspen growing on the edge. Within 150 feet, the trail winds around a strange pine tree, growing horizontally, parallel to the ground. The trail then continues over a bridge to return to the trailhead.

A Trip to the Moon

The lava flow at Sunset Crater Volcano National Monument was one of the training sites for the Apollo 17 astronauts, who explored the surface of the moon in December 1972. Among other training activities, the astronauts tested their lunar vehicle, called a rover, on the rugged terrain here in the national monument.

51. WUPATKI PUEBLO TRAIL

Distance ▪ 0.5-mile loop
Difficulty ▪ Easy
Features ▪ A loop trail through the largest prehistoric pueblo in the Flagstaff area
Starting elevation ▪ 4915 feet
Highest elevation ▪ 4920 feet
Total climb ▪ 90 feet
Location ▪ Wupatki National Monument
Map ▪ USGS Wupatki
Hiking season ▪ Year-round

Getting there: The trail is in Wupatki National Monument. From Flagstaff, take US 89 north 16 miles to Forest Road 545, turn right, and continue about 26 miles, through Sunset Crater Volcano National Monument (see Lava Flow Trail, Hike 50) and into Wupatki National Monument. Stop first in the visitor center to see the exhibits about the peoples who lived here. The trail to

Wupatki Pueblo begins just outside the visitor center. Restrooms and drinking water are available at the visitor center; a trail guide is available at the trailhead.

This easy walk through a prehistoric pueblo provides a firsthand look at how people lived in the Southwest almost a thousand years ago, and if nothing else, it should make us more appreciative of the modern conveniences we have today. It is a fun (and even educational) hike for children. This hike can easily be done along with several other hikes at this national monument and nearby Sunset Crater Volcano National Monument, and all in a day trip from Flagstaff, or as a change of pace before or after a visit to Grand Canyon National Park.

Built into a sandstone outcropping, Wupatki Pueblo was made of the materials at hand—slabs of red sandstone, blocks of pale beige limestone, and chunks of brown basalt, cemented together with clay. Beams were made from fir and pine trees from the nearby mountains and roofs were covered with brush, bark, and mud. Rooms at ground level had no doorways, but were entered through roof openings using ladders, and the rooms were aligned south and east to take advantage of the warming winter sun.

Although Wupatki is generally considered an archeological site from the prehistoric Sinaguan culture, there is evidence of the presence of other peoples of the day. Archeologists have discovered traditional Sinagua undecorated reddish-brown pottery, but have also found more than one hundred other types of pottery. The architecture of the pueblo itself is a mixture, with masonry work and T-shaped doorways common to Ancestral Puebloan builders, a ball court that looks a lot like those the Hohokam built, and a circular amphitheater one would expect at a Sinaguan pueblo.

Construction began about 1106, with more rooms added every twenty to forty years, until, for reasons not yet explained, the residents left about 1250. It's believed that some of its residents relocated to other Sinaguan communities to the south, while others joined the Hopi and Zuni cultures to the east. The name Wupatki is a Hopi word that means "long cut house."

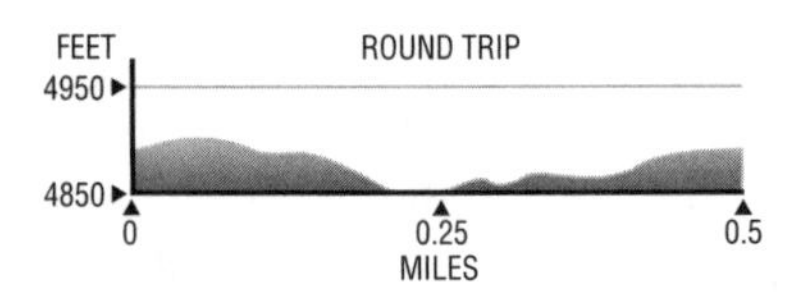

The trail is paved, with some steps and hills. It is wheelchair accessible to an overlook, and accessible for its entire length with assistance. About 300 feet from

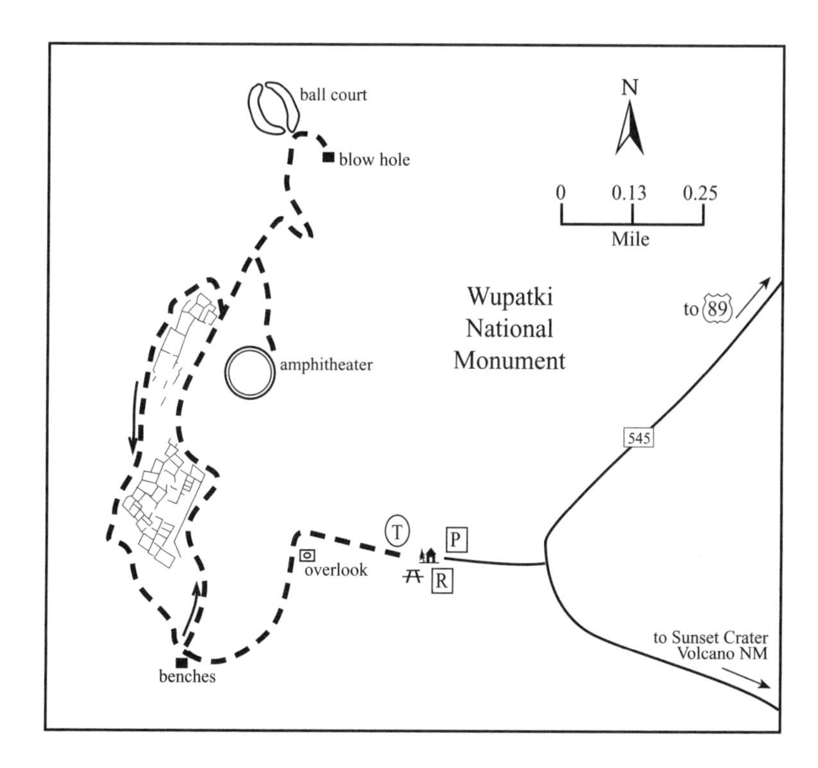

the trailhead, the asphalt trail makes a sharp left turn at an overlook that provides a view of the entire site. The trail widens for an intersection at 0.1 mile, with benches to the left. Take the trail to the right as it descends past multiroom ruins.

The rooms are extremely small by today's standards, but were probably used only for sleeping and in bad weather; the rest of the time the residents would have been outdoors. The pueblo stood three stories high in places, with about one hundred rooms, and in the 1100s was the largest man-made structure for at least 50 miles in any direction. You now continue past some unexcavated sections of the pueblo and a reconstructed circular structure that resembles a great kiva.

At an intersection at the end of the ruins, you can either begin looping back to the trailhead or continue straight to descend to the amphitheater and ball court, which are well worth the brief detour.

The amphitheater was used for meetings and ceremonies, but archaeologists believe that the gatherings included trading partners and visitors from faraway villages, in addition to Wupatki's inhabitants. The exact game played in the ball field is a mystery, but it is believed to be derived from, if not exactly the same as, a game played in Mexico during the same period. Its mere existence provides convincing evidence that the people of Wupatki had contact with other people far away.

Enter the round amphitheater through the opening to discover a stone bench built around its entire circular interior. A fire in the middle would provide the perfect atmosphere to tell stories of adventures. The oblong ball court, downhill from the amphitheater, is enclosed by 6-foot-high stone walls with openings on each end.

On the same level as the ball court, there is a natural phenomenon called a blow hole. The hole in the ground provides passage to a subterranean vault of unknown dimensions, formed by an earthquake or by the dissolving of the underlying limestone. High external atmospheric pressure causes air to rush into the hole, while low atmospheric pressure forces air out of the hole. On warm afternoons you can often feel and even hear air being blown out the hole, while at cooler times air is sucked in.

A prehistoric pueblo

Now return to the intersection at the edge of the ruins and continue the loop, passing additional rooms, until you arrive back at the trailhead. We strongly recommend that you also visit the other archeological sites at Wupatki—all are easily accessible—and also hike the Doney Mountain Trail (Hike 52).

We've Seen This Place Before

Ever been to the movies? Then you've likely seen northern Arizona. The wonderful 1939 classic western *Stagecoach*, which gave unknown actor John Wayne his big break, was filmed in Monument Valley, north of Navajo National Monument along the Arizona-Utah border, with scenes also shot near Kayenta and in the Phoenix area. Lake Powell, near Page, also along the Arizona-Utah border, portrayed the barren future in both the 1968 and 2001 versions of *Planet of the Apes;* scenes in *Forrest Gump*, the 1994 film starring Tom Hanks, were shot in Flagstaff. Flagstaff is also the birthplace of old-time western actor and TV kids' show host Andy Devine—he was called Jeremiah Schwartz then—and actor Ted Danson, who was born in San Diego but grew up in Flagstaff.

52. DONEY MOUNTAIN TRAIL

Distance ▪ 1 mile round trip
Difficulty ▪ Easy to moderate
Features ▪ A hike to the top of two volcanic cinder cones, offering panoramic views
Starting elevation ▪ 5360 feet
Highest elevation ▪ 5500 feet
Total climb ▪ 230 feet
Location ▪ Coconino National Forest
Map ▪ USGS Wupatki
Hiking season ▪ Year-round (may be closed for short periods after snowfall)

Getting there: The trail is in the Peaks Ranger District of Coconino National Forest, just outside Wupatki National Monument. From Flagstaff, take US 89 north 16 miles to Forest Road 545, turn right,

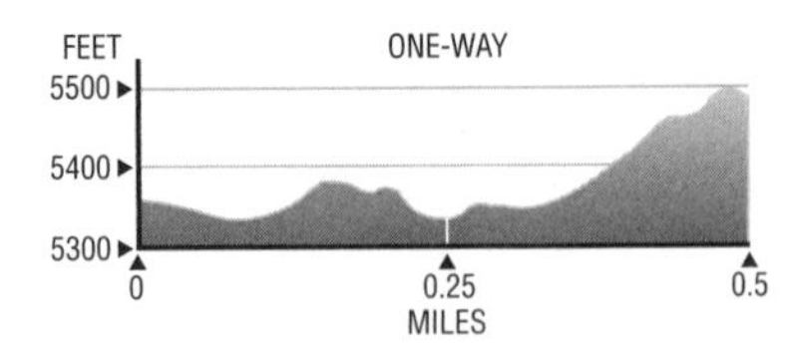

and continue about 26 miles, through Sunset Crater Volcano National Monument (see Lava Flow Trail, Hike 50) and into Wupatki National Monument. After stopping at the visitor center and seeing Wupatki Pueblo (see Wupatki Pueblo Trail, Hike 51, above), continue just outside the monument's boundary to the Doney Picnic Area and the parking lot for the marked trailhead. There are restrooms but no drinking water at the trailhead.

Although the main reason for visiting this area is the well-preserved remains of the homes of prehistoric Puebloans in Wupatki National Monument, it is also well worth coming here to see its geologic features, and especially to climb to the top of the cinder cones that form Doney Mountain, where you'll be rewarded with splendid views of the surrounding countryside.

Four cinder cones, collectively known as Doney Mountain, formed when molten magma blasted from cracks in the ground, spewing high into the air where it cooled to form particles of varying sizes, then fell back to earth in large piles. The trail to the top of two of the hills winds from the black cinders of the flat ground to the brown cinders of one hill, then back to the red cinders of the other. Sparse vegetation of sagebrush, some grasses, and small junipers demonstrates the harshness of the environment, and yet there are ruins of a field house from long-ago farmers.

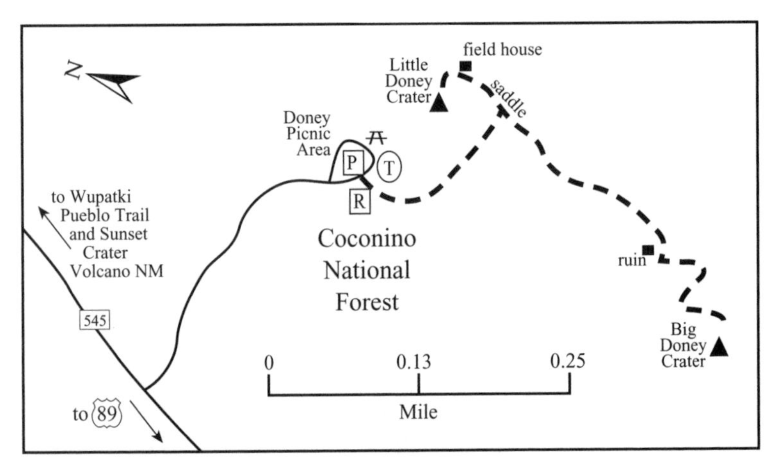

The well-worn trail has interpretative signs describing the geology and human history of the area. It begins with a seemingly endless landscape of black cinders, sprouting juniper and a spiky shrub called Mormon tea, and continues to an intersection, in a saddle between two cinder cones at a little over 0.1 mile. From here you'll notice the occasional light-colored rocks with rounded, smooth edges that are not volcanic and seem somewhat out of place, until you realize that the lava and cinder deposited by the eruptions lie on a base of limestone, sandstone, and sedimentary rock laid by ancient oceans.

The two branches of the trail lead to the two cinder cones. Take the trail to the left to Little Doney Crater. As the trail climbs about 100 feet, the color of the cinders changes from black to brown. The cinders range in size from tiny specks of dust to massive boulders—known as bombs—with the largest rocks making up the cone. This is because as cinders fell back to earth from the eruption, the larger ones fell straight down, close to the source, to form the cone, while the smaller, lighter particles were carried away by the wind.

A sign at 0.2 mile points out a stack of rocks that formed a field house for prehistoric farmers. Many similar rock piles are found throughout the area because the inhabitants ranged far and wide to grow crops on any available fertile land. Just 100 feet after the sign, a circle of rocks and a bench mark Little Doney Crater's top. This is a good vantage point from which to admire the expanse of pale colors of the Painted Desert to the southeast.

From here, return to the trail intersection, then continue straight to climb Big Doney Crater. The trail passes another ruin—a partially excavated pit house—on the right at about 0.4 mile. Here you will also notice a change in the terrain. Volcanic stones are being broken down by erosion to form soil, which supports juniper, sparse grasses, and some wildflowers.

The trail makes a continuous but moderate climb through switchbacks over hard-packed dirt and, in some places, cinders. The climb ends at about the 0.5-mile point at the top of Big Doney Crater, where the surrounding plains are dotted with plants, and a large white crack exposes a streak of limestone in the Wupatki plain below. The cone is covered with red cinders, tinted by iron oxide during the eruption. To the southwest you can see the towering San Francisco Peaks, which were also formed by volcanic action.

Return to the trailhead along the same path.

53. SANDAL TRAIL

Distance	1 mile round trip
Difficulty	Easy
Features	A walk through a pygmy forest to views of a prehistoric cliff dwelling
Starting elevation	7260 feet
Highest elevation	7284 feet
Total climb	215 feet
Location	Navajo National Monument
Map	USGS Betatakin Ruin
Hiking season	Late spring through early fall

Getting there: The trail is located in Navajo National Monument, which is on the Navajo Nation, 30 miles west of Kayenta via US 160 and AZ 564. It's about 140 miles northeast of Flagstaff. The monument is operated by the National Park Service. The trail starts from the patio behind the national monument's visitor center, where drinking water, restrooms, and information are available.

This paved trail leads through an open woodland to an overlook offering good but distant views of the ruins of the Betatakin cliff dwelling, constructed about 1250. The cliff dwellings are somewhat dwarfed by the huge sandstone arch 450 feet overhead; take binoculars for a better view. (Binoculars are also available at the overlook.) A 300-millimeter telephoto lens on a 35-millimeter camera also works well.

The name of the national monument is somewhat misleading. Although the Navajos live here now, the cliff dwellings that are the monument's main attraction were constructed centuries before the Navajo's arrival by a group of Ancestral Puebloan people called the Kayenta, who are believed to be the ancestors of today's Hopi and other Pueblo people. The monument's visitor center contains displays on the Kayenta and Navajo cultures, with exhibits of pottery, stone tools, and numerous other artifacts excavated here. There is also a replica of an Ancestral Puebloan home and an exhibit on tree-ring dating techniques.

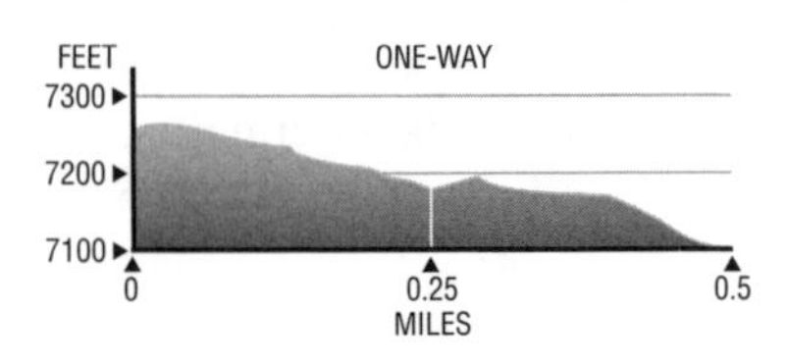

After checking out the exhibits in the visitor center, begin the hike by walking out the center's back door. Among the first things you'll see are replicas of a traditional fork-stick Navajo hogan,

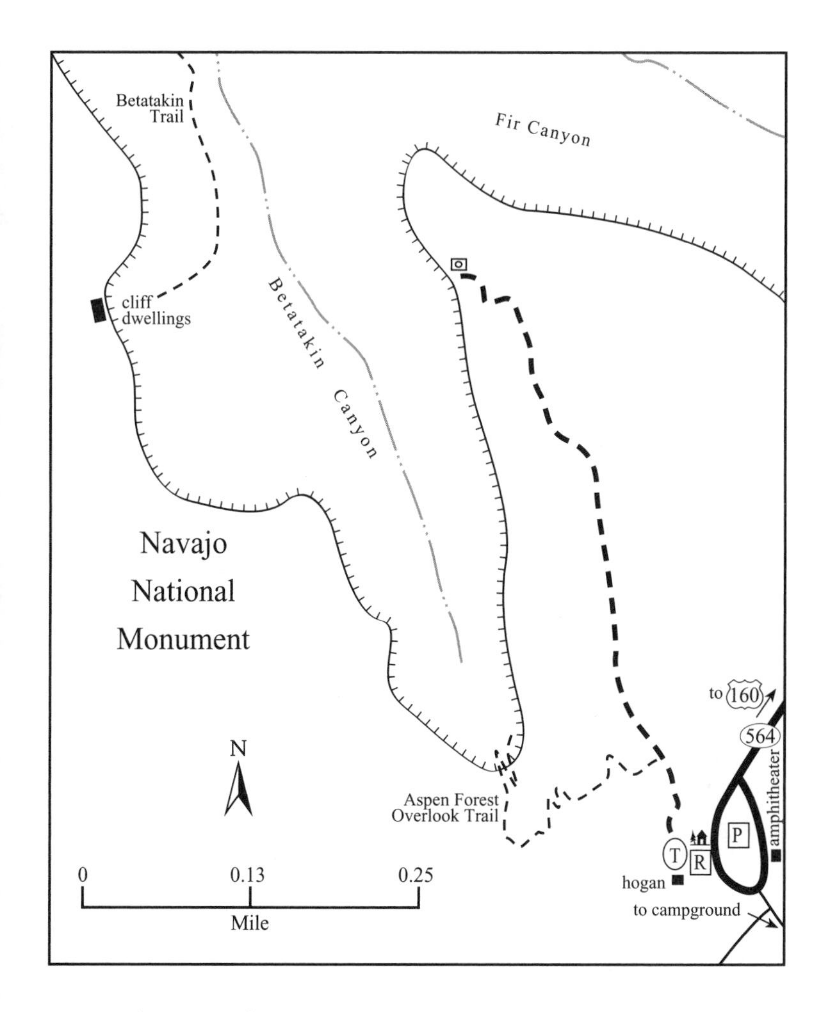

a sweat house, and a wagon that was among those built in the early 1900s specifically to be sold to Navajos at area trading posts. At about 400 feet, the Aspen Forest Overlook Trail (see Hike 54) branches off to the left. Continue straight ahead for the Sandal Trail.

The trail is mostly downhill—elevation at the overlook is 7067 feet—and consists of large stretches of solid stone dotted with islands of soil that supports a pygmy conifer forest of piñon pine and Utah juniper. These miniature trees grow among pincushion and grizzlybear prickly pear cacti, Mormon tea, broadleaf yucca, cliff rose, and other desert plants. Wooden bridges span the natural ditches that carry rainwater to the thick forest at the bottom of the canyon. Occasional

Good, but distant views of the ruins of the Betatakin cliff dwelling

signs along the trail identify plants such as yucca, buffaloberry, and cliff fendlerbush and explain how they were used by the native peoples of Betatakin, or "Talastima," as the Hopis say.

The edges of the steep cliffs that form the canyon are visible from the trail, but the bottom is seen only from the overlook at the terminus. Erosion has rounded the red sandstone along the trail, but the circular pattern evident in the rock occurs not by erosion alone but because of the way the sandstone was formed. The cliffs are ancient, solidified sand dunes that erode along the swirling patterns of the once-windblown sands. Springs seeping out at the base of the cliffs form round alcoves where the rock has been washed away. The trail ends at a fenced overlook on the edge of a cliff, providing a good view of the cliff dwelling across the canyon. *Betatakin*, a Navajo word for "ledge house," perches in a large protective alcove in a canyon wall. Occupied from about 1250 to 1300, at its peak Betatakin may have housed 125 people. Why these well-built structures were abandoned after only fifty years is unclear, although archeologists say it may have been at least partly due to changes in weather patterns that made the Kayenta's farming existence unproductive.

Looking down, you'll notice that the forest of full-size Douglas firs and quaking aspens in the bottom of the canyon is a drastic contrast to the sparse, pygmy forest above. A sheltered bench provides rest and shade before you start the easy ascent back to the visitor center. *Note: Those who want to hike all the way to the cliff dwellings can do so only on a ranger-guided hike on the moderate-to-strenuous Betatakin Trail, Hike 55, discussed below.*

54. ASPEN FOREST OVERLOOK TRAIL

Distance	1 mile round trip
Difficulty	Moderate to strenuous
Features	A deep canyon with a forest of aspen and fir
Starting elevation	7260 feet
Highest elevation	7260 feet
Total climb	300 feet
Location	Navajo National Monument
Map	USGS Betatakin Ruin
Hiking season	Spring through fall

Getting there: This trail is in Navajo National Monument, located on the Navajo Nation, 30 miles west of Kayenta via US 160 and AZ 564, which is operated by the National Park Service. It's about 140 miles northeast of Flagstaff. The trail starts from the patio behind the national monument's visitor center, where drinking water, restrooms, exhibits, and information are available.

Like a visit to a forgotten land, the Aspen Forest Overlook Trail leads from the barren tops of sandstone cliffs down a winding switchback to a viewpoint of a lush forest at the bottom of Betatakin Canyon. As the trail descends, the vegetation changes from sparse, drought-resistant plants to tall conifers and quaking aspens, as though nature forgot to tell them that they live in a desert. Signs describe the vegetation along the trail, providing plant names in English, Navajo, and Hopi.

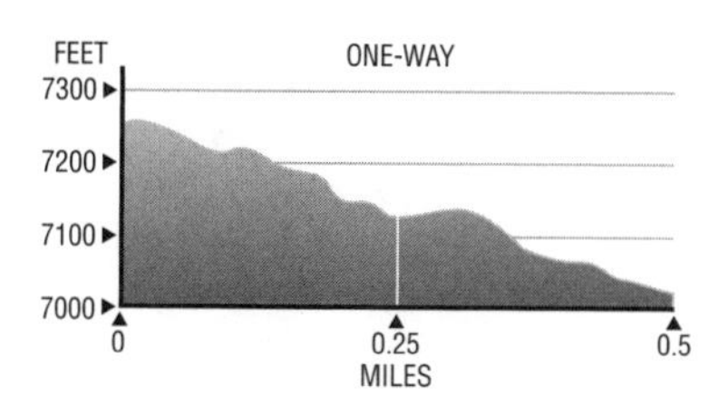

This trail may be short but it is very steep in spots, with handrails to provide support. If possible, take the hike in the rain, so you can see the 300-foot waterfalls careening down the canyon walls.

From the patio, follow the paved Sandal Trail, Hike 53, described above, about 400 feet past small stunted trees to the dirt trail turnoff on the left marked by a sign. Even before the Aspen Forest Overlook Trail turns to descend a short flight of stairs, the desert plants, similar to those on the top of the cliff, grow more abundantly.

A few more steps and the trail is completely isolated from the world above as it drops into the Betatakin box canyon. Only 0.25 mile down the path, just past a bridge over a natural gully, the plant life changes from pincushion and prickly pear cactus to Gambel oak and small fir trees growing at the base of a short cliff. The tops of tall trees from the canyon bottom are visible.

At about 0.3 mile, just past the second bridge at the top of a flight of stone steps, the 75- to 100-foot-tall Douglas firs come into full view. The trail continues to drop as it hugs a red sandstone cliff formed by an ancient, solidified sand dune. Switchbacks, with numerous stone steps, wind past wildflowers and box elder until at the 0.5-mile point, the overlook is reached. The last 400 feet or so is the steepest part of the trail.

The complete picture of the canyon shows black willow, dogwood, aspens, and other deciduous plants only at the closed end of the box canyon, while desert life dominates the rest. The forest is shielded from harsh elements by the high sandstone cliffs. The alcove that houses the Betatakin Ruin cannot be seen from the overlook.

From the overlook, the only way back to the trailhead is the way you came, a steep but short trek.

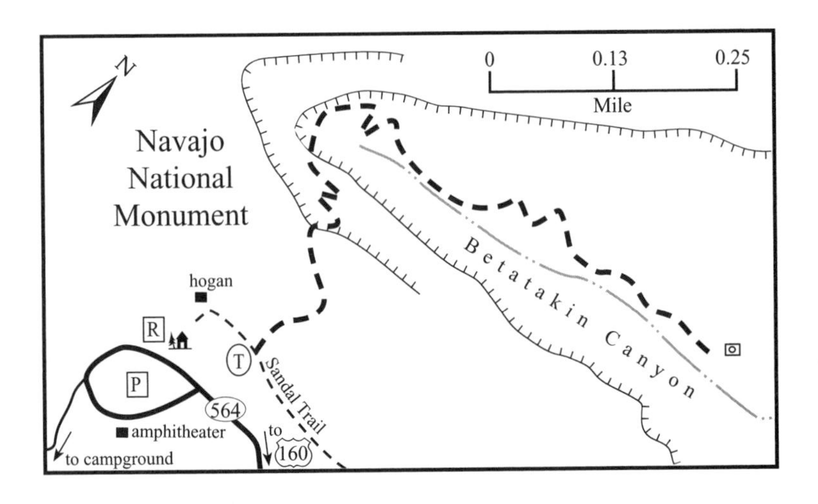

Good views of a forest at the bottom of Betatakin Canyon

No Romance in Mistletoe

Kissing under the mistletoe, such as that seen along the Betatakin Trail, at Christmastime may be a fun holiday tradition, but mistletoe itself is anything but romantic. In fact, this plant is a parasite whose roots grow into tree branches, and it lives off the tree's life-giving sap. Eventually the mistletoe can kill its host.

55. BETATAKIN TRAIL

Distance	5 miles round trip
Difficulty	Strenuous
Features	A ranger-led hike to well-preserved prehistoric cliff dwellings
Starting elevation	7070 feet
Highest elevation	7070 feet
Total climb	700 feet
Location	Navajo National Monument
Map	USGS Betatakin Ruin
Hiking season	Primarily spring through fall; year-round weather permitting

Getting there: The trail is in Navajo National Monument, located in the Navajo Nation, 30 miles west of Kayenta via US 160 and AZ 564. It's about 140 miles northeast of Flagstaff. The hike can only be done as a ranger-guided tour. There are two hikes daily from June through September, and one daily the rest of the year. There is a limit of twenty-five people per tour. Hikers, led by the ranger, drive from the parking area in front of the visitor center onto a dirt road to the trailhead 0.75 mile away. The visitor center has drinking water, restrooms, exhibits, and information.

Well-preserved cliff dwelling ruins, pictographs, petroglyphs, stairs cut in stone, noisy piñon jays, soaring turkey vultures, and tall mushroom-shaped rocks are the highlights of this hike, which can be taken only as a free ranger-led trek. The hike takes you from the barren cliff tops to the lush canyon bottom and finally into the spacious stone alcove that houses the cliff dwellings. The hike includes steep switchbacks and should not be undertaken by anyone with health problems. It takes between 3 and 5 hours, with no water along the way, so carry all that is needed. Rangers recommend that hikers take at least two liters of water and a snack.

The cliff dwellings that are this trail's main attraction were constructed by a group of Ancestral Puebloans called the Kayenta, who are believed to be the ancestors of today's Hopi and other Pueblo peoples. Occupied from about 1250 to 1300, at its peak Betatakin may have housed 125 people. Why these well-built structures were abandoned after such a short period of time is unclear, but archeologists suggest that it may have been at least partly due to changes in weather patterns that made the Kayenta's farming existence unproductive.

The first 0.9 mile of the trail follows a wide dirt road that descends slowly over Navajo tribal lands past a series of box canyons. The tops of the cliffs form the flat Colorado Plateau, which stretches as far as the eye can see, while the canyons lie where sheer cliffs cut 600 feet downward. The red-colored terrain supports juniper, piñon, barrel cactus, and other plants that can survive the searing summer heat. Sandstone boulders near the road display the round and swirling erosion pattern of stone formed from ancient sand dunes. The overlooks of the many canyons reveal the same mesmeric, circular pattern in their large, vertical walls, while some reveal the beginnings of alcoves.

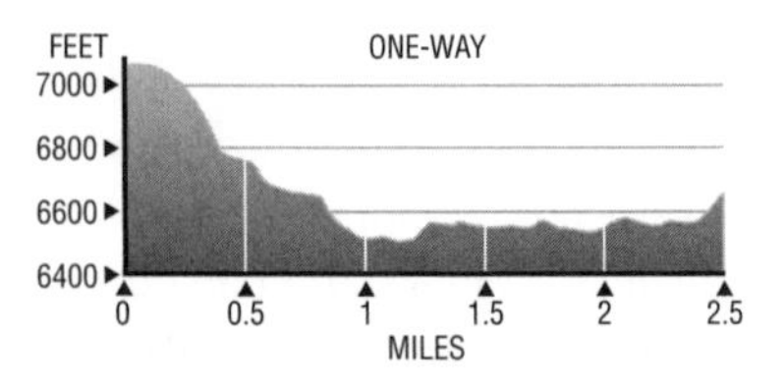

The dirt road ends at about 0.9 mile at Tsegi Point and a foot trail passes through a large groove in the stone to a seemingly endless flight of stairs. These were cut directly in the natural rock in

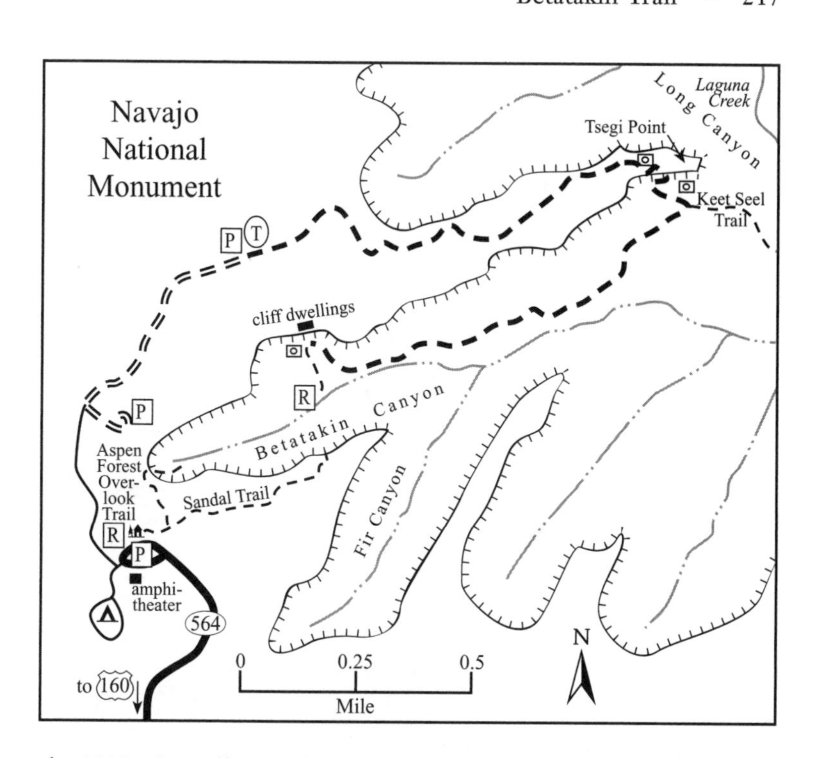

the 1930s. A small petroglyph is carved into the wall at about 1.1 miles, about 8 feet above the stairs, which descend another 0.2 mile before reaching the base of steep cliffs. The now-flat trail passes through juniper and piñon pine to an intersection at 1.3 miles; the trail to the left goes to Keet Seel, another preserved ruin. You'll follow the right fork for Betatakin.

At this trail junction, look back toward the base of the stairs to see cliffs shaped like two tall mushrooms. Notice also the mistletoe growing on some of the juniper trees. The trail slowly descends around tall red cliffs. The large wash at just over 2 miles shows how the topsoil is swept from the canyon bottoms by heavy water flow, leaving only bare rock.

From the intersection at about 2.3 miles, the soaring Betatakin alcove is visible through the thick trees of the canyon bottom. Each step of the climb toward the cliff dwelling reveals more of the alcove—the small doors, the round wooden beams supporting the roofs, and the pole ladders between the different levels. Green, horizontal lines of plant life around the alcove's interior shows that it formed as water seeped from the top of the cliff, through the porous sandstone, and out the cliff face, carrying rock with it.

Original grinding stones (Photo by Lawrence Letham)

The buildings on the left side of the alcove are more complete than those on the right, caused when a stone ledge high in the alcove broke off, obliterating half the village. Inside the ruins, small steps lead to close looks at the remains on the right half of the village. The entire site, including the grinding stones and corn cobs, is original except for the pole ladders and the carved steps. Be sure to see the pictographs painted on the exterior of the alcove.

Hikers can return to the trailhead at their own pace or with the ranger. Going up the innumerable steps is tiring, so be prepared to make a few rest stops.

THE SEDONA AREA

There are a lot of beautiful locations in the American West, and anytime anyone puts together a list of the best of them, Sedona's there, either at or near the top. The town's main claim to fame is the spectacular beauty of the surrounding red-rock formations—an abundance of pillars, mesas, buttes, cliffs, and canyons. The rock gets its color from hematite—iron oxide—so what we're admiring here is essentially rusty rocks. Nearby is the splendid Oak Creek Canyon, which combines striking red-rock cliffs and formations with a lush

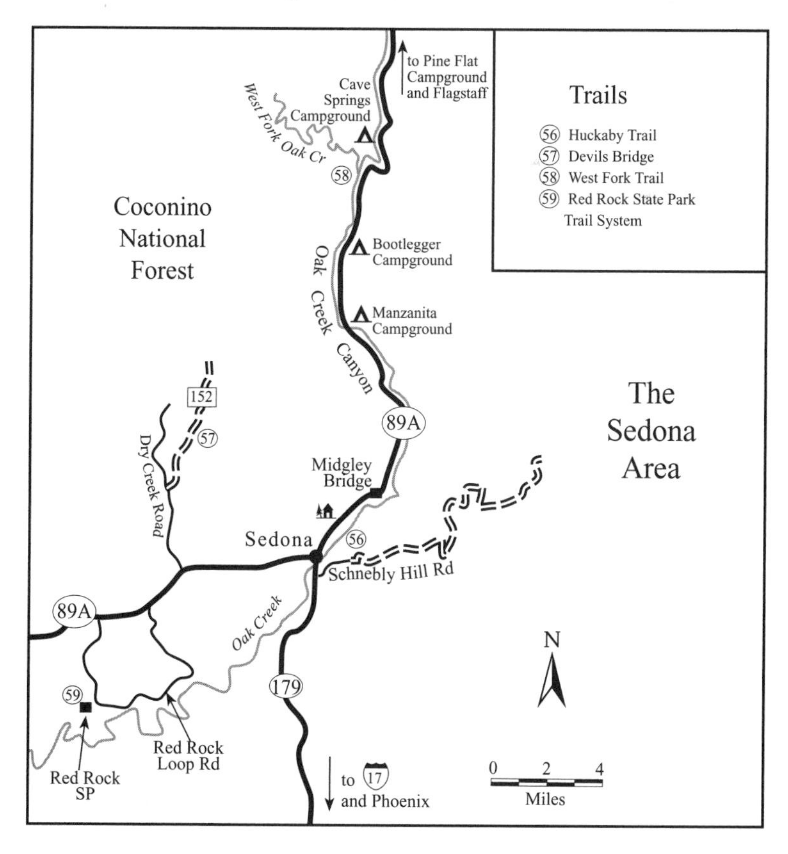

Sedona is known for its dramatic red rock formations.

river valley of oak, maple, box elder, ferns, and myriad wildflowers. Elevation in Sedona is about 4400 feet.

The Sedona area has numerous hiking trails, and you can also see the wondrous red-rock scenery here on horseback, by four-wheel-drive vehicle, and by air (airplane or hot air balloon—take your choice). Or simply take a drive around town—the views are spectacular in all directions. An especially good vantage point is from Schnebly Hill Road, which heads northeast from downtown Sedona off AZ 179.

However, this is an extremely popular tourist destination, so be prepared for crowds and traffic jams, especially during school vacations—summer weekends are usually the busiest times. Parking areas at trailheads are sometimes full and parking along the roadsides is prohibited in some areas. A Red Rock Pass is required to park at many of the popular trailheads; it can be purchased for a moderate fee at visitor centers in Sedona and in Oak Creek Canyon.

Where, you might ask, did the name Sedona come from? Well, it seems that one of the area's first pioneers, Carl Schnebly, wanted to establish a U.S. Post Office, and submitted two possible town names to federal postal officials—Schnebly Station and Oak Creek

Crossing. But the officials said those names would be too long to fit on a postal cancellation stamp, so Schnebly's brother, another settler, suggested the town be named for Carl's wife, Sedona. Carl liked the idea, and the government liked the name, too. After all, it fits nicely on a cancellation stamp.

The Uptown Gateway Visitor Center, staffed by the U.S. Forest Service and local chamber of commerce, is located at the northeast edge of Sedona in what is called Uptown Sedona, at 331 Forest Road, at its corner with AZ 89A. There is also a visitor center on AZ 179 in the village of Oak Creek, and two along AZ 89A in Oak Creek Canyon. For additional information, contact the various government agencies mentioned below, as well as the Sedona-Oak Creek Canyon Chamber of Commerce. You'll find complete contact information in the appendix at the back of this book.

Sedona's Spiritual Side

A number of visitors to Sedona come to experience what are called Vortex Sites—energy centers that exude power that enhances meditation and prayer. Area bookstores and visitor centers can provide information on the specific locations of these sites. Many are in the national forest and forest service officials ask that visitors to the sites help to protect the spiritual and scenic beauty of the landscape by not disturbing them by moving rocks or branches, by being as quiet as possible, and generally by "leaving no trace."

CAMPGROUNDS

There are several commercial campgrounds with RV hookups, hot showers, and all the usual amenities in Sedona. In addition, there are quite a few U.S. Forest Service campgrounds in Oak Creek Canyon, in the Red Rock Ranger District of the Coconino National Forest. All the forest service campgrounds make good base camps for hiking the Sedona area, but only Cave Springs has showers, and none have RV hookups or dump stations. They all have plenty of shade and offer a forest camping experience, and all charge a moderate nightly fee. Generally, those closest to Sedona fill first.

Moving north from Sedona along AZ 89A, from its intersection with AZ 179, **Manzanita Campground** at 6.4 miles is open year round, has drinking water and toilets, 18 sites, and does not permit trailers. At 9.1 miles north of the intersection, **Bootlegger Campground** is open spring through fall, has toilets but no drinking water, 10 sites, and also does not permit trailers. Our favorite campground in Oak Creek Canyon, at 11.9 miles from the intersection, is **Cave Springs Campground,** which with 80 sites lets campers get back farther from the highway. It can accommodate RVs and trailers up to 36 feet long, has drinking water, showers, and toilets, and is open from spring through fall. At 12.9 miles north of the intersection, **Pine Flat Campgrounds** have a total of 58 sites on both sides of the highway. Both are open from spring through late fall, have drinking water and toilets, and permit RVs and trailers up to 36 feet long. A limited number of reservation sites are available at Cave Springs and Pine Flat; see the appendix in the back of this book.

56. HUCKABY TRAIL

Distance ▪ 5.8 miles round trip (2.9 miles with a shuttle)
Difficulty ▪ Moderate
Features ▪ Panoramic views of Sedona, plus a walk along scenic Oak Creek
Starting elevation ▪ 4400 feet
Highest elevation ▪ 4550 feet
Total climb ▪ 600 feet
Location ▪ Coconino National Forest
Map ▪ USGS Munds Park, Munds Mountain, Sedona
Hiking season ▪ Year-round

Getting there: The trail is located just northeast of Sedona in the Red Rock District of the Coconino National Forest. From the intersection of AZ 89A and AZ 179, go south on AZ 179 to Schnebly Hill Road, turn left, and go about 0.9 mile to a large parking area. The trailhead is on the north side of the lot. There are restrooms but no water at the trailhead. An alternative is to start the hike at Midgley Bridge, north of Sedona on AZ 89A, or arrange for transportation at either end and hike one way only.

This trail combines some of the best of what the Sedona area offers: panoramic views of the town and surrounding red-rock formations,

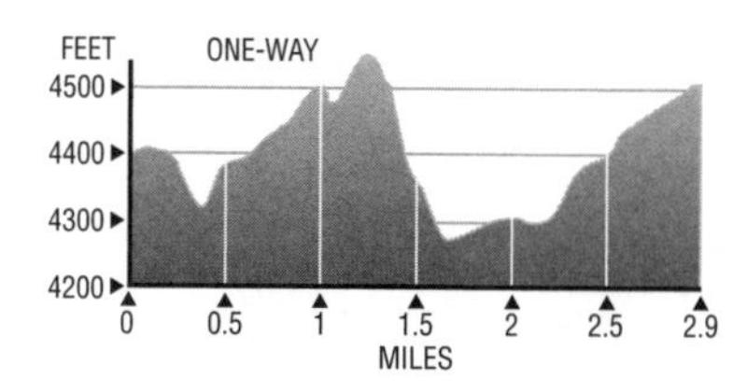

plus a trek along pretty Oak Creek. Although it can be hot during the summer, the sections along the stream are shady and you can always take your shoes off and cool your toes in the water.

Starting from Schnebly Hill Road, the trail begins with spectacular panoramic views of the red-rock formations over Sedona. The packed dirt trail starts out heading west and quickly drops into Bear Wallow Canyon, following a wagon road that dates to the late 1800s. After about 0.5 mile the trail tops a ridge, offering splendid distant views. As you walk along the ridge you can see Oak Creek in the canyon below. The trail switchbacks down through an open woodlands of piñon and juniper, and you reach Oak Creek at about 1.5 miles.

The trail now follows Oak Creek, on its east side, through a riparian area of pines, sycamores, and cottonwoods; then crosses the creek just after mile 2. You'll have to hop from rock to rock or wade in the shallow creek. Here the terrain is similar to the West Fork Trail (Hike 58) with lush greenery highlighting the towering reddish brown canyon walls. There are numerous delightful spots for a picnic lunch or just a moment of contemplation along the creek before the trail starts to switchback up the side of the canyon.

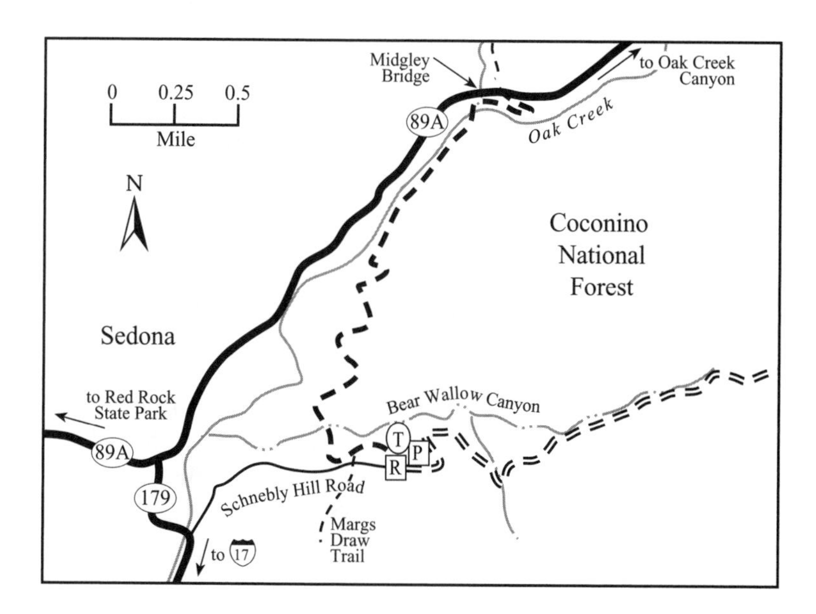

Panoramic views from the trail

Eventually the trail gets to a viewpoint at the base of Midgley Bridge—a great view of the section of Oak Creek you just left—and then you can walk under the bridge to a parking area on AZ 89A, convenient if you happened to leave a vehicle there or arranged to have someone waiting for you. If that's not the case, return to Schnebly Hill Road along the same route.

A Beautiful Woman in a Beautiful Landscape

Actress Gene Tierney, whom legendary Hollywood producer Darryl Zanuck called "the most beautiful woman in movie history," had tall competition from Mother Nature in the 1945 melodrama *Leave Her to Heaven*. This Technicolor extravaganza, which won an Academy Award for best cinematography, does a splendid job of capturing the magnificent red-rock country of the Sedona area, with one of its most dramatic scenes—Gene Tierney's character on horseback speeding away to spread the ashes of her late father—filmed on Schnebly Hill. In typical Hollywood fashion, names have been changed, so in the film Sedona becomes the fictional community of Jacinto, New Mexico.

57. DEVILS BRIDGE TRAIL

Distance ■ 1.8 miles round trip
Difficulty ■ Moderate
Features ■ A scenic hike to a wondrous natural stone arch
Starting elevation ■ 4600 feet
Highest elevation ■ 4950 feet
Total climb ■ 400 feet
Location ■ Coconino National Forest
Map ■ USGS Wilson Mountain
Hiking season ■ Year-round

Getting there: The trail is northwest of Sedona, in the Red Rock District of the Coconino National Forest. From the intersection of AZ 89A and AZ 179, go about 3 miles south on AZ 89A to Dry Creek Road, turn right, and follow it for about 1.9 miles to Forest Road 152 (also called Dry Creek Road), which is dirt. Turn right onto the forest road and follow it for about 1.5 miles to a small parking lot and a sign for the trailhead. There are no restrooms or drinking water.

The red-and-white striated mountains of Sedona are the backdrop to Devils Bridge, the largest natural arch in the Sedona area. In addition, a side trail leads to views of the forest surrounded by Sedona's famous red-rock mountains, and a weathered sandstone overhang is a graphic example of how the wind sculpts solid stone. Juniper, manzanita, and cypress offer occasional shade along the trail.

The gravel trail is wide and well maintained, and begins among juniper trees and prickly pear cactus. It then winds between two mountains—a mostly red mountain on the left (north) and a mostly white one on the right (south), although both have colored bands of red and white. The red sandstone was deposited by ancient seas, and the yellow-white Coconino sandstone is from desert sand dunes from long ago. Millions of years ago, the area alternated between inland sea and desert dune, resulting in the red and white bands.

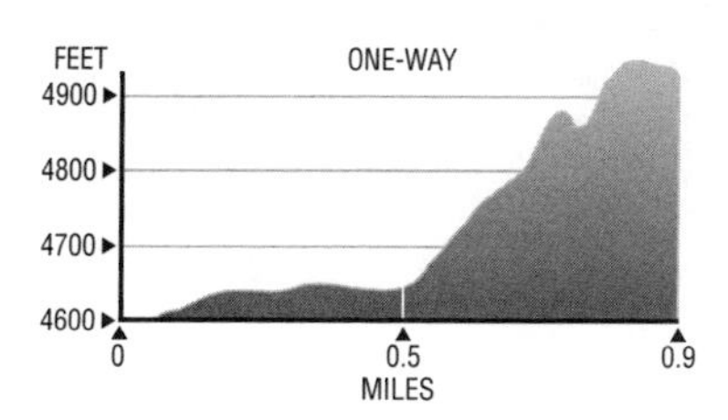

At about 0.1 mile, the trail turns to the right toward the white mountain, where a large boulder balances on the top. It is visible for much of the hike. Piñon trees and sotol agave dot the landscape, and except for the green plants, everything else along the trail is red: red rocks, red dirt, and even the branches of the manzanita are red. The trail is relatively flat until it comes to a wash at 0.4 mile. Although it first appears that the trail will follow the wash to the left, it actually goes to the right up some large, flat stones that look like stairs. Look for the cairn at the top. As the trail climbs, it is easier to see the colored bands on the mountains.

The trail narrows at approximately 0.65 mile, as it passes a large rock that is black on the top from rain and red on the bottom. Shade lies just ahead under the thick trees where the trail comes to an intersection at about 0.75 mile. Continue to the left on the main trail to Devils Bridge. Just past this intersection, another side trail to the right leads to overviews of the entire valley. The view is worth the effort to hike the small incline. Return to the main trail after enjoying the view.

Just past the side trail, the main trail passes under an overhang of weathered sandstone, the result of wind erosion. As the trail continues, it looks like it is about to dead-end into a tall wall of black, solid stone,

Layered red and white mountains (Photo by Lawrence Letham)

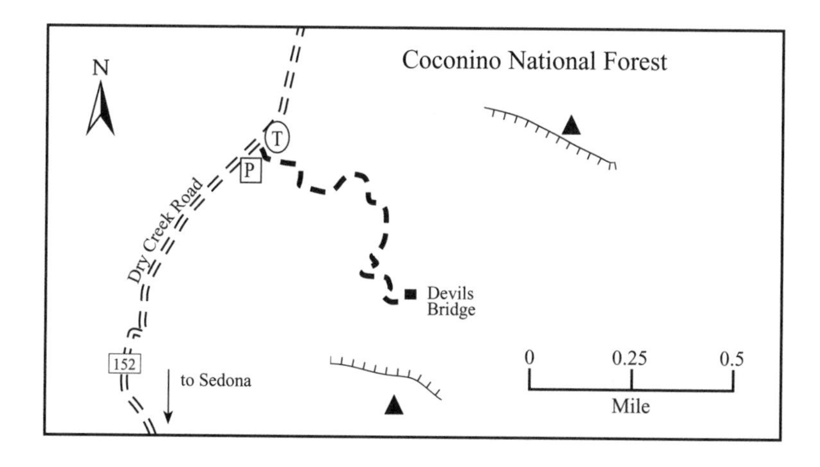

but at the last second it veers to the left around a large pine tree. The sandstone arch soon comes into view only a few hundred feet ahead. The 50-foot arch rises from two highly sculpted, red sandstone bases and stands in front of a shallow box canyon in the solid cliff. Hike behind the arch to get a wonderful view of blue sky and red mountains through the opening.

Return along the same route.

58. WEST FORK TRAIL

Distance	6.8 miles round trip
Difficulty	Moderate
Features	A pretty hike along (and across) a creek, set in a beautiful canyon
Starting elevation	5350 feet
Highest elevation	5500 feet
Total climb	1145 feet
Location	Coconino National Forest
Map	USGS Munds Park, Wilson Mountain, Dutton Hill; USFS trail guide
Hiking season	Year-round

Getting there: The trail is located in Oak Creek Canyon, about 11 miles north of Sedona, in the Red Rock District of the Coconino National Forest. The well-marked trailhead is on the west side of AZ 89A, and a parking fee is charged. There are restrooms but no drinking water. A trail guide is also available for a small fee.

A very pleasant change of pace in mostly arid Arizona, this popular trail follows the West Fork of Oak Creek through a riparian area of Gambel oak, box elder, canyon maple (also called bigtooth maple), pines, and ferns. There is also a variety of colorful wildflowers, including white nightshade, red skyrocket, deep pink wild geraniums, yellow and white pearly everlasting, yellow brown-eyed Susan and common monkey flower, pure white sacred datura, and bluish purple monkshood.

Hikers should be prepared to cross the creek a number of times. In most cases you'll be able to step from rock to rock, although depending on water levels, you may need to wade briefly in ankle-deep water. Also be aware that poison ivy—with its shiny leaves in clusters of three—is abundant along the trail.

This busy trail begins as an easy walk through the woods, and if you happen to be there in the fall, the first thing you may notice is the smell of apples from the numerous apple trees that were planted here in the late 1800s. At about 0.25 mile the ruins of Mayhews Lodge appear along the trail. The lodge incorporated three existing cabins, including one built in the 1870s by "Bear" Howard, who reportedly got his name for using a knife to kill four bears at various times during his life. The lodge was developed in the 1920s and operated until 1968 when the property was bought by the U.S. Forest Service. A fire destroyed much of the lodge in 1976.

Shortly after passing the lodge ruins you'll reach a fork, where you'll go right and then sign in at the wilderness register. From here the trail follows the river through the shady canyon, and the rock-hopping begins. The trail is mostly packed sand and dirt, with some rock and occasional tree roots. The canyon is lush with vegetation, with tall ponderosa pines and Douglas firs, and picture-perfect red sandstone cliffs sculpted by the forces of water and wind.

At about the 2-mile point—you've crossed the stream at least a half-dozen times by now—the trail seems to go in three different directions. Take the middle fork. Cairns mark the few spots where you might go wrong. In this area there is an abundance of Gambel oaks, but also a variety of evergreens, including one huge ponderosa pine that the trail circumnavigates.

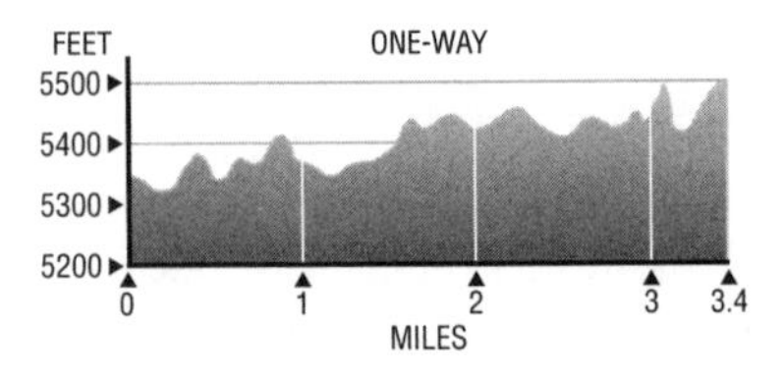

There is a wonderful natural

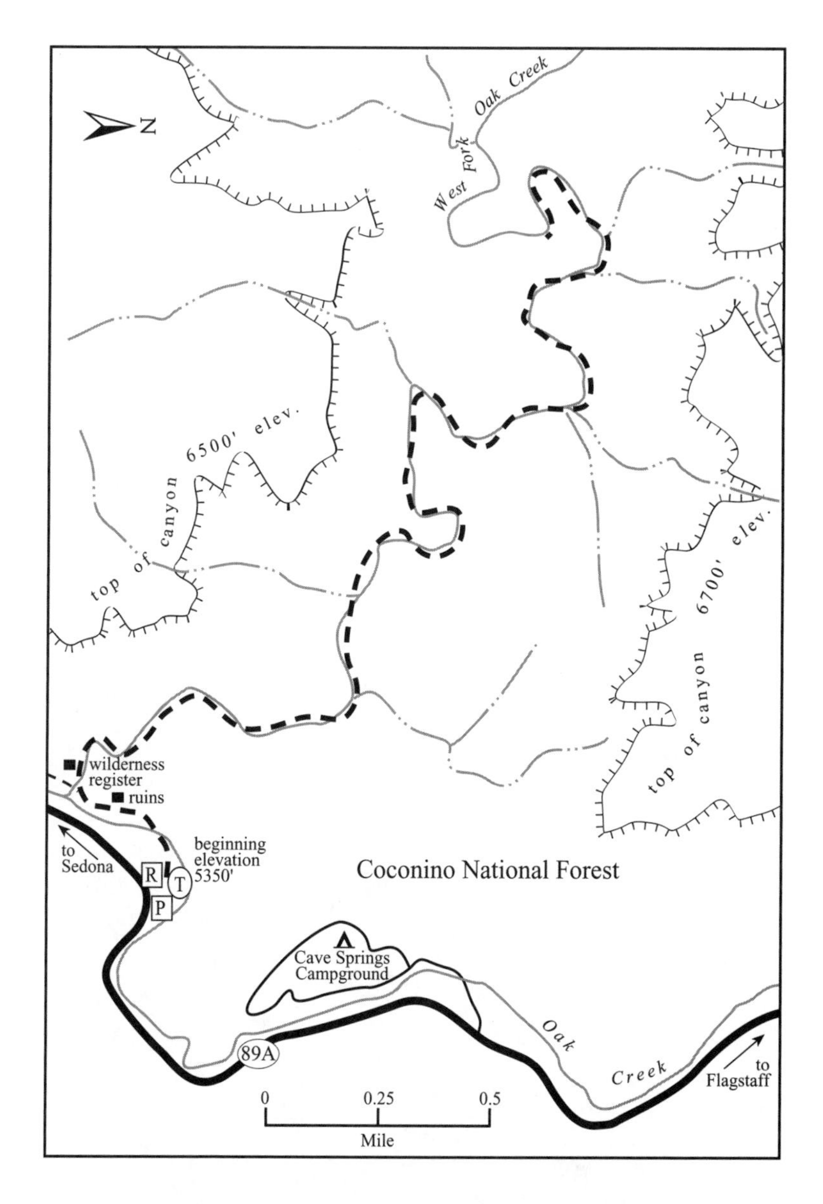

rest stop at about 3 miles, with smooth flat rocks conveniently located for sunbathing or just relaxing and watching kids and dogs play in the water. Some guides consider this the end of the trail, but it does continue, and in our opinion this is where it gets serious.

From this point the trail is increasingly steeper and rockier, as it climbs up, around, and back down to a point where the canyon walls close in, and except in extremely dry years, this is where the trail ends—at an especially scenic spot reminiscent of The Narrows in Zion National Park in southern Utah.

Most hikers will spend a bit of time here, having lunch or a snack, before heading back to the trailhead via the same route.

Hiking the West Fork Trail

West Fork Trail Being Loved to Death

The delightful West Fork Trail is among our favorite hikes in this area, and apparently we're not the only ones who feel that way. Forest Service officials say it is the most popular trail in the Coconino National Forest, and its heavy use, especially on summer weekends, is hurting its plant and animal life. A permit system to limit use is being considered, but in the meantime there's a lot that hikers can do to minimize human impact on both the canyon and fellow hikers: Be quiet on the trail (loud noises are upsetting the canyon's owls); keep dogs leashed; do not take any rocks, plants, or even autumn leaves; stay on the established trail; don't throw rocks; and of course don't leave any litter. Also, if possible avoid hiking the trail on summer weekends. During warm weather, weekday mornings get the least use. The quietest time on the trail, though, is in winter, when ice crystals and icicles are beautiful and a blanket of snow turns the canyon into a winter wonderland.

59. RED ROCK STATE PARK TRAIL SYSTEM

Distance ■ 1.9 miles round trip
Difficulty ■ Easy to moderate
Features ■ Interconnecting trails along Oak Creek and to overlooks offering panoramic views of red-rock country
Starting elevation ■ 3900 feet
Highest elevation ■ 4010 feet
Total climb ■ 300 feet
Location ■ Red Rock State Park
Map ■ USGS Sedona; Red Rock State Park brochure
Hiking season ■ Year-round

Getting there: To get to Red Rock State Park from Sedona, drive 3 miles southwest on AZ 89A to Lower Red Rock Loop Road, turn left, and continue several miles to the park entrance station, then continue to the visitor center, where drinking water and restrooms are available. Swimming or wading in Oak Creek

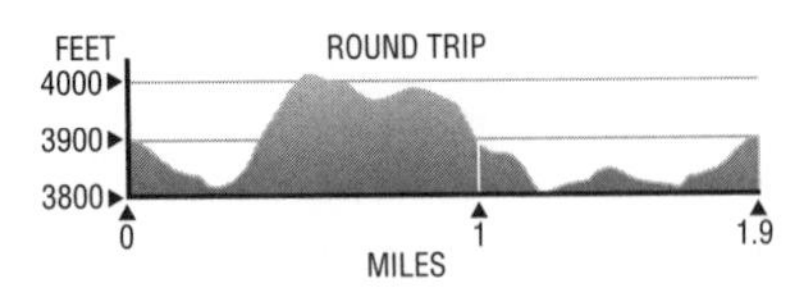

is prohibited, and pets are not permitted in the park. A moderate day-use fee is charged; there is no camping.

Offering both a lush riparian area along a picturesque stream and panoramic views from red sandstone cliffs, Red Rock State Park is a place to be explored leisurely. Pack a lunch, grab your binoculars and camera, and plan to spend the day. It's worth it.

All together there are ten short interconnected trails. Individual trails range in length from less than 0.5 mile to almost 2 miles, round trip from the visitor center, but most hikers combine sections of different trails. We particularly recommend two trails—Eagles Nest and Kisva—but you won't go wrong with any of the trails here. A visit should start at the visitor center to see the various displays and get information on all the park's trails.

If it is a warm day, we suggest you start with the park's most challenging hike—Eagles Nest Trail—a 1.9-mile loop that climbs about 200 feet to the park's highest point, providing great panoramic views of the red-rock cliffs. This somewhat rocky trail provides less shade than trails along the creek, so wear a hat and carry drinking water. To get to the

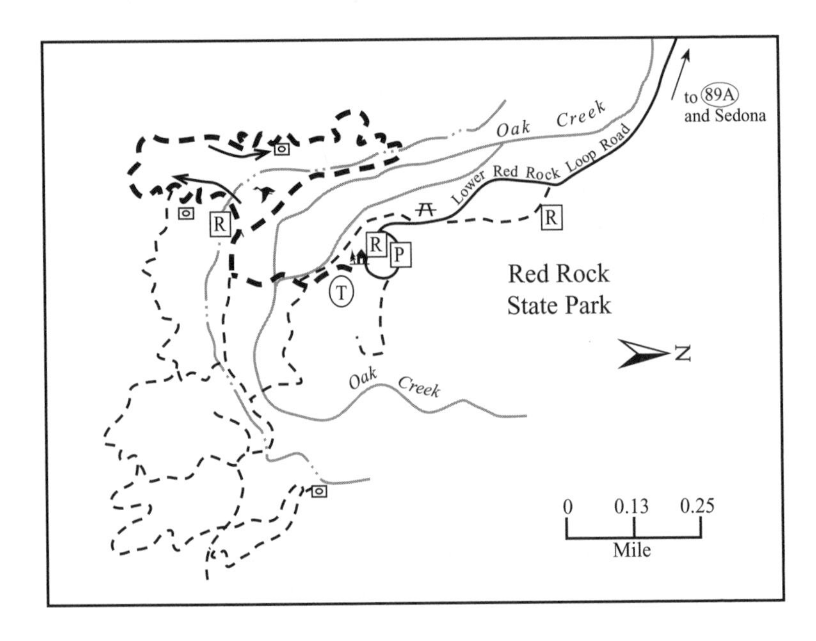

Good advice for those hiking the Red Rock State Park Trail System

Eagles Nest Trail, follow the access trail from the visitor center, cross Oak Creek on a bridge, turn right onto the Kisva Trail, and follow it a short way to a well-marked intersection where you turn left onto Eagles Nest Trail. Follow the Eagles Nest Trail up several short switchbacks and up onto a ridge. The trail then loops back down to again intersect with the Kisva Trail, which offers a very pleasant change of pace.

Measuring 1.7 miles (to and from the visitor center), the Kisva Trail meanders through the riparian area along picturesque Oak Creek, beneath tall cottonwoods, sycamores, and willows, offering close-up views of the wetlands. There is an abundance of plants and wildlife, plus splendid views not only along the creek but also panoramas of the park's namesake red-rock cliffs. A section of the Kisva Trail has numbered signs identifying plants and discussing other natural aspects of the park, with booklets available at the visitor center.

Because of the riparian environment here, you are almost guaranteed to see a variety of birds at any time of year, especially along the Kisva

Trail and other trails in the wetlands. Species seen here include about four dozen year-round residents, among them great blue herons, great horned owls, northern cardinals, Cooper's hawks, greater roadrunners, Anna's hummingbirds, belted kingfishers, red-naped sapsuckers, black phoebes, canyon wrens, and lesser goldfinches. In summer watch for northern mockingbirds, turkey vultures, white-throated swifts, violet-green swallows, and hooded orioles. Black hawks may be nesting in the park from spring through summer. Species that often spend winters here include the bald eagle.

The park is operated primarily as a nature center, and numerous guided hikes, talks, and bird-watching walks are offered. Ranger-led nature walks are given year-round, usually twice daily; and guided bird walks, which often include areas of the park not usually open to the public, are given several mornings a week year-round.

PETRIFIED FOREST NATIONAL PARK

This easily reached national park, right along I-40 in northeastern Arizona, offers a delightful display of colorful petrified wood, as well as the Painted Desert, ancient fossils, and archeological sites. The park can be appreciated for its fascinating geology or for the beauty of the petrified wood, especially magnificent just after a rainstorm. It has a good scenic drive, walking and hiking trails, and visitor centers/museums.

The processes that created the petrified wood here began about 225 million years ago, when this region was quite a bit different than it is today, with tropical forests teeming with tall conifers. As the trees died, they were washed into the shallow waters of a floodplain, where

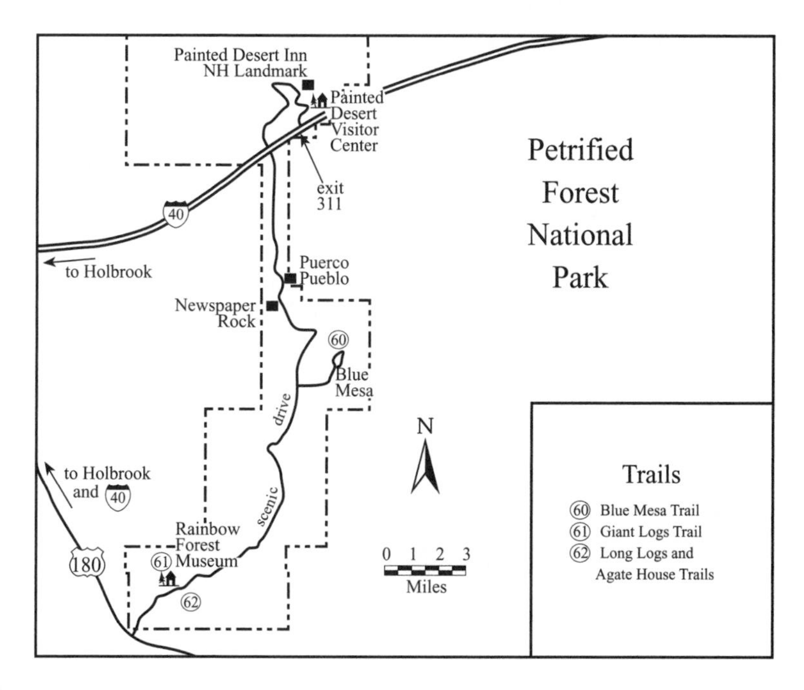

they were buried by mud and silt, plus ash from distant volcanoes. This covering drastically reduced the amount of air getting to the trees, thereby bringing the decaying process to a halt. Silica from the volcanic ash replaced the wood's organic material, eventually leaving quartz crystals in its place. Iron, manganese, and other minerals then streaked the quartz with shades of red, yellow, brown, green, blue, and purple.

The park also is a repository of fossils, since the same sediments that buried the trees preserved the other plants and animals as well. In addition, there are splendid views of the Painted Desert, with its badlands in shades of red, orange, maroon, tan, and gray. There is also evidence that people have lived here for thousands of years, including the Ancestral Puebloans, the predecessors of the modern Pueblo tribes, who occupied this area from the 1100s through 1300s and made tools and even houses from the petrified wood.

Large chunks of petrified wood against a backdrop of barren badlands

A 28-mile scenic drive leads to viewpoints as well as short trails, which offer close-up views of the petrified wood. Several of these trails are discussed below. These trails are paved and leashed pets are permitted. From an overlook you can see Newspaper Rock, with hundreds of petroglyphs including an image of the famous humpbacked flute player, Kokopelli, and a bit farther along the road is a short trail to the remains of a one hundred-room pueblo occupied between 1250 and 1380 by the Ancestral Puebloans. There are also overlooks of the Painted Desert.

Petrified Forest National Park is 117 miles east of Flagstaff via I-40. The north entrance is 25 miles east of Holbrook on I-40; the south entrance is 20 miles east of Holbrook on US 180. Holbrook sits along I-40.

For additional information, contact the park office. The park has no campgrounds, but commercial campgrounds are available nearby in the community of Holbrook, with information available from the Holbrook Chamber of Commerce. You'll find complete contact information in the appendix at the back of this book.

Historic Landmark Being Restored

The Painted Desert Inn National Historic Landmark, which overlooks the desert from Kachina Point, near the park's north entrance, once served as a lunch counter and trading post for early travelers on Route 66. After the National Park Service purchased the inn in 1936, workers in the Civilian Conservation Corps (CCC) rebuilt it in the Southwestern style, not so cleverly covering some of the building's original petrified-wood walls with stucco. Inside, they installed oak floors and hand-painted glass ceiling tiles, and added six guest rooms, each with a fireplace. Upon completion in 1940, the twenty-eight-room inn became an immediate hit with travelers. After World War II, the Fred Harvey Company managed the building as a visitor center and restaurant until 1963.

In 1947, renowned Hopi artist Fred Kabotie painted several murals inside the inn, including one that depicted the coming-of-age journey of the Hopi to the sacred Zuni salt lake. Kabotie's murals may have helped save the building, which had severe structural problems that almost resulted in its demolition. The inn was declared a National Historic Landmark in 1987. In recent years it has housed a museum, but in 2004 a massive rehabilitation project began, which includes new electrical wiring and plumbing and extensive repairs and renovations. Long-range plans also call for the restoration of some of the Fred Harvey-era traveler's amenities, including a guest room and lunch room, as they would have looked in 1948.

60. BLUE MESA TRAIL

Distance ■ 1-mile round trip
Difficulty ■ Moderate
Features ■ A hike through intriguing badlands littered with petrified wood
Starting elevation ■ 5623 feet
Highest elevation ■ 5623 feet
Total climb ■ 90 feet
Location ■ Petrified Forest National Park
Map ■ USGS Adamana
Hiking season ■ Year-round

Getting there: Petrified Forest National Park is 117 miles east of Flagstaff via I-40. The north entrance is 25 miles east of Holbrook on I-40; the south entrance is 20 miles east of Holbrook on US 180. Holbrook sits along I-40.The trailhead begins at the Blue Mesa sun shelter. It's located at the north edge of the 3-mile Blue Mesa Loop Road, which is accessed from a turnoff about 16 miles south of the north entrance to the park along the park's 28-mile scenic drive. There are no restrooms or drinking water at the trailhead.

An otherworldly landscape of blue, purple, brown, and white rock, dotted with chunks of reddish brown petrified wood, helps us understand why this inhospitable terrain is called the badlands. There is no water and very little grows here. The trail is mostly paved, and although it is only 1 mile long it's steep in spots, with practically no shade. The trail, half of which is a loop, has numerous interpretive panels, spaced to give you a chance to catch your breath as you walk.

From the trailhead, you almost immediately drop off the mesa as the trail loops among some of the baddest badlands we've ever seen, descending to the valley floor. The first views out over the stark hills of the badlands—composed primarily of bentonite clay—appear somewhat eerie but distant, but as you begin to walk among the hills, after about 0.35 mile, the landscape takes on an otherworldly appearance and you feel very much alone regardless of how many other people are on the trail.

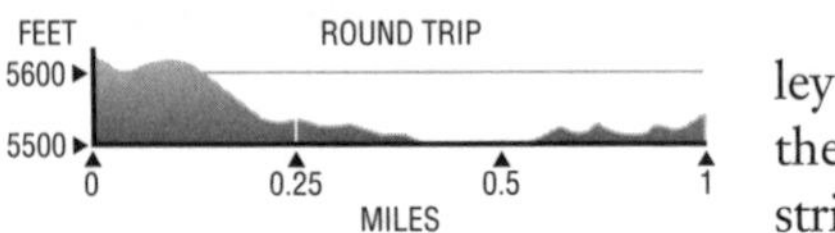

Once you're down on the valley floor it's an easy walk among the silent, barren hills of stone, striped in shades of blue, gray, and

A hiker stops to take a photo along the trail.

white. You may notice that it's hard to determine the size of the hills, an effect caused by the fact that there is almost no vegetation or other clues that would help provide a sense of scale. At the bottom, you can observe how the different colors of these hillsides streak and blend where the clay has washed into drainages. Look for small plant fossils, abundant in the area, but please do not remove them.

After another 0.35 mile or so the trail begins its climb back to the top of the mesa and the trailhead.

An Ancient Calendar

The Ancestral Puebloans may not have had the Weather Channel or even Benjamin Franklin's *Poor Richard's Almanack* to guide them, but they developed a method that marked the longest day of the year, and that was extremely important in helping them to know exactly when to plant their crops. Around the time of the Summer Solstice, which occurs about June 21, the sun shines through a natural crack in a rock, directing a beam of light onto a smaller boulder beside it. This beam gradually moves down the edge of the rock to a small circular petroglyph that had been painted by prehistoric people, and it touches the center of the petroglyph precisely on the Summer Solstice. The petroglyph is at Puerco Pueblo, along the scenic drive a little over 11 miles south of the north entrance, and during a two-week period around the Summer Solstice, park rangers meet with visitors daily from 8:00 to 10:00 AM at the petroglyph to discuss this ancient calendar.

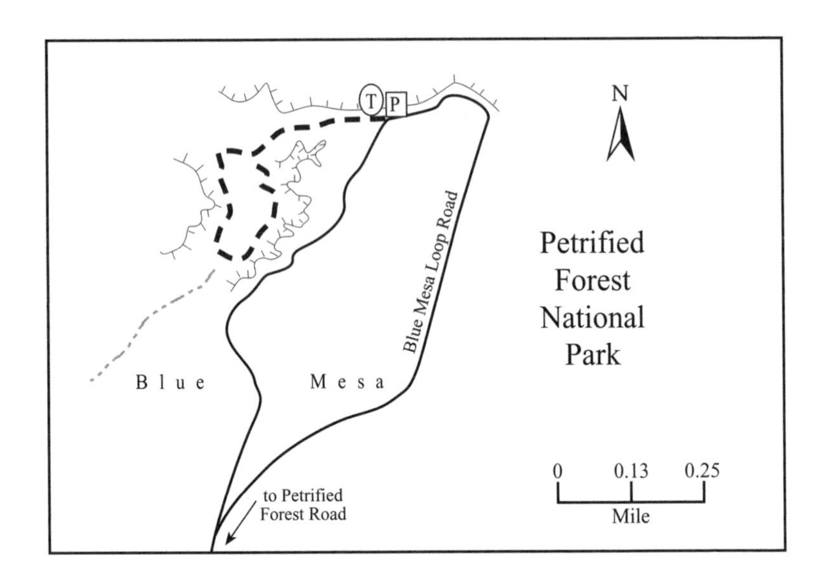

61. GIANT LOGS TRAIL

Distance	0.4-mile loop
Difficulty	Easy
Features	A paved trail where you'll see colorful petrified wood and get distant views
Starting elevation	5479 feet
Highest elevation	5509 feet
Total climb	30
Location	Petrified Forest National Park
Map	USGS Agate House
Hiking season	Year-round

Getting there: Petrified Forest National Park is 117 miles east of Flagstaff via I-40. The north entrance is 25 miles east of Holbrook on I-40; the south entrance is 20 miles east of Holbrook on US 180. Holbrook sits along I-40.The trailhead is behind the Rainbow Forest Museum near the south entrance to the park. After browsing the museum, exit through the back door and the trailhead is straight ahead.

This is a fun way to learn about petrified wood and to see some of the largest and most colorful logs in the park, including "Old Faithful,"

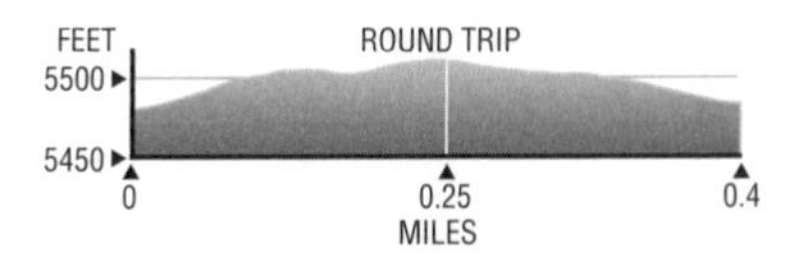

almost 10 feet across at its base, which was named by the wife of the park's first superintendent.

Constructed in the 1930s by the Civilian Conservation Corps, the paved trail has some steps and hilly sections, so those in wheelchairs will need help getting around it. Before leaving the museum, however, be sure to pick up a copy of the trail guide, available at the door just inside the museum. The museum has restrooms and drinking water. The trail has 11 stops, each corresponding to a page in the guide, and at each stop you'll find out about the trees or the area's geology. The trail guide is free if you return it at the end of your hike; otherwise, a small fee is charged.

From the museum, follow the trail in a counterclockwise direction. It begins by going up a gentle incline to what looks like a jumble of oddly shaped rocks and boulders. Then you realize they are log-shaped, and indeed once were trees. The trail continues to meander among many different-sized petrified logs with dissimilar colors and designs. Look out at the sandstone formations in the badlands that surround the park. These are part of what is called the Chinle Formation, deposited more than 200 million years ago during the Triassic Period.

Soon the trail comes to a bronze marker honoring Stephen T. Mather, the first director of the National Park Service. His firm belief

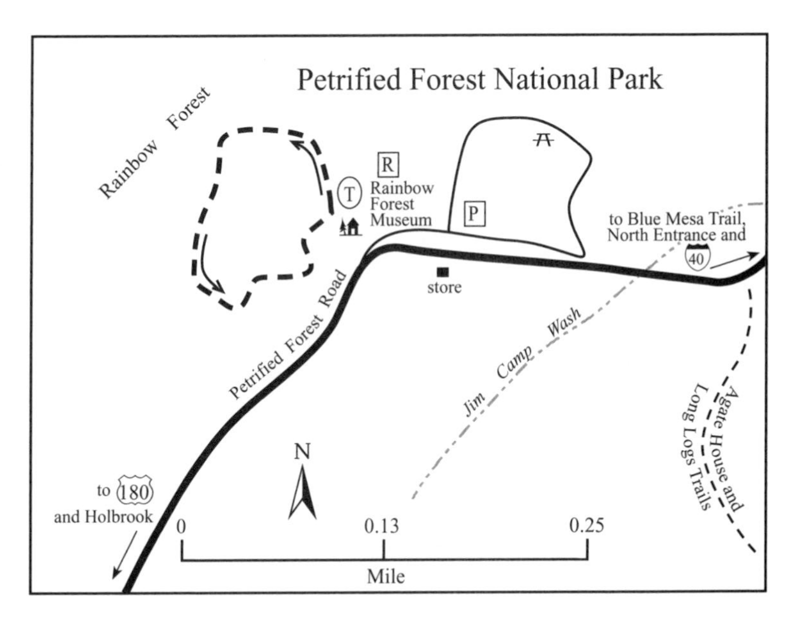

in development of services for visitor enjoyment and comfort, along with park preservation and conservation, laid the foundation for a long-lasting workable park service.

At just over the halfway point, at the top of the trail, is "Old Faithful," one of the largest petrified logs in the park. It's 35 feet long, with a base diameter of almost 10 feet and a weight estimated at about forty-four tons: a behemoth in any language. In the early 1960s "Old Faithful" was fractured by a lightning strike and mended with cement, an act that would not take place in today's philosophy of noninterference with nature.

The trail meanders around and down into a wash before returning to the museum.

69. LONG LOGS AND AGATE HOUSE TRAILS

Distance	3 miles round trip
Difficulty	Moderate
Features	Numerous petrified logs and a prehistoric dwelling made of petrified wood
Starting elevation	5464 feet
Highest elevation	5517 feet
Total climb	175 feet
Location	Petrified Forest National Park
Map	USGS Agate House
Hiking season	Year-round

Getting there: Petrified Forest National Park is 117 miles east of Flagstaff via I-40. The north entrance is 25 miles east of Holbrook on I-40; the south entrance is 20 miles east of Holbrook on US 180. Holbrook sits along I-40. Park at the Rainbow Forest Museum parking area near the park's south entrance. A visit to this museum is very worthwhile, and you'll also find restrooms and drinking water here. From the parking area, walk 0.5 mile east to the trailhead.

Both the Long Logs Trail and the Agate House Trail begin at the same trailhead, and combining them creates an enjoyable and varied hike to see one of the largest concentrations of petrified wood in the national park plus a small pueblo built of petrified wood. These

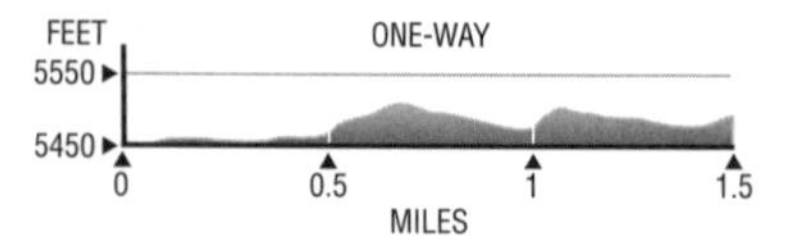

walks also provide panoramic views and a sense of serenity.

We like doing the Long Logs loop first, meandering among a seemingly unlimited quantity of petrified logs, and leaving Agate House, which we consider the most interesting part of these two hikes, for the end.

Follow the sign for the Long Logs Trail, which is a 0.6-mile loop, and fairly level, although it does have a few steps. The trail seems to aimlessly wander among some wonderful examples of petrified wood,

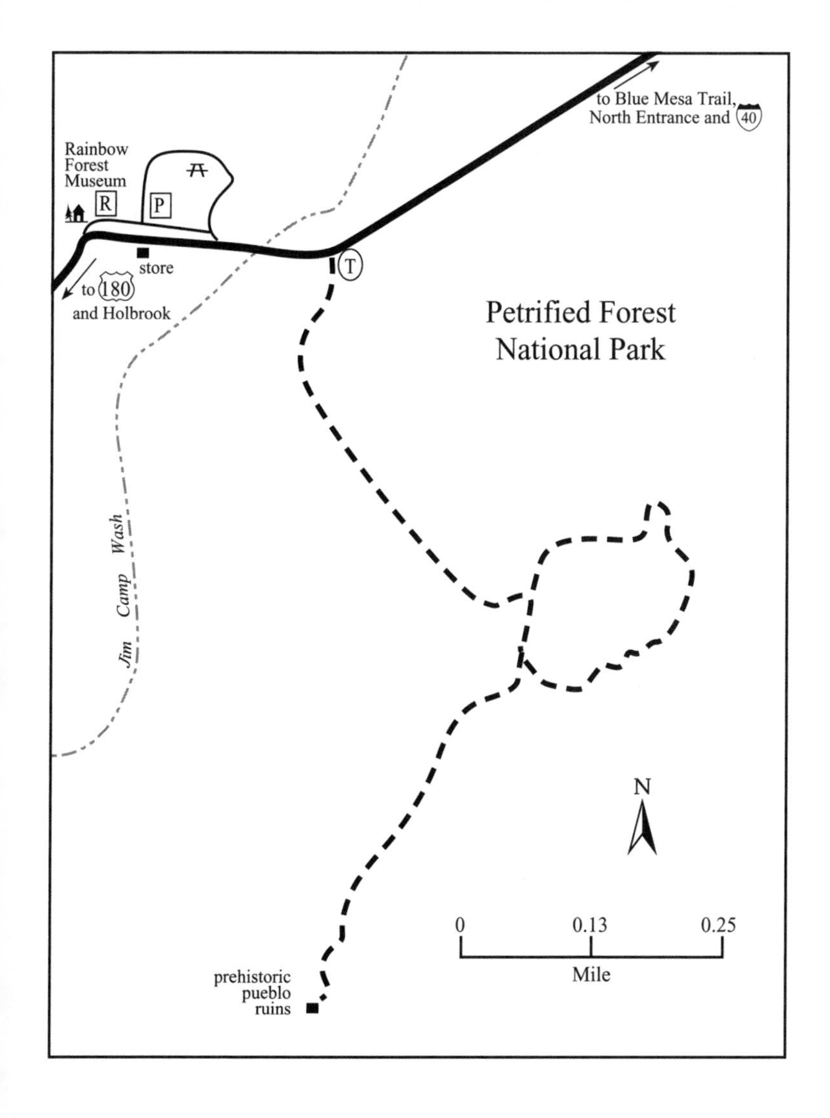

Partially restored prehistoric pueblo made of petrified wood

some quite large. The general landscape reminds us of the surface of the moon—barren and quite forbidding—with the monotony broken by the numerous bright reddish-brown logs of stone. Scientists say the abundance of petrified wood here suggests a prehistoric logjam, likely created by ancient rivers. In the distance are the multicolored rock formations of the badlands.

The Long Logs Trail returns you almost to where you started, with a shortcut to the Agate House Trail, which runs 0.4 mile one-way. The walk up the gentle slope to a knoll overlooking the desert is similar to the Long Logs Trail, with colorful bits of petrified wood along the sides of the path, although there are not as many large petrified logs as along the Long Logs Trail.

Agate House, however, is fascinating. This is a partially restored prehistoric pueblo constructed of petrified wood cemented together with mud. Archaeologists believe this eight-room structure was built in the twelfth century, but they say it was likely only a brief occupation because there is no ceremonial chamber and very little "cultural debris," or what we might call trash, in the area. Possibly the building was used as a seasonal shelter for farmers or traders.

The pueblo's largest room was reconstructed by workers in the 1930s, and that apparently is how it acquired a window, something the original Ancestral Puebloan dwelling never had.

From Agate House, head back down the way you came to the trailhead and then continue on to the Rainbow Forest Museum parking area.

APPENDIX: INFORMATION SOURCES

NATIONAL PARK SERVICE

Chiricahua National Monument
1306 East Bonita Canyon Road
Willcox, AZ 85643-9737
(520) 824-3560; *www.nps.gov/chir*

Coronado National Memorial
4101 East Montezuma Canyon Road
Hereford, AZ 85615
(520) 366-5515; *www.nps.gov/coro*

Grand Canyon National Park
P.O. Box 129
Grand Canyon, AZ 86023
(928) 638-7888; *www.nps.gov/grca*

Navajo National Monument
HC 71, Box 3
Tonalea, AZ 86044-0704
(928) 672-2366; *www.nps.gov/nava*

Organ Pipe Cactus National Monument
10 Organ Pipe Drive
Ajo, AZ 85321-9626
(520) 387-6849; *www.nps.gov/orpi*

Petrified Forest National Park
P.O. Box 2217
Petrified Forest, AZ 86028
(928) 524-6228; *www.nps.gov/pefo*

Saguaro National Park
3693 South Old Spanish Trail
Tucson, AZ 85730-5601
(520) 733-5100; *www.nps.gov/sagu*

Sunset Crater Volcano National Monument
6400 North U.S. 89
Flagstaff, AZ 86004
(928) 526-0502; *www.nps.gov/sucr*

Tonto National Monument
HCO2, Box 4602
Roosevelt, AZ 85545
(928) 467-2241; *www.nps.gov/tont*

Tumacácori National Historical Park
P.O. Box 67
Tumacacori, AZ 85640
(520) 398-2341;
www.nps.gov/tuma

Walnut Canyon National Monument
6400 North U.S. 89
Flagstaff, AZ 86004
(928) 526-3367; *www.nps.gov/waca*

Wupatki National Monument
6400 North U.S. 89
Flagstaff, AZ 86004
(928) 679-2365;
www.nps.gov/wupa

U.S. FOREST SERVICE

Southwestern Region
333 Broadway Southeast
Albuquerque, NM 87102
(505) 842-3292; *www.fs.fed.us/r3*

Coconino National Forest

1824 South Thompson Street
Flagstaff, AZ 86001
(928) 527-3600;
www.fs.fed.us/r3/coconino

Mormon Lake Ranger District
4373 South Lake Mary Road
Flagstaff, AZ 86001
(928) 774-1147

Peaks Ranger District
5075 North U.S. 89
Flagstaff, AZ 86004
(928) 526-0866

Red Rock Ranger District
P.O. Box 300
Sedona, AZ 86339-0330
(928) 282-4119

Coronado National Forest

300 West Congress Street
Tucson, AZ 85701
(520) 388-8300;
www.fs.fed.us/r3/coronado

Douglas Ranger District
3081 North Leslie Canyon Road
Douglas, AZ 85607
(520) 364-3468

Nogales Ranger District
303 Old Tucson Road
Nogales, AZ 85621
(520) 281-2296

Santa Catalina Ranger District
5700 North Sabino Canyon Road
Tucson, AZ 85750
(520) 749-8700

Kaibab National Forest

800 South Sixth Street
Williams, AZ 86046
(928) 635-8200;
www.fs.fed.us/r3/kai

North Kaibab Ranger District
P.O. Box 248
Fredonia, AZ 86022
(928) 643-7395

Tusayan Ranger District
P.O. Box 3088
Grand Canyon, AZ 86023
(520) 638-2443

Tonto National Forest

2324 East McDowell Road
Phoenix, AZ 85006
(602) 225-5200;
www.fs.fed.us/r3/tonto

Mesa Ranger District
5140 East Ingram Street
Mesa, AZ 85205
(480) 610-3300

STATE PARKS

Arizona State Parks
1300 West Washington Street
Phoenix, AZ 85007
(602) 542-4174; *www.azstateparks .com* or *www.pr.state.az.us*

Catalina State Park
P.O. Box 36986
Tucson, AZ 85740
(520) 628-5798

Lost Dutchman State Park
6109 North Apache Trail
Apache Junction, AZ 85219
(480) 982-4485

Patagonia Lake State Park
HC2 Box 273
Nogales, AZ 85621
(520) 287-6965

Picacho Peak State Park
P.O. Box 275
Picacho, AZ 85241
(520) 466-3183

Red Rock State Park
4050 Red Rock Loop Road
Sedona, AZ 86336
(928) 282-6907

Tonto Natural Bridge State Park
P.O. Box 1245
Payson, AZ 85547
(928) 476-4202

Tubac Presidio State Historic Park
P.O. Box 1296
Tubac, AZ 85646
(520) 398-2252

CITY AND COUNTY PARKS

Phoenix Parks and Recreation Department
Phoenix City Hall
200 West Washington Street, 16th Floor
Phoenix, AZ 85003
(602) 262-6862; *www.phoenix .gov/parks/mntparks.html*

Tucson Mountain Park
Pima County Natural Resources, Parks and Recreation Department
3500 West River Road
Tucson, AZ 85741
(520) 883-4200 (direct to park)
(520) 877-6000 (Pima County); *www.co.pima.az.us/pksrec /natres/tucmts/tumtpk.html*

Usery Mountain Regional Park
Maricopa County Parks and Recreation Department
411 North Central Avenue, Suite 470
Phoenix, AZ 85004
(602) 506-2930; *www.maricopa .gov/parks/usery*

NATURE CONSERVANCY

Patagonia-Sonoita Creek Preserve
The Nature Conservancy of Arizona
27 Ramsey Canyon Road
Hereford, AZ 85615
(520) 394-2400;
www.nature.org/arizona

CONVENTION AND VISITORS BUREAUS AND CHAMBERS OF COMMERCE

Flagstaff Convention and Visitors Bureau
211 West Aspen Street
Flagstaff, AZ 86001-5399
(800) 842-7293 or (928) 779-7611; *www.flagstaffarizona.org*

Grand Canyon Chamber of Commerce
P.O. Box 3007
Grand Canyon, AZ 86023
www.grandcanyonchamber.com

Greater Phoenix Convention & Visitors Bureau
400 East Van Buren Street, Suite 600
Phoenix, AZ 85004
(877) 225-5749 or (602) 253-4415; *www.phoenixcvb.com*

Holbrook Chamber of Commerce
100 East Arizona Street
Old Court House
Holbrook, AZ 86025
(800) 524-2459 or (928) 524-6558; *www.ci.holbrook.az.us*

Metropolitan Tucson Convention & Visitors Bureau
100 South Church Avenue
Tucson, AZ 85701
(800) 638-8350 or (520) 624-1817; *www.visittucson.org*

Sedona-Oak Creek Canyon Chamber of Commerce
P.O. Box 478
Sedona, AZ 86336
(800) 288-7336 or (928) 282-7722; *www.sedonachamber.com*

Willcox Chamber of Commerce & Agriculture
1500 North Circle I Road
Willcox, AZ 85643
(800) 200-2272 or (520) 384-2272; *www.willcoxchamber.com*

OTHER INFORMATION SOURCES

Arizona Office of Tourism
1110 West Washington Street, Suite 155
Phoenix, AZ 85007
(866) 275-5816 or (602) 364-3700; *www.arizonaguide.com*

Arizona Public Lands Information Center
222 North Central Avenue
Phoenix, AZ 85004
(*Note:* move expected in 2005)
(602) 417-9300;
www.publiclands.org

Navajo Nation Tourism Department
P.O. Box 663
Window Rock, AZ 86515
(928) 871-6436;
www.discovernavajo.com

CAMPGROUND RESERVATIONS

National Park Service
(800) 365-2267;
http://reservations.nps.gov

U.S. Forest Service
(877) 444-6777;
www.reserveusa.com

Xanterra Parks & Resorts (Grand Canyon's Trailer Village)
(888) 297-2757 or (928) 638-2631;
www.grandcanyonlodges.com

SUGGESTED READING

Carline, Jan D., Steven C. Macdonald, and Martha J. Lentz. *Mountaineering First Aid: A Guide to Accident Response and First Aid Care*, 5th ed. Seattle: The Mountaineers Books, 2004.

Chronic, Halka. *Roadside Geology of Arizona*. Missoula, Mont.: Mountain Press Publishing, 1983.

Epple, Anne Orth. *A Field Guide to the Plants of Arizona*. Helena, Mont.: Falcon Press Publishing, 1997.

Fleming, June. *Staying Found: The Complete Map and Compass Handbook*, 3rd ed. Seattle: The Mountaineers Books, 2001.

Henry, Marguerite. *Brighty of the Grand Canyon*. New York: Aladdin Books, Macmillan Publishing Co., 1991.

Laine, Barbara and Don. *Little-Known Southwest: Outdoor Destinations Beyond the Parks*. Seattle: The Mountaineers Books, 2001.

Laine, Don and Barbara. *New Mexico & Arizona State Parks: A Complete Recreation Guide*. Seattle: The Mountaineers Books, 1998.

Lauer, Charles D. *Tales of Arizona Territory*. Phoenix: Golden West Publishers, 1995.

Letham, Lawrence. *GPS Made Easy: Using Global Positioning Systems in the Outdoors*, 4th ed. Seattle: The Mountaineers Books, 2003.

INDEX

ABOUT THE AUTHORS

Residents of northern New Mexico since 1970, **Don** and **Barbara Laine** have spent countless hours exploring the Southwest's mountains, deserts, lakes, rivers, and plains. Their interests include hiking, photography, wildlife viewing, and visiting historic sites, as well as loafing in a shady campground. Don spent more than twenty years in radio and newspaper journalism before turning to travel writing and photography full time in the early 1990s, and his articles and photographs have been published in regional and national newspapers and magazines. Barb's background includes work as a draftsman in a land surveying office, which she continues to do part-time, and she has also worked in administration at a nonprofit arts organization and a small private school.

Together Don and Barb have authored more than a dozen travel guides, including *Little-Known Southwest: Outdoor Destinations Beyond the Parks* and *New Mexico & Arizona State Parks: A Complete Recreation Guide*, both published by The Mountaineers Books. They have also written *The New Mexico Guide*, published by Fulcrum Publishing, and a number of Frommer's travel guides, including *Frommer's National Parks of the American West* and *Frommer's Utah.*

Lawrence Letham worked in the electronics industry as an electrical engineer for twenty years. He is now a registered patent agent and law student at Arizona State University. When he is not writing patents or studying, he hikes and camps with his wife and six children. He lives in Arizona.

Don and Barb Laine (Photo by Allan Davies)

Lawrence Letham (Photo by Allan Davies)

THE MOUNTAINEERS, founded in 1906, is a nonprofit outdoor activity and conservation club, whose mission is "to explore, study, preserve, and enjoy the natural beauty of the outdoors. . . . " Based in Seattle, Washington, the club is now the third-largest such organization in the United States, with seven branches throughout Washington State.

The Mountaineers sponsors both classes and year-round outdoor activities in the Pacific Northwest, which include hiking, mountain climbing, ski-touring, snowshoeing, bicycling, camping, kayaking, nature study, sailing, and adventure travel. The club's conservation division supports environmental causes through educational activities, sponsoring legislation, and presenting informational programs.

All club activities are led by skilled, experienced instructors, who are dedicated to promoting safe and responsible enjoyment and preservation of the outdoors.

If you would like to participate in these organized outdoor activities or the club's programs, consider a membership in The Mountaineers. For information and an application, write or call The Mountaineers, Club Headquarters, 300 Third Avenue West, Seattle, WA 98119; 206-284-6310. You can also visit the club's website at *www.mountaineers.org* or contact The Mountaineers via email at *clubmail@mountaineers.org*.

The Mountaineers Books, an active, nonprofit publishing program of the club, produces guidebooks, instructional texts, historical works, natural history guides, and works on environmental conservation. All books produced by The Mountaineers Books fulfill the club's mission.

Send or call for our catalog of more than 500 outdoor titles:

The Mountaineers Books
1001 SW Klickitat Way, Suite 201
Seattle, WA 98134
800-553-4453
mbooks@mountaineersbooks.org
www.mountaineersbooks.org

The Mountaineers Books is proud to be a corporate sponsor of The Leave No Trace Center for Outdoor Ethics, whose mission is to promote and inspire responsible outdoor recreation through education, research, and partnerships. The Leave No Trace program is focused specifically on human-powered (nonmotorized) recreation.

Leave No Trace strives to educate visitors about the nature of their recreational impacts, as well as offer techniques to prevent and minimize such impacts. Leave No Trace is best understood as an educational and ethical program, not as a set of rules and regulations.

For more information, visit *www.LNT.org*, or call 800-332-4100.

OTHER TITLES YOU MIGHT ENJOY FROM THE MOUNTAINEERS BOOKS

100 Classic Hikes in Arizona, 2nd Edition, *Scott Warren*
The gorgeous full-color format has made this one of Arizona's most popular hiking guidebooks.

Best Hikes with Dogs: Arizona, *Renée Guillory*
Where to hike with Fido: all trails recommended as dog-friendly and dog-fun!

Hiking the Grand Canyon's Geology, *Lon Abbott and Teri Cook*

Hiking Arizona's Geology, *Ivo Lucchitta*
The only guides to Arizona's wild places that combine hiking and geology. Unlock the mysteries of the landscape, step by step.

Hiking the Southwest's Canyon Country, 3rd Edition, *Sandra Hinchman*
This popular hiking guide includes trip itineraries with day-by-day suggestions.

Day Hiker's Handbook: Get Started with the Experts, *Michael Lanza*
Experts at *Backpacker* magazine explain how to begin a hiking hobby—from finding companions to selecting comfortable gear.

Desert Sense: Camping, Hiking & Biking in Hot, Dry Climates, *Bruce Grubbs*
How to make your way safely in the desert.

Available at fine bookstores and outdoor stores, by phone at 800-553-4453 or on the web at *www.mountaineersbooks.org*

THE MOUNTAINEERS BOOKS